American Gangster Cinema

Crime Files Series

General Editor: **Clive Bloom**

Since its invention in the nineteenth century, detective fiction has never been more popular. In novels, short stories, films, radio, television and now in computer games, private detectives and psychopaths, prim poisoners and overworked cops, tommy gun gangsters and cocaine criminals are the very stuff of modern imagination, and their creators one mainstay of popular consciousness. Crime Files is a ground-breaking series offering scholars, students and discerning readers a comprehensive set of guides to the world of crime and detective fiction. Every aspect of crime writing, detective fiction, gangster movie, true-crime exposé, police procedural and post-colonial investigation is explored through clear and informative texts offering comprehensive coverage and theoretical sophistication.

Published titles include:

Hans Bertens and Theo D'haen
CONTEMPORARY AMERICAN CRIME FICTION

Anita Biressi
CRIME, FEAR AND THE LAW IN TRUE CRIME STORIES

Ed Christian (*editor*)
THE POST-COLONIAL DETECTIVE

Paul Cobley
THE AMERICAN THRILLER
Generic Innovation and Social Change in the 1970s

Lee Horsley
THE NOIR THRILLER

Fran Mason
AMERICAN GANGSTER CINEMA
From *Little Caesar* to *Pulp Fiction*

Susan Rowland
FROM AGATHA CHRISTIE TO RUTH RENDELL

Crime Files
Series Standing Order ISBN 0–333–71471–7 (hardcover)
Series Standing Order ISBN 0–333–93064–9 (paperback)
(*outside North America only*)

You can receive future titles in this series as they are published by placing a standing order. Please contact your bookseller or, in case of difficulty, write to us at the address below with your name and address, the title of the series and the ISBN quoted above.

Customer Services Department, Macmillan Distribution Ltd, Houndmills, Basingstoke, Hampshire RG21 6XS, England

American Gangster Cinema

From *Little Caesar* to *Pulp Fiction*

Fran Mason

First published 2002 by
PALGRAVE MACMILLAN
Houndmills, Basingstoke, Hampshire RG21 6XS and
175 Fifth Avenue, New York, N.Y. 10010
Companies and representatives throughout the world

PALGRAVE MACMILLAN is the global academic imprint of the Palgrave
Macmillan division of St. Martin's Press, LLC and of Palgrave Macmillan Ltd.
Macmillan® is a registered trademark in the United States, United Kingdom
and other countries. Palgrave is a registered trademark in the European
Union and other countries.

ISBN 10: 0-333-68466-4 paperback
ISBN 13: 978-0-333-68466-5 paperback

This book is printed on paper suitable for recycling and made from fully
managed and sustained forest sources.

A catalogue record for this book is available from the British Library.

Library of Congress Cataloging-in-Publication Data
Mason, Fran, 1962-
    American gangster cinema: from Little Caesar to Pulp Fiction/Fran Mason.
       p. cm.
    Includes bibliographical references and index.
    ISBN 0-333-67452-9 – ISBN 0-333-68466-4 (pbk.)
    1. Gangster films–United States–History and criticism. I. Title.

PN1995.9.G3 M37 2002
791.43′655–dc21

                                                            2002026948

10 9 8 7
11 10 09 08

Printed and bound in Great Britain by
Antony Rowe Ltd, Chippenham and Eastbourne

Contents

Preface

The American film gangster is an iconic figure of the industrial twentieth century in both its modern and postmodern forms, representing a culture of mobility, urban space, excess, and individual licence. He is also, however, an anti-social figure within this context because he is the focus for a liberation from hierarchy and from the past (in his embrace of the modern) that society and ideology wish to repress. One of the iconic images of the gangster genre is of a sharply dressed gangster holding a gun appearing out of the shadows with himself either silhouetted against a wall or throwing a shadow forward. This image enacts the gangster's problematic status. He is a figure of a shadowy world of crime that legitimate ideological society wishes to deny but whose shadow falls across official society's world of honest toil, discipline, order, and contained individuality, threatening to dominate or displace it with his own ideology of the pleasure principle, excess, chaos, and individual self-gratification.

The film gangster, therefore, represents a seminal figure in the history of twentieth-century culture, forming the focus for a range of tensions that have dominated the discourses of industrialised society. These range from the role of the individual within an increasingly rationalised society, the impact of urban space (and its association with the fracturing discourses of modernity and postmodernity), the tension between tradition and the modern, the opposition between labour and pleasure, and particularly the relationship between ideology and freedom. The gangster genre forms a focus for these tensions in its representation of the individual in opposition to society and represents an attempt to engage with the actuality of twentieth-century culture through the displaced persona of the gangster so that, even though he represents concerns that may appear to be predominantly masculine, he also articulates wider tensions and contradictions that attach to the simple act of living everyday life in the modern period. What follows in this account of the American gangster film is an attempt to understand how the gangster is located within these tensions and contradictions and how audiences are attracted to the genre because it offers, in its fantasies of gangster criminality and individual liberation, an alternative to living ideologically that, in the content of the films, provides a spectacle of pleasure and freedom otherwise unavailable.

Acknowledgements

Thanks are due to several of my colleagues at King Alfred's College. Much of the groundwork for this book was laid in conversation with Alasdair Spark whom I would also like to thank for providing research support throughout this project. Thanks are also owed to Leighton Grist for his help in tracking down copies of difficult to obtain movies and to Andrew Blake and Carol Smith for their encouragement throughout the writing of this book. My thanks also go to Kathy Parkes and Lyn Black who provided much needed administrative help, particularly in the final stages of writing.

I would also like to thank Clive Bloom, of Middlesex University, for his perceptive comments on the manuscript as well as my editors at Palgrave, Rebecca Mashayekh and Emily Rosser, for their patience and help over the course of writing this book. Thanks are also due to Martin Humphries at the Ronald Grant Archive and Nina Harding at the BFI Stills Archive for their kind assistance and advice.

A Chronology of the Gangster Film

The following forms a select filmography of the gangster film since 1912 with the name of the director in parentheses followed by annotations in bold to offer some sense of the concerns or sub-genre attached to each film.

1912 *Musketeers of Pig Alley* (D.W. Griffith) **silent gangster**
1914 *The Gangsters and the Girl* (Thomas Ince) **silent gangster**
1915 *Regeneration* (Raoul Walsh) **gangster melodrama**
1927 *Underworld* (Josef von Sternberg) **silent melodrama**
1928 *The Racket* (Lewis Milestone) **cops-and-robbers**
1929 *Alibi* (Roland West) **smalltime hood**
1930 *Doorway to Hell* (Archie Mayo) **rise and fall of the big shot**
      Little Caesar (Mervyn Le Roy) **classic/rise and fall of the big shot**
1931 *Quick Millions* (Rowland Brown) **racketeering/rise and fall**
      The Public Enemy (William Wellmann) **classic/foot soldier**
      Smart Money (Alfred E. Green) **gangster–gambler**
      Taxi (Roy Del Ruth) **urban tough**
1932 *Scarface* (Howard Hawks) **classic rise and fall of the big shot**
      Three on a Match (Mervyn Le Roy) **gangster melodrama**
1933 *Lady Killer* (Roy Del Ruth) **comedy gangster**
      Blondie Johnson (Ray Enright) **female gangster**
1934 *Manhattan Melodrama* (W.S. Van Dyke) **Cain and Abel**
1935 *G-Men* (William Keighley) **G-Man**
      Confidential (Edward L Cahn) **G-Man/racketeering**
1936 *Bullets or Ballots* (William Keighley) **G-Man**
      The Petrified Forest (Archie Mayo) **social/melodrama**
1937 *Dead End* (William Wyler) **social gangster**
      The Last Gangster (Edward Ludwig) **big shot**
      Marked Woman (Lloyd Bacon) **gangster melodrama**
1938 *Angels with Dirty Faces* (Michael Curtiz) **social/Cain and Abel**
      I Am the Law (Alexander Hall) **G-Man**
      Racket Busters (Lloyd Bacon) **racketeering**
1939 *The Roaring Twenties* (Raoul Walsh) **gangster epic**
      Each Dawn I Die (William Keighley) **prison drama**
      Invisible Stripes (Lloyd Bacon) **social/prison**
1940 *Brother Orchid* (Lloyd Bacon) **comedy gangster**
      Johnny Apollo (Henry Hathaway) **star vehicle**
1941 *High Sierra* (Raoul Walsh) **bandit/death of the big shot**
      Out of the Fog (Anatole Litvak) **family in peril**
      Lady Scarface (Frank Woodruff) **female gangster**
1942 *The Big Shot* (Lewis Seiler) **death of the big shot**

1961   *Underworld USA* (Sam Fuller) **syndicate**
       Pretty Boy Floyd (Herbert J. Leder) **biopic**
1967   *Point Blank* (John Boormann) **one man against the mob**
       Bonnie and Clyde (Arthur Penn) **retro/revisionist**
       The St Valentine's Day Massacre (Roger Corman) **retro/revisionist**
1971   *Shaft* (Gordon Parks) **blaxploitation**
1972   *The Godfather* (Francis Ford Coppola) **gangster epic**
       Across 110th Street (Barry Shear) **black gangster**
       Shaft's Big Score (Gordon Parks) **blaxploitation**
1973   *Mean Streets* (Martin Scorsese) **gangster–loser**
       The Outfit (John Flynn) **gangster–loser**
       Charley Varrick (Don Siegel) **gangster–loser**
       The Friends of Eddie Coyle (Peter Yates) **gangster–loser**
       Black Caesar (Larry Cohen) **black gangster**
       Dillinger (John Milius) **biopic**
       Lucky Luciano (Francesco Rosi) **biopic**
1974   *The Godfather, Part II* (Francis Ford Coppola) **gangster epic**
1975   *Lepke* (Menahem Golan) **biopic**
1976   *The Killing of a Chinese Bookie* (John Cassavetes) **gangster–loser**
1980   *Gloria* (John Cassavetes) **one woman against the mob**
1981   *Thief* (Michael Mann) **one man against the mob**
1983   *Scarface* (Brian De Palma) **revisionist/big shot**
1984   *Once Upon a Time in America* (Sergio Leone) **gangster epic**
       The Cotton Club (Francis Coppola) **nostalgia**
       City Heat (Richard Benjamin) **comedy/nostalgia**
1985   *Prizzi's Honor* (John Huston) **parody**
1986   *Tough Guys* (Jeff Kanew) **nostalgia**
       Wise Guys (Brian de Palma) **comedy**
1987   *The Untouchables* (Brian De Palma) **nostalgic G-Man**
1988   *Married to the Mob* (Jonathan Demme) **comedy**
       Eight Men Out (John Sayles) **nostalgia**
1990   *Goodfellas* (Martin Scorsese) **foot-soldier**
       Miller's Crossing (Joel Coen) **postmodern retro**
       The Godfather, Part III (Francis Ford Coppola) **gangster epic**
       King of New York (Abel Ferrara) **big shot**
1991   *Boyz'n the Hood* (John Singleton) **gangsta**
       New Jack City (Mario Van Peebles) **gangsta**
       Diary of a Hitman (Roy London) **assassin**
       Billy Bathgate (Robert Benton) **nostalgia**
1992   *Reservoir Dogs* (Quentin Tarantino) **postmodern pastiche**
1993   *True Romance* (Tony Scott) **gangster loser**
       Carlito's Way (Brian De Palma) **postmodern 'realism'**
       A Bronx Tale (Robert de Niro) **family vs the gang**
       Menace II Society (The Hughes Brothers) **gangsta**
1994   *Pulp Fiction* (Quentin Tarantino) **postmodern gangster**
       Romeo Is Bleeding (Peter Medak) **Russian gangster**
       Little Odessa (James Gray) **Russian gangster**
       Leon (Luc Besson) **assassin**
1995   *The Usual Suspects* (Brian Singer) **postmodern heist/suspense**

Introduction

Film genre is ostensibly an area with an unproblematic sense of how to define the parameters of its study. Grant, in his introduction to the second volume of *The Film Genre Reader*, articulates the apparent ease with which genre films can be understood as 'those commercial feature films which, through repetition and variation, tell familiar stories with familiar characters in familiar situations. They also encourage expectations and experiences similar to those of similar films we have already seen' (Grant, 1995: xv). Implicit within this view of genre, despite the mention of 'variation', is that a genre is a common set of practices that can be identified by its iconography, narrative formulae and semiotic codes. In these terms, a text that is generic can be located and understood within its genre no matter when and where it is produced, so that texts from different societies, cultures and historical periods can all be understood within the same parameters of signification. A genre operates under the rule of a taxonomy or metanarrative that unites its various manifestations and binds them within the same field of operation by effectively imposing a set of codes which limit their meanings to those made available by the generic boundaries. Although theories of film genre have been problematised by studies that focus on their production in terms of the creation by the classical Hollywood studio system of a range of discursive practices which enabled them to identify and market film as a standardised product with a predictable audience and set of viewing positions (Neale, 1980), the focus on the organisation of films into categories from the point of view of their textual similarities and consumed meanings has formed a common view of genre. When turning to gangster film this tendency is even more evident. The gangster film, like the western, is almost the epitome of easily recognised iconographies and narrative conventions, Cowie noting that it has 'a limited set of narrative themes or problematics' (1993: 127) in opposition to the variety and fracturing that characterises *film noir*, while Mitchell comments on the necessity of understanding its formulations as part of larger generic articulations of 'repetitive patterning' (1995: 203). In these articulations, the gangster film becomes a generic paradigm of generic paradigms.

The creation of the gangster genre metanarrative is the result of two things. First, the early years of genre criticism in the 1970s, when genre was identified in its consistency of iconography, narrative, and ideology, produced several books on the gangster film (McArthur, 1972; Shadoian, 1977 and Rosow, 1978) which sought to give legitimacy to their study by refining the genre into a structured arrangement of elements. The second reason for the view that the gangster genre is united by a dominant set of conventions and semiotic codes is that a group of films all produced in the early 1930s and usually referred to as the 'classic' narrative (*Little Caesar*, *The Public Enemy*, and *Scarface*) have been given a privileged position within the study of the genre as paradigmatic examples of its iconography. The result is that these films have been allowed to set the domain within which the gangster genre has been studied, so that when a critic, such as Cowie, states that a gangster film works within a defined set of parameters what they are talking about is the parameters of the classic narrative, not the genre as a whole. The intention of this account of the gangster genre is to question the view that it can be understood simply as a set of conventions created in the early 1930s which are then replicated or slightly varied during the course of its 70-year history. Adopting this latter position produces a host of difficulties in the study of the genre, the least of which is that the pre-sound gangster film is ignored or regarded as a 'precursor' to the gangster genre proper (Neale, 2000: 79). The major difficulty is that the variety and flexibility of the manifestations of the gangster genre are repressed in taking the view that the gangster film simply maps an obligatory set of iconographies (the city, guns, technology, sharp suits, the speakeasy), ideological frameworks (the inversion of the American Dream) or narrative structures (the rise and fall of the gangster). If the 'rise and fall narrative' is a necessary requirement for a film to enter the genre, then the first two parts of *The Godfather* trilogy are not strictly gangster movies.

The approach taken here seeks to redress this position, albeit offering the same kind of selective process that Neale identifies in his criticism of accounts which focus on the classic narrative at the expense of other variations. In order to do justice to as many texts as possible while also retaining a sense of the historical development of the genre, some areas have received more attention than others. This study of the genre also rather unfairly neglects the silent gangster movie while 'couple on the run' movies also do not receive much attention, principally because it is felt that they are closer in spirit to the road movie in their concerns but also because there is a question as to whether a couple constitutes a gang. The overall aim, however, has been to offer as wide-ranging an account as possible in order to draw attention to the variety and mut-ability of the gangster genre without falling into the trap of simply cataloguing every different type of gangster film or crime cycle. The position taken here is that although the gangster film may share a set of iconographic features and narrative patterns these are multiple and cannot be reduced to those found in the classic narrative. The approach to genre, as an abstract form, is that rather than being a structure of identifiable patterns with one iconographic, ideological, and narrative framework, is that it is best understood as a field of operations which makes available a range of textual tropes, semiotic codes and narrative patterns and that it is a site of possibility or a space that allows things to happen, rather than a reified codification of delimited conventions. Thus, this account is not an attempt to identify a single dominant theme which characterises all gangster films, but an attempt to study the variety and flexibility of the gangster form. *American Gangster Cinema* explores the development of the post-sound gangster genre through its many incarnations and asks whether the gangster film can be seen as a unitary genre or whether it should be treated as a set of variations or sub-genres. While it may have certain thematics, such as the relationship between the individual and society, industrialisation and the experience of everyday life in modernity and postmodernity, concerns with spatiality and territorialisation (both of physical territory and of screen space), as well as wider cultural concerns with masculinity, identity, and power, the variations within it do not always utilise iden-tical thematic articulations nor adopt the same ideological and narrative patterns as all the other variations or sub-genres.

The genre can seen as analogous to a Venn diagram with both areas of overlap and areas of distinctiveness and it is the aim of this study to draw attention to both aspects in the study of the gangster film's generic development. In this respect, the intention is to envision the gangster genre as having the same flexibility and variety in its manifestations as Cowie identifies with *film noir*, a flexibility that expresses the transforma-tive qualities of the genre as it responds to shifts in historical, cultural, and production paradigms over the course of its history. The approach taken here also partakes of unashamed textual analysis, seeking to ana-lyse specific manifestations of the genre in order to not only avoid falling into the trap of imposing a restrictive and unworkable taxonomy on to resistant texts but also to study specific film texts as a way of highlighting their concerns and how they encapsulate, vary or contravene the param-eters of the genre as a whole, the sub-genre they operate within, the culture they refract, and the matrix of their production. *American Gangster Cinema* thus has as a particular concern the range of meanings that gangster movies put into circulation and the tensions that are created in their variation or re-definition, particularly how these tensions operate within textual manifestations and in their cultural and social articulations. Chapter 1 locates the early sound gangster film within the context of a dramatisation of modernity and its tensions, not only the contradictions of modernity as a space of both constraint and liberation, but also as the genre maps the tensions between the persistence of re-sidual ideology and the modern transgressions that threaten the stability of social hierarchy. This dialectic is not only mapped within the film texts, but also in the production process in the prohibitions imposed on the gangster genre by both the studios and the Production Code Adminis-tration which can be seen as attempts to censor both the representation and embrace of modernity that the excess of the gangster movie seemed to articulate. Chapter 2 explores the post-Code gangster film in the 1930s, after the Hays Office moratorium on gangster movies in 1935, exploring the ideological flexibility the genre displayed in response to its censorship while also identifying the textual variation of the genre in its first post-'classic' phase. The chapter argues that the late 1930s is not a period of derivative replication, as has often been argued, but one that foregrounds the fact that not only is the 'classic' cycle not the only incarnation of the gangster genre, but that its succeeding phases cannot be understood solely within the generic parameters it apparently embodies. The late 1930s, despite, or because of, uncertainties over the options available to the gangster genre can be seen as a period of experimentation and one that carries forward into the 1940s as new variations and sub-genres develop either in response to changing patterns of production or cultural transformations. Chapter 3 covers the period of the 1940s in the fractur-ing of the genre and its development of new variations such as the 'death of the big shot' formula, a continuation of the cycles and sub-genres created in the late 1930s in, for example, the Cain and Abel, social gangster, or G-Man variations.

Chapter 3 forms an interface between the pre-war and post-war incar-nations of the gangster genre and traces the changing function of the gangster and the gang as the genre responds to cultural circulations of ideology, particularly the paranoias over the death of the individual that are found in the early post-war gangster cycles: gangster *noir*, the heist movie, and the syndicate film. Chapters 4 and 5 explore these new variations or sub-genres as they articulate this issue in the context of contradictory fears over both the systematisation and corporatisation of society represented by the 'rackets' (gangster *noir* and syndicate) and the simultaneous fragmentation of everyday life (the heist film). Chapter 4 focuses on *noir* inflections of the gangster genre and investigates articulations of masculinity and their perversion as well as the perceived critique of capitalism in its corporatised or rationalised versions that this particular sub-genre seems to offer. Whether this critique is of capitalist economics and ideology as a whole is open to question, not least because many *noir* films identify corporatism as a perverted form of capitalism (for example, the much cited anti-capitalist *Force of Evil*) with the result that they adopt, even if inadvertently, a nostalgic bourgeois recuperation of capitalist production in its classic forms. The same tendency can be seen in the syndicate film in the 1950s, which is discussed alongside the heist movie in Chapter 5, but which in the context of both the McCarthy and Kefauver hearings, is also refracted through wider paranoias about secret organisations (both Communist and criminal) which produces a multiform gangster sub-genre that articulates a range of cultural meanings. The syndicate movie and the heist movie, however, represent antithetical visions of society. Although both shift attention away from the individual gangster hero, effectively making the 'gang' the main character in their narratives, they do so with different perspectives, the one suggesting a society dominated by systems and restrictions, the other a fragmented culture of nomadic and empty individuals cut adrift from social structures.

The contradictions found within the syndicate and heist variations foreground the fracturing of the gangster genre's ideological and iconographic operations, a process that is exaggerated in the post-classical and postmodern phases of the genre which are explored in the final two chapters. Chapter 6 covers the period of the 1960s and 1970s from the cycle of nostalgic biopic films that ended the 1950s and began the 1960s to the creation of a new wave of gangster films in the early 1970s, tracing the way in which films of the period utilised existing conventions either as part of a renewal of the genre in their articulation within new ideological, cultural, or narrative forms or as part of what might be considered a nascent postmodern replication of generic codes. That gangster films in the period of the 1960s and 1970s often present both replication and revision within the same film text (for example, *The St Valentine's Day Massacre*) generates an ambiguous dialectic that places this phase of the genre interestingly between a modernist avant-garde aesthetic and a postmodern loss of critical distance. The final chapter covers the period from the 1980s to the end of the 1990s with particular attention given to the resurgence of the gangster movie at the beginning of the 1990s. The chapter loosely articulates its concerns under the rubric of the postmodern gangster film, but also covers alternative textual practices and perspectives such as, for example, the urban realism of the 'gangsta' film. The purpose is to trace both the conflicting responses to contemporary culture and the fragmentation of the genre in a period of generic hybridity, concluding with the question whether the gangster genre has reached a point where it can still be said to display generic distinctiveness in the identifiable form of the postmodern gangster film or whether it blurs into the generality of postmodern film in the mixing of codes and collapse of generic boundaries.

1
Modernity and the Classic Gangster Film

Silent and early sound contexts for the 'classic' cycle

Although the classic gangster cycle of *Little Caesar*, *The Public Enemy*, and *Scarface* was initiated with *Little Caesar* in 1931 it did not spring into life fully formed, like Athene out of Zeus' head. The gangster genre already had a history by 1931, not only in silent and sound cinema, but also in the theatre. One reason for the rise of the gangster film was the popularity of gangster dramas on Broadway from 1927 onwards which provided ready-made scripts for Hollywood during its flurry of gangster activity between 1930 and 1932. The silent era was not without its interest as far as the gangster genre was concerned, most notably producing *The Musketeers of Pig Alley* (D. W. Griffith, 1912), generally regarded as the 'first genre-oriented gangster film' (Everson, 1998: 227), *The Gangsters and the Girl* (Thomas Ince, 1914), *Regeneration* (Raoul Walsh, 1915), *Underworld* (Josef von Sternberg, 1927) and *The Racket* (Lewis Milestone, 1928).[1] Most of these films, however, narrativise their gangsters within the frame of Victorian melodrama with its easily identifiable moral categories and gender constructions (the male villain and the duped female victim). *The Musketeers of Pig Alley* is a good example of this with a plot that involves a gangster, the Snapper Kid (Elmer Booth), attempting to corrupt the virtuous Little Lady (Lillian Gish) by tempting her away from the husband who has left her, in order to make his fortune out of town, with the promise of a life of pleasure (exemplified by the 'Gangster's Ball') that his criminal earnings can give her. The film represents him as a parasite, not only in his approaches to the abandoned Little Lady and in his mock chivalry at the gangster's ball, but particularly in the fact that the money which he uses to tempt Little Lady away from honest toil is stolen from her musician husband on his return. The

Snapper Kid leaches off official society, but the film is muted in its criticism of him in that he escapes punishment for the theft of the money, is given an alibi for the gang war in which he is involved and is finally even rewarded for allowing Little Lady and her husband to keep the money he has stolen by being given a wad of banknotes by a hand that mysteriously appears from offscreen. Despite its attempt to portray the reality of crime in the slums, with its authentic locations (albeit confined to one alley) and its representation of gangs, gang warfare, and corrupt police, the film is thus quite artificial in its narrative structure and retains its basis in melodrama. The Snapper Kid, however, is quite a modern looking gangster, in his sharp suit, particularly in comparison to other figures in the film who look as if they have stepped off a Victorian stage, whether it is the frock coated husband or the snarling gangster thugs; while, ideologically, Little Lady could be any virtuous hardworking damsel in distress from the theatre.

Raoul Walsh's *Regeneration*, one of the first full length gangster films, is another interesting blend of old fashioned melodrama and modern values. The former is present in the clear opposition between good (the virtuous Marie) and evil (the unrepentant gangster Skinny) and in the film's narrative of redemption while the latter can be seen in the way that the film attributes criminality to a social environment of deprivation, indicated in the opening scenes that show a world of tenements, poverty, drunkenness, and people wearing rags for clothes. Within this, the film traces the creation of a gangster, Owen Conway (Rockliffe Fellowes), and his redemption through contact with the saintly Marie, blurring the melodramatic oppositions even while it works within the melodrama's generic conventions. Conway is neither good nor evil, and although he is designated as a gangster he is not shown committing any acts of criminality beyond street fighting. He is represented more as a street tough who spends his time drinking and gambling, an indigent waiting to be saved. Indeed, his potential for 'regeneration' is shown throughout the film not only in a series of chivalric acts where he either rescues children or saves underdog characters from a beating, but also in a scene in a music hall where the image of him as a child eating an ice cream is transposed over an image of him drinking a glass of beer. This not only indicates the innocence he has lost but also that he can return to this state of grace, something the the film maps as Marie's love for him draws him away from crime. Despite a lapse into gang life when he protects Skinny from discovery by the police (which is actually the result of his sense of honour for a debt he owes), he is redeeemed when he refuses to kill Skinny in revenge for the death of Marie. With this ending the film reverts to a melodramatic ideology of heroism , a reversion which is also seen narratively in the race-against-time finale as Owen and the police try to rescue Marie from the clutches of the villainous Skinny.

Many silent gangster films shared this opposition between the melodramatic and the modern and even as late as Josef von Sternberg's *Underworld* in 1927 the same process can be seen at work. The film follows the life of gang boss Bull Weed (George Bancroft) and his relationships with his flapper moll, Feathers (Evelyn Brent), and a down at heel lawyer he befriends and nicknames 'Rolls Royce' (Clive Brook) because of the associations of class that attach to him. The film has many modern elements in representations of speakeasies, nightclubs and gang rivalries but mixes these with elements that are either anachronistic (the rather fanciful Gangster's Ball), stylised (the artificial settings of the film) or which mimic *Regeneration*'s invocation of the conventions of melodrama, such as Bull's final redemption. There is also an opposition between the illegitimate gangster and his legitimate friend which forms an easy identification of good and evil, not only for the audience but for the character of Feathers who chooses the upright Rolls Royce over the criminal Bull Weed, a choice that also maps a class based designation of morality and immorality typical of melodrama where the former is associated with the bourgeoisie and the latter with the working class. The film, however, partially blurs these categories in showing the apparently upright Rolls Royce working for a mobster, firstly by sweeping floors in a night club and then later as a frontman for Bull's organisation. The film also reverses *Regeneration*'s melodrama narrative by showing the love of the gangster moll rescuing the middle class Rolls Royce from this environment, a union that is legitimated not by conventional morality but by the gangster Bull who, at the end of the film, allows the two to escape rather than exacting vengeance for what he perceives as an act of betrayal, although this act still works within bourgeois morality because it signals Bull's redemption in sacrificing himself in order to allow Feathers and Rolls Royce to escape from a police raid on his hide-out. Similarly, despite realising the error of his ways, the film ends with Bull being taken off to be punished by death for his crime of murdering rival gang boss, Buck Mulligan.

Although strongly based in melodrama, gangster films of the silent era had an impact on the sound gangster film, not only in their urban setting but also thematically in motifs such as the gangster as both hero and villain (*Regeneration* and *Underworld*), the undercover narrative (*The Gangsters and the Girl*), and the cops-and-robbers formula (*The Racket*). Similarly, individual films also directly influenced later sound incarnations of the genre: *The Roaring Twenties* shares the same romantic narrative as *Underworld* while the narrative of the saintly woman redeeming the gangster can be seen in films such as *Johnny Eager* and *Force of Evil*. Early examples of the sound gangster movie also tended to retain the silent era's melodramatic structures, but developed a more distinctive form for the genre because they more clearly placed themselves within a modern industrialised urban world. The addition of sound is key in the development of the genre because the diegetic sounds of gangster language, gunshots, and the screeching of tyres, as well as the background noises of the city environment, more fully evoked the modern world that the gangster inhabited than the dark backstreet slums of the silent gangster film. The addition of sound also meant that there was no need for dialogue to appear on screen with the effect that editing and action in the gangster genre could move more quickly from shot to shot and scene to scene, establishing a faster pace for the narrative that more fully evoked the pace of modern society. Of particular importance to the sound gangster film is the noise of the gunshot. Silent movies had guns but could not effectively represent the power or menace of the gangster because they could only show that a shot had been fired in the image of the ballooning puff of smoke appearing from the barrel of the gun. Ironically, it is the addition of sound to the rendering of violence that created the gangster as a film spectacle and represented his uncontainability within the ideological structures of reform and redemption mapped in the silent gangster melodrama. The gangster's transgressive and excessive elements are more immediately evoked in the sound era and he comes to be an embodiment of the threat of the modern, not only in the literal threat of the violence of the gun, but in his mobility, which challenged the established hierarchies that the ideological messages of the sound gangster film often tried to defend. In this respect, the gangster is a seminal figure in modern cinema not only because he embodies modernity but also because the gangster film becomes a site for a set of tensions that have dominated the twentieth century. Firstly, the gangster film articulates power relations in terms of the individual's relation to society, particularly the opposition between tradition or residual ideology and social change, in which the gangster becomes a figure who dramatises fears of social anarchy and fragmentation in the perceived paranoia over the liberation of the individual and desire through new labour patterns and forms of consumption. Secondly, in their ideological attempt to repress the modern desires and freedoms that the gangster symbolised, the studios (particularly through the Production Code) inadvertently helped to foreground the tension between residual ideology and contemporary change enacted in modernity. As a consequence of this, the gangster film became the site of opposing ideologies, one nostalgic evoking order, hierarchy, and discipline (and represented by the family), the other foregrounding the excess and chaos of modernity (represented by the gang).

The reason the films of the classic cycle are so important in the early development of the gangster genre is that they establish these contradictions and tensions more fully than other early sound examples, such as *Alibi* (Roland West, 1929), *Doorway to Hell* (Archie Mayo, 1930) and *Quick Millions* (Rowland Brown, 1931). Outside the classic gangster narrative, the gangster film tended to re-iterate the melodramatic form and ideology of the silent gangster film. *Alibi*, for example, directed itself toward representing its unrepentant gangster as obviously 'unmanly' in the cowardice he displays at the end of the film. Nor does *Alibi* offer a convincing modern setting for its representation of crime because, apart from one street scene showing a robbery and numerous scenes of night club acts, it articulates its vision of the gangster world as one that predominantly takes place in tastefully decorated art nouveau drawing rooms. *Doorway to Hell* and *Quick Millions* are more authentically located within an urban setting and a gangster world of racketeering, but they too envisage the triumph of ideology and hierarchy as opposed to the classic gangster's unrepentant illegitimacy. Both films focus on the desires of their heroes, Louis Ricarno (Lew Ayres) and Bugs Raymond (Spencer Tracy) to assimilate, the former through his desire to retire and through the gentlemanly education he gives his brother and the latter by assimilating into high society through marriage. In both cases, although the films more obviously focus on the modern world and its technology (cars and Tommy guns), modernity itself is perceived as a chaotic place to escape from into the stability of legitimate society and the fact that the gangsters have helped to create the urban anarchy they seek to escape implies their repentant realisation of the error of their ways.

The 'classic' cycle in its critical context

Despite these early versions of the gangster genre, critical discussion of the 'classic' cycle of *Little Caesar*, *The Public Enemy* and *Scarface* has often seen them not only as a dominant early variation of the gangster film but as a defining moment which created the rules, conventions, and iconography of the genre as a whole. The classic gangster movie becomes an 'ur-text' for all other gangster movies and later films either replicate its themes, iconography, and ideology or they are deviations away from the gangster norm and thus not properly within the gangster genre (Shadoian, 1977: 18). A counter position to the dominant view articulates the classic formula as a variation not a dominant because it locates the classic style within the Hollywood production process which released films in terms of 'cycles', not genres.[2] Maltby, for example, sees the gangster film not as a genre but as 'what the production industry understood as a cycle... the product of a single season (1930/31) and [which], at least, within the industry's operating definitions, comprised no more than 23 pictures' (1995: 111). Despite this view of the classic narrative as a cycle, criticism has still given it a privileged position in the genre's development because it is seen to define and shape the iconography of the genre. In this view, the classic cycle creates a generic taxonomy which is actually a product of the criticism that privileges its position. Warshow's 'The Gangster as Tragic Hero', which focused on films from the classic phase, has a particular place in the creation of a taxonomy for the genre and many critics have followed Warshow in identifying common themes within this period which have come to be seen as timeless dominants of the entire genre.[3] These major themes are: the dominant rise and fall narrative (Warshow, 1977); the gangster as a tragic figure trapped in an urban nightmare but who is also a mythic and archetypal figure living out of his time (Schatz, 1981); a dominant narrative opposition between the family (and its identification with the law) and gang (and its transgressions against official society) in which the Oedipal narrative is reworked through the killing of the 'father' to produce improperly sexualised and socialised males (Gledhill, 1985); a historical basis in the society of Prohibition which is characterised by a cultural and ideological structure that mirrors and inverts the American Dream (Shadoian 1977; Rosow, 1978, Bergman 1992); and finally a clear iconography that makes a gangster movie easily recognisable (McArthur, 1972). The effect of presenting a taxonomy of the gangster genre based on the early classic films has thus had the effect of reducing it to a reified ahistorical system of conventions rather than a mutable and flexible form capable of changing in response to shifts in ideologies and social and cultural practices. Of particular importance in this reification is the paradoxical view that the classic gangster is both a mythic or archetypal figure and a product of a twentieth-century urban and capitalist environment.

   The tragic or mythic account of the gangster film was introduced by Warshow who argued that the gangster movie is tragic because, as Gledhill notes: 'its rise and fall structure contains within it the failure of the struggle for individual self-assertion with which we identify, but which we also know society cannot allow' (1985: 89). The gangster transcends existing economic conditions in achieving the American Dream in a perverted form but is brought down because his inversion of the American Dream is a challenge to official ideology. Like tragic heroes of old the gangster tries to achieve individuality (which American ideology promises its citizens) but is destroyed by a larger system (ideology itself) because his actions put a strain on this system. Schatz follows Warshow in seeing the gangster as a tragic figure but his view also attaches elements of the Epic to the gangster hero when he writes that the gangster's 'death is the consummate reaffirmation of his own identity' (1981: 90). Here the gangster is very similar to a Romantic hero who transcends the social order for a brief period and becomes archetypal because he refuses to bow down to the systems of law and ideology which ultimately destroy him. This position is ideological itself because it posits the myth of the 'subject-outside-history' in enunciating the idea that it is possible for a person to become a self-determined individual free from social constraint. That the gangster film ends with the death of the gangster, however, demystifies this ideology by giving proof that the gangster is a 'subject-inside-history' which is potentially the classic cycle's most radical and contradictory feature. In recuperating the legitimacy of the moral and legal order of society, the ideological demands of society – as expressed through their articulation within the Hollywood system of production – inadvertently foreground the mythic qualities of the self-determined 'subject-outside-history' by bringing him back inside social and historical constraints. This paradox can be seen in the critical accounts which focus on the historically specific period in which the gangster lived in their discussion of his embodiment of the American Dream, itself a product of modern industrialised society, but one which implies transcendence of social and historical forces. Rosow and Bergman both discuss the gangster movie in terms of the American Dream's myth of opportunity by mapping Andrew Carnegie's maxims about success and self improvement on to the gangster narrative while identifying the gangster as an illegitimate inversion (Rosow, 1978:28–9; Bergman, 1992:7–10). That the gangster embodies ideology locates him within history, but the illegitimate means he uses create the threat of an alternative cultural economy outside the parameters of historical action allowable by society.

The contradictions are particularly exposed in the oppositions between ideology and the gangster within the classic cycle. *The Public Enemy*, for example, is structured around a tension between the family and the gang, in which the family is coded as the norms of behaviour ideology finds acceptable but which are threatened by the desires unleashed by the gangster's involvement with the surrogate family of the gang. As a surrogate family the gang is also torn apart by the gangster's desires as he embarks on the road to money and power, often destroying the gang 'family' before he is destroyed by society. Tony Camonte in *Scarface*, for example, kills Guino Rinaldo, who has been his gang 'brother' throughout the film, before he too is killed by the police. The destruction of the family unit in the classic phase initiates an endless cycle of destruction of surrogate families and the descent into the chaos of gang war which is itself a conflict between 'families'. The gangster becomes a symbol of endless disruption and his actions re-define the family-gang opposition so that it also entails an opposition between tradition (residual ideology) and modernity (social change). The family is articulated in terms of old certainties, hierarchy and eternal values while the gang is coded as the permissive and licentious society allowable with the onset of an industrialised and capitalist modernity and the technologies and forms of consumption it makes available. This is often dramatised in terms of a tension 'between the old, agrarian European societies...and the heartless, wide-open world of the American city' (McArthur, 1997: 29). That this is a *tension* between history and modernity, rather than a displacement of the former by the latter, however, can be seen in *Scarface* in which Tony Camonte embraces the modern world with gusto but imposes the values and traditions of the family and community on his sister Cesca by attempting to refuse her a place in the permissive society he occupies. Narratively, therefore, the classic gangster film is located at the interface between traditional systems of restraint, discipline and hierarchy and the chaos and excess of modernity.

Little Caesar: an untypical 'classic'

Of the three major classic gangster films of the early 1930s *Little Caesar* best exemplifies these tensions at work. It is also the film that has most often been seen as paradigmatic in the creation of the classic gangster metanarrative, Shadoian commenting that it 'is to the gangster movie what *Oedipus Rex*, in Aristotle's analysis, is to Greek tragedy' (1977: 21). *Little Caesar* establishes the narrative of the rise and fall of a gangster, the Italian Rico Bandello (Edward G Robinson), beginning with his humble non-Anglo origins. The film also maps the gangster narrative in terms of the American Dream with Rico leaving the provinces, in true Horatio

Alger style, to make it in the big city where he will achieve, for a short time, the power and status he desires. He rises, through excessive violence, to the top of the gangster hierarchy, but causes his own downfall by turning on the best friend, Joe Masara (Douglas Fairbanks Jr), who he believes has betrayed him. The metanarrative that *Little Caesar* maps can be seen in the opening two scenes of the film which virtually form a microcosm of the paradigms of the gangster genre. The film opens in long shot showing a gas station with a car parked outside. Three shots are heard and two figures run to the car. The next scene takes place inside a diner and the film introduces the two characters who have just held up the gas station and presumably murdered someone. The two characters, Rico and Joe, discuss a newspaper item which leads the latter into a tribute to the pleasures of the city where money, clothes, dancing, and women can be found. Rico, however, is dismissive of such talk: 'Money's all right, but it ain't everything.' For him the city is the opposite of the small town, a place where power can be achieved and where 'nobodies' like themselves can 'be somebody, know that a bunch of guys will do anything you tell 'em, have your own way or be nothin' '.

These opening scenes set out several things that are paradigmatic within the critical metanarrative of the gangster genre. First, the gangster's desire for power is established as well as the violent means with which his power is achieved. Secondly, the gangster's immigrant background is set out as is his lack of opportunity within ideological parameters because of his immigrant status. Thirdly, the structural devices that are often present in gangster movies are also established here in Rico's relationship to Joe who has two functions in the film. Joe is the subservient male partner who accompanies the gangster on his rise (though this role is taken on later by Otero) but also has a more problematic role as the honest broker who either functions in direct opposition to the gangster as a representation of official ideology or as a 'fellow traveller' who wishes to escape the world of the gangster into the world of honest work, but is held to the gangster by loyalty or shared guilt. This latter aspect is not established immediately, but is implicit in Joe's view of what the city holds for them (legitimate success) and is soon put into practice when they reach the big city because while Rico goes in search of the nearest gang, Joe gets a job as a dancer in 'The Bronze Peacock'. The opening scenes also thus introduce the opportunities made available by modernity and the city, in opposition to the smalltown which is associated with parochial tradition and hierarchy. The film, however, problematises the metanarrative view of the gangster as an illegitimate incarnation of the American Dream, because Rico's desire for success is for power, not material gain, and because Rico is as disciplined as any honest worker in his route to the top, abjuring the pleasures that Joe embraces. His illegitimacy is in the excess he displays and in his use of violence, and not in his desire for success. Joe, as the 'honest broker' is as aberrant as Rico in his view of pleasure as a sign of the achievement of the American Dream and the film maps the paradoxical space of modernity in articulating their two visions of what it allows: success (the ideology of opportunity) and pleasure (modern licentiousness).

The relationship between Joe and Rico also establishes a further aspect of the gangster metanarrative in its representation of masculine bonding. The role of the male pair who spend more time with each other than with women generates a subtext of homo-eroticism that sets the gangster genre outside of the usual Oedipal trajectory. In *Little Caesar*, the relationship between Rico and Joe is frequently that of a couple and Rico's anger when Joe avoids the gang is more because Joe has found a new partner, Olga, than because Joe is being disloyal to the gang. As Shadoian suggests, however, the relationship between Rico and Joe is less explicitly erotic than that between Rico and Otero. When Rico has become a powerful figure Otero admires him in his new clothes and there is a scene after Rico has driven the rival gangster, Arnie Lorch, from town, where Rico lounges on a bed while Otero sings his praises. Otero then falls on the bed and although this signifies Otero's subservience the scene is also very obviously coded as an expression of his desire for Rico. Similarly, when Rico and Otero confront Joe over his betrayal it is Otero who tries to shoot him in order to eliminate his rival for Rico's love (Shadoian, 1977: 30). The male pair also functions in gangster films at a more mundane level to create a narrative around loyalty and betrayal, in which the gangster accomplice either dies with the gangster as an act of loyalty (*Invisible Stripes*), is killed by the gangster (*Scarface*), or betrays the gangster (*Angels with Dirty Faces*). *Little Caesar* creates two of these narratives: Otero dies out of loyalty, while Joe – through Olga, his dancing partner and lover – betrays Rico.

Little Caesar, however, is as untypical as it is typical. Little Rico is as aberrant as a gangster as he is as a citizen. Even in the gangster world he is an outsider. The opening scenes present Rico as a smalltown hood dreaming of glory and recognition but this is presented as radically different to the desires of the gangsters he finds in the big city. Rico is shown to be an outsider when he joins Sam Vettori's outfit because Vettori sees Rico as both provincial and outmoded in his violent impulses: 'No rods. That's old stuff.' In the scene where Rico tries to join

Vettori's mob, his marginality is represented by his position at the edge of the screen when he talks to a more centrally positioned Vettori but also occurs when he is introduced to the other members of the gang. The camera dollies and drops as it moves from one gangster to another while Vettori announces their names and although this is a version of the subjective camera in which the mob are introduced through Rico's eyes it also codes Rico as an outsider because he is outside the circle the gang make around the card table. He occupies no space on the screen and unlike Vettori, at this point, he has no control of the screen space, his inability to territorialise the screen a signal that he is a minor figure. The fact that Rico is effectively offscreen also codes Rico as different to the gang. Not only is he not an accepted member of the gang but also he does not share the same values or desires: they are content to be foot soldiers whereas Rico is not.

The representation of the gangster as untypical is compounded by the function of the gangs in the film. Although *Little Caesar* establishes the gangster motif of the division of territories and gang wars (the war over the Northside between Lorch and Vettori) the territories have already been carved up when Rico arrives in the big city and a sort of peace exists between the gangs and the police. In this, the film is untypical as is the fact that no references to bootlegging or protection rackets are made, a gangster motif principally established in *The Public Enemy*. The gangs of *Little Caesar* are gangs of robbers who perform heists and raids from behind their front organisations (a trope borrowed from the silent gangster film), all of which are under the central control of 'Big Boy'. In some respects this is typical of the cinematic gangster world, but the desire to maintain the peace is unusual. Vettori and Diamond Pete want to maintain the status quo, and avoid the celebrity status that Rico desires, because this would mean police interest in their affairs. Rico's desires for status and power however disrupt this equilibrium and code him as an aberrant gangster: he is represented as a force for chaos and excess whereas the gangs themselves represent restraint and discipline. The relationship of Rico to the gang, however, establishes one of the gangster film's dominant motifs. Rico is the individual gangster acting out his own desires in an unrestrained and excessive way in opposition to the gang system and its disciplining of individual desires. This is complemented by Rico's desire for celebrity status which figures the gangster movie as a world of excess characterised by display and spectacle, of which his violence is a part. From *Little Caesar* on the gangster film's protagonist is someone who not only makes violence a spectacle by turning it into a performance but who also displays the wealth and status that it provides. In wishing to remain in the shadows Arnie Lorch and Vettori are the aberrant gangsters and in his desire to display his status (as in the banquet in celebration of his success and when he walks the street to display his power) Rico becomes typical.

Rico's relationship with the gang also introduces issues of space and territory. Unlike *The Public Enemy* the gang in *Little Caesar* is not a masculine brotherhood where each man can rely on the other. It is a place of both adoration (Otero) and disloyalty (Pete) held together by Rico's command and not a compact and loyal organisation. Rico's impact on the gang creates this instability because he sees the gang simply as a group of people for him to control and who will provide the means for his advancement. Rico is a loner who, although he rises to control the gang through strength of will, is not fully part of it. This is represented in Rico's position in the streets of the city. Unlike Tom Powers in *The Public Enemy* Rico is ill at ease on the streets. While Tom Powers is a *flaneur* figure Rico is more comfortable in small rooms and protected places. Rico's world is a secret domain of back rooms and even the banquet scene, which Rico feels is public recognition of his power and status, takes place in a private room above the public space which is open to all. Rico is most often seen in small concealed rooms which are exclusive places signalling that a person is on the inside of the gangster power system, but they are also hiding places, fortresses protected from the outside that give the impression that Rico's power is very fragile. This is most obviously represented in the scene after the robbery of Lorch's club. The police arrive to question Vettori and Rico and the scene cuts between the outer office where the police interrogate the former and a secret room attached to it where Rico is seen with a gun and bag of money in each hand leaning towards the wall listening to what Vettori says. Rico is both protected by the room and trapped. He cannot come out into the 'public' space of the office but his access to the secret inner room symbolises his power and the fact that it is Rico who is in the inner sanctum, rather than Vettori, implies that he has already taken over the gang because Vettori is left outside to act as a foot soldier providing a buffer between the police and the gang leader.

Rico's occupation of the public space of the street, on the other hand, is characterised by tension. The street is where Rico is under threat, as when rival gangsters in a milk van attempt to shoot Rico with a machine gun. The film's ending represents this more obviously. At the flophouse where he ends up after his downfall, Rico is not really part of the crowd and, indeed, is represented as scruffier and drunker than the other hoboes while his walk through the streets after he has been goaded into revealing his whereabouts to Flaherty only shows how vulnerable he is. As he walks aimlessly around the streets a long shot reveals him to be a tiny figure against the vastness of the street space and it is on the streets where Rico dies, trying to hide behind the sign advertising Joe's first film, a poor defence that cannot substitute for the walls of the fortress space he usually occupies. It is in the ending that the film shows its uncertainties about Rico's status, in terms of both morality and power. Schatz writes that Rico's dying words ('Mother of Mercy, is this the end of Rico?') 'reflect our own disbelief that this heroic, willful, urban demigod ever could be destroyed' (Schatz, 1981: 87), implying that he has defied morality and controlled society. While Rico's death certainly represents his defiance at the hands of his nemesis (Flaherty) in true tragic form it also however sees him as a powerless figure, isolated and without a gang to protect him, a powerlessness made evident by his inability to force more than $150 out of the $10,000 he has entrusted to Ma Magdelena. In representing him as a tiny figure during his random walk along the streets he is seen as insignificant and coded in this sequence as a minor disturbance that the city has suffered rather than the big shot he thought he was: he did, after all, only control Northside and not the whole city. There are also questions around moral issues in Rico's death. Rico dies not for the moral education of the audience, as later gangsters were to die, but as an act of political expediency and revenge on the part of Flaherty. He is killed for his disruptive influence and his excessive behaviour, not for any moral reasons. Similarly, Joe goes unpunished for his part in the robbery and murder at the gas station at the beginning of the film and, although it might be said that he redeems himself by informing on Rico, Joe himself is unwilling to do this and it is Olga who actually denounces Rico to the police.

The gangster and modernity

Although *Little Caesar* can be seen as an articulation of the opposition between traditional ideologies and their dissolution in modernity, it also expresses the contradictions of modernity itself. The sign under which Rico dies is for a film called *Tipsy Topsy Turvy* and although its presence is a comment on Rico's rise and fall it can also be read as a comment on the turmoil of a modern society that has no conviction in its values, social structures, and ideologies. Modernity is not only fractured by the persistence of residual structures and ideologies into its own emergent social arrangements, but, as Berman has argued, is itself a cultural logic where nothing is stable (Berman, 1983). The cultural logic of modernity maps a tension between order and chaos, between liberalisation and control of desires and between excess and discipline.[4] Modernity developed out of the eighteenth century Enlightenment project which was primarily concerned with the liberation of knowledge from superstition and religion through the development of rationality and the consequent liberation of the individual through both knowledge of the world and through knowledge of the self. This would also lead to social liberation in which traditional forms of hierarchy and ideology (such as serfdom and religion) would be revealed to be irrational and new more rational forms of social and cultural structure would come into existence. This project, however, was troubled by the technological and economic changes that began in the nineteenth century in which industrial production moved to the division of labour in order to increase the output of commodities and thereby maximise a company's profits. The end result of this is the Fordist or Taylorist conveyor belt mode of production in the twentieth century in which specialisation becomes paramount and each worker performs only one function. This process of rationalisation created a social order in which workers became functional cogs in the machine of industrial production and which was extended through the twentieth century into social and cultural spheres, generating increasing fears over the loss of individuality. In modernity, the individual is simply one among many and the crowd, in which people are anonymous undirected atoms, becomes one of the defining images of modern experience. The individual is either randomly moving around space (as in a crowd) or directed within a system not of his or her own making (Fordist production). The paradox of modernity is that it encompasses a systematised economic life built on an ideology of freedom in which individual experience is actually one of fragmentation and alienation rather than structure, freedom or purpose. One of the key aspects of this experience is the city which encompasses these tensions. It is the place of industry and Fordist production, where dwellings are mass produced and 'echo machine production' (Jones, 1990: 72). The city, however, also allows an anonymity that provides more freedom than rural life and where the individual has more freedom to consume because the rationalisation of production has led to a greater number of products to choose from. The iconic figure of the modern city is the *flaneur*, the wandering citizen who moves freely about the urban landscape observing and mapping the city, its buildings, inhabitants, and culture.[5]

The city, the iconic space of modernity, is also the place of the gangster who, onscreen, finds himself to be part of the same tensions of modernity detailed above. The gangster movie is located in a city of the industrial and technological, where traditional morality has become lax or non-existent, where the pleasure-principle and an easier enactment of sexuality and desire are possible (as represented by the night club and the speakeasy), where rationalisation and routinisation are dominant motifs (in the systematisation of gang life into corporate structures and the routinisation of violence), and where commodities, consumerism and money form the desiring network in which the gangster locates himself. The gangster figure is characterised by an urge towards individual freedom and the fulfillment of his desires (through violence or consumption) and who not only moves around the city freely like the *flaneur* but who also controls territory rather than simply subjecting the city to his gaze. As a *flaneur* the gangster is a free-floating entity who lives his desires through the uncontrolled movement around both the city and the culture of modernity. An example of the gangster-as-*flaneur* is the figure of Tom Powers in *The Public Enemy* who, as a foot soldier, is most often presented moving around the city enforcing the gang's protection racket. He is represented as having the freedoms of the *flaneur*, most obviously presented in the scene when he tries out his new car and meets Gwen, who acts as a sexual object for him to observe. It is the lack of constraint that this mobile *flaneur* quality represents that signals the gangster's dangerous place in modernity as he comes to symbolise the unlimited and excessive modes of action and desire-fulfillment that modernity allows. The freedom of spatial movement also suggests his danger as his transgression of the physical boundaries is also coded as both freedom of movement around society and transgression of hierarchy. The gangster gives no acknowledgement to boundaries and his ease of access into the physical spaces of legitimate society and of the rich represent his cultural danger to fixed social structures.

Ultimately, although the gangster experiences freedom in his mobility around the cultural spaces of modernity he is also subjected to its controls, whether this is within the gang system or in his punishment by another gang or the police (usually resulting in his death) for the excessive freedom his uncontrolled desires have engendered. The gangster is effectively disciplined by the imposition of a constraining structure upon him, which introduces a key opposition that works as one of the underlying narrative engines in the classic gangster movie, but which also recurs at various points in the genre's history: the opposition between discipline and excess. An example of this at a textual level occurs in *Quick Millions* when Bugs Raymond has his bodyguard killed because he is excessively violent and has become a liability to the gang. It is not therefore just the police or the FBI that discipline the gangster. Self-discipline is a key element of the classic gangster movie and often works in conjunction with excess to create success for the gangster and the gang. For example, Tom Powers in *The Public Enemy* shows discipline in enforcing the gang's sales (with the act of enforcement itself being an act of discipline) but is excessive in the means he uses to effect this. The relationship between discipline and excess is founded in the opposition between the gangster's individual desire and society's attempt to curtail it, but it also entails the re-entry of socialised restrictions either in the form of the gang or in the gangster's own superego. The gangster film can thus be seen, in Freudian terms, as a site of struggle similar to that which occurs in the ego, between the desires of the id and the containing strategies of the superego, but mapped socially as well as in the psyche. The relationship between work and leisure figures strongly in the gangster movie, particularly in the refusal of official work sanctioned by ideology. The gangster creates an alternative economy of excess in which modernity's separation of work and desire (in the Fordist mode of production where the worker does not do what he desires but works for others' desires) is obliterated by the gangster. The gangster circumvents the rationalising systems that the official economy of American capitalism demands in labour and production and as such threatens the puritan work ethic of self-discipline and hard work even as he also enacts it in a criminal economy, but in a form of discipline that advances his own desires.

The Public Enemy: modernity, space, and masculinity

Although in production at the same time as *Little Caesar*, *The Public Enemy* (William Wellman, 1931) was released shortly after. It is often paired with *Little Caesar* in the study of the classical gangster movie but the two films are very different, not only narratively but also in visual style and in the representation of the cultural space the gangster inhabits. *Little Caesar*, despite such fast paced scenes as the killing of Tony and the heist, has a fairly static episodic narrative and is shot in a stilted, expressionistic style. In *The Public Enemy* the lighting is more naturalistic, the editing crisper and, although episodic overall, there is a stronger sense of continuity between scenes. *The Public Enemy* also has Jimmy Cagney in the role of Tom Powers and he provides a more human and vital gangster figure than Robinson's Rico with his performance helping to give the film a sense of movement and fluidity that *Little Caesar* doesn't have. Cagney's embodiment of the urban tough guy, in conjunction with Wellman's surer direction, means that the film is faster paced and has more striking and memorable scenes. These include one of the best remembered scenes in gangster cinema in which Cagney pushes a grapefruit in Mae Clarke's face but the film also has a host of others: the shooting of the horse that kills Nails Nathan, the machine gunning of Matt, the beer-keg on the family table after Mike's return from War, Tom spitting beer in a barman's face, his little dance of joy after arranging a date with Gwen (Jean Harlow), the image of Tom collapsing in the gutter after a shoot-out as the rain cascades around him, and the final scene in which, wrapped in bandages like a mummy or a baby, he collapses through the door of the family home. The film has an exuberance that is also absent from *Little Caesar* and more obviously embraces the modern society in which it is set, despite the more obvious presence of residual ideology in the form of Tom's family. The film can be seen as a clearer enactment of modernity, not only because it focuses on the cultural experiences of mobility, technology, and urban space, but also because it maps the tensions between residual hierarchy and ideological structures of stability and the emergent logic of transformation and contestation that characterise the modern period.

The film also differs from *Little Caesar* in its representation of a gangster who is more at home on the streets than in back rooms, expressed most notably when Tom is unable to remain restricted indoors, after his gang are force to hide out, and ventures forth into the street thus indirectly causing Matt's death. The street is the paradigmatic experience of modernity, a place of movement, change, and consumption, and *The Public Enemy*'s emphasis on the street as a site of narrative action expresses its embodiment of modern principles. Tom's ease with the streets also serves as the centre point for the film's narrative and ideological structure: the relationship between the family and the gang. *The Public Enemy* is the story of a foot soldier who finds liberation from the restrictive space of the home in his entry into the street-life of the gang. It is the street where the film starts in 1909, during Tom and Matt's youth as the two begin their road towards crime. The opening scene establishes the relationship between Tom and Matt: Matt wants a kiss from a girl while Tom wants to get to business. In the next scene they are seen running through a store with the watches they have stolen and sliding down the elevator rail to elude capture. This scene shows their facility in moving around the public spaces of the city, a motif that returns constantly throughout the film and is opposed to their uncertainties in closed spaces, as in the first robbery they embark on which

fails not only because they are inexperienced but also because they are
ill at ease in the restricted place of the interior of the fur warehouse. This
is not the case when they escape as they acrobatically slide down drain-
pipes, their ease in the open street signalled by Tom's killing of the beat
cop who is ostensibly the person appointed to control urban space. The
family narrative is introduced shortly after when Tom is strapped by his
father for his wrongdoings, an act that establishes the home as a puni-
tive place similar to a prison. Although the father does not reappear in
the film, his place is taken by Tom's older brother, Mike, who acts as the
ideal family man governed by morals and the work ethic in opposition
to the easy money and freedoms that Tom finds in the gang, in which
the family symbolises traditional ideologies and social structures and
the gang the uncontrolled culture of modernity which threatens to
displace them. The other part of the family narrative is Tom's mother
who is weak willed and indulgent towards Tom. Her presence in the film
also establishes Tom as someone who has not been properly socialised in
her continual references to Tom as her 'baby'. Tom's crime becomes
identified with immaturity and irresponsibility whereas Mike is identified with maturity and duty, an inflection that also ideologically represents modernity as a desiring economy based on childish feminine wish
fulfilment, while tradition and hierarchy are coded as rational masculine and mature.

Tom's position in the family, however, is complicated by the fact that
he has a criminal surrogate father in Putty Nose, a Fagin figure who
controls a group of young criminals and who helps plan the fur heist.
When it goes wrong, however, he flees town and leaves Tom and Matt in
the lurch, suggesting he is an inadequate father. Tom's relationship with
Putty Nose also establishes his relationship with gang-life, which, because of Putty Nose's aberrance, is typed as a deviant alternative to the
family. This is signalled not only by Putty Nose abandoning Tom and
Matt, but also by the homosexual connotations of Putty Nose's interest
in Tom. In the 1909 segment when Tom and Matt come to sell the
watches, Putty Nose tentatively strokes Tom's face which is coded as a
perversion of the masculine code of the gang, transforming its basis on
loyalty to one based on desire, one of many images in the film which, in
identifying the gang with modernity, enunciates both as uncontrolled
and dangerous places. Putty Nose also helps to show them their initial
powerlessness. When they return to the headquarters to find that he is
gone their position on the outside of the gang is indicated by the fact
that they are locked out and spoken to only by a face at the grille. In this
respect, the film signals that ability to move freely on the streets does

not bring power; power is only gained when you are part of the gang and are able to move freely between different spaces, to transgress boundaries as if there were no exclusion zones. This is signalled in the second, successful, heist which takes place in 1920 during Prohibition. In this raid Tom and Matt siphon alcohol out of kegs inside a warehouse and pump it through a pipe in the wall to a waiting gasoline truck. Gang life allows them to obliterate inside/outside barriers and use space as if there were no obstacles in their way. In the gangster film, as a whole, the ease with which barriers are transgressed is usually coded through the metaphor of the door of the speakeasy through which the gangster can pass easily but which, with its grille, acts as a barrier and a surveillance device for others. Spatiality has conventionally been a way of mapping social hierarchy in cities but in Tom's transgression of spatial boundaries the gangster becomes a paradigm for the threat to both existing social hierarchy and its physical territorial expressions. The breach of spatial power relations in the gangster film becomes more than just an act of crime because it represents the mobile transformative qualities of modernity which threaten to dissolve all ideology and hierarchy.[6] Tom's embrace of the gangster life can therefore be seen as an embrace of social change which, while it may transgress traditional morality and legality, is not itself a moral choice. It begins to take on the aspect of a cultural choice in his expression of modernity's new freedoms and in this respect Tom's danger is not his criminality, but his challenge to existing power structures in the release of his uncontrolled male desires into society.

Tom finds the gangster life to be one where he has freedom of movement, but this is juxtaposed to the life of the family and social ideology. In the form of Mike, the family has a patriarchal figure who represents official ideology and work. Mike has a job on the streetcars, works at night school, has a steady girlfriend, and volunteers to serve his country in World War One while Tom stays at home. He represents all that society desires of its citizens: he works hard and is restrained in his desires and behaviour. However, although Mike acts as the voice of restraint and discipline the film is not kind in its portrayal of him. Mike is a rigid figure and although he disciplines Tom at two points in the film by punching him to the floor, seemingly indicating his superior morality and masculinity, he comes off badly in comparison to Tom overall. He is the voice of tradition who has been left behind by modernity and his belief in the usefulness of education is debunked by Tom when he says that in going to night school Mike is 'learning how to be poor'. The scene where the opposition between the family and gang is made clearest in the film, but which also shows how alienated Tom is from the home, despite his mother's affections, is the beer-keg scene. The Powers' family have a dinner to celebrate Mike's return from the War to which Tom brings a keg of beer which throughout the scene looms large, placed as it is in the centre of the table. It not only draws attention to itself but because of its size is in everyone's direct eyeline and causes the characters to peer round it to talk to each other. It acts as a metaphor for the invasion of the home by the gangster world of bootlegging and crime and causes Mike to erupt in anger when Tom pours drinks from it. This, however, has as much to do with the fact that the beer-keg also acts as a metaphor for power and masculinity and Mike's anger is at the way in which his honest life of toil has effectively emasculated him while Tom's life of excess and crime has empowered and embodied him as a man because of his place within the gang's masculine brotherhood.

Gang life in *The Public Enemy* is made attractive because it offers this achievement of masculinity but also because its fluidity allows independence and freedom to live a life of excess. After the disaster of Putty Nose's gang Tom and Matt team up with Paddy Ryan, but his mob is a much more free floating arrangement than the usual gang. Where the rival gang of Schemer Burns is organised, Paddy Ryan's mob is part of an alliance with Nails Nathan which is represented as more an organisation of friends or a brotherhood than a hierarchy. The gang is much more flexible and does not depend on a rigid structure with a gang boss to be obeyed or supplanted. *The Public Enemy* therefore focuses on the everyday life of the enforcer rather than the rise to the top as in *Little Caesar* and *Scarface*. Although Tom is a foot soldier or henchman his life is one that is characterised by freedom of movement and action. Tom takes orders from Nails but there is little restraint or discipline involved meaning that Tom is content to remain a foot soldier because it brings him all the money, pleasure and action that he needs. Despite the fluidity of the gang, territory is still an issue and Tom principally acts as an enforcer in the gang, making sure that the local bars take Paddy's beer. Enforcement is, however, as much about lifting restrictions on the gang's freedom as it is about making money and helps to ensure that the gang can move freely around the space of the city. *The Public Enemy* has very few police officers and nothing like the Nemesis figure that *Little Caesar* has in Flaherty. The gangs are the law and their freedom of movement is virtually unopposed in the film with a particular emphasis on night clubs and speakeasies which metonymically represent the gangster's control of space. The control of space or territory is usually only temporary because the gang is not interested in carving out a territorial empire, with the result that control of space is strongly allied with the presence of the body of the gangster

Control of space becomes an expression of masculinity which becomes an index of identity in the film and its achievement is associated with creating a place for the self in society. Tom's murder of Putty Nose, for example, is an attempt to achieve an unquestioned masculinity. Nails has doubted Tom's ability and willpower because he has not punished Putty Nose for running out on him, but the murder of Putty Nose is also a way of exorcising the implications of homosexuality that Putty Nose represents. The murder therefore becomes a sign of masculinity as both a personal and public proof of virility. Tom must murder Putty as a spectacle of maleness, to prove to Nails that he is capable of being part of the brotherhood. Masculinity is measured by toughness and ruthlessness, but also measured by comparison to other members of the gang. As a contrast to Tom, Matt is less of a masculine force because he is an observer in the killing of Putty Nose, but also because of his romantic involvement with Mamie. Tom, on the other hand, uses women (Kitty and Gwen) to express his masculine control, although often this control is expressed more in terms of an excessive violence (as with the grapefruit scene) rather than sexually. This is particularly the case with Gwen with whom Tom has an unsuccessful relationship. Late on in the film Gwen offers him the chance to consummate their affair 'to please your boyfriends' (which also however implies a homosexual bond with the other gangsters) but Tom leaves before it can be taken further, forsaking pleasure for business. Gwen is simply a trophy for Tom, a sign of his virility even if the actuality is rather different.

The final scenes of the film bring home the relationships between masculinity and space. These scenes show the gang hiding out from Schemer Burns' mob, Tom and Matt leaving the hideout, Matt's death as he is pinned against a wall by a machine gun, Tom's revenge (in which Schemer Burns' mob is also presented as trapped, this time against the windows of a warehouse), and finally, the scene in the hospital where Tom comes to some form of repentance before being delivered home by the Burns' mob wrapped in bandages. In these scenes, the space of the city is presented more as a trap than a place of freedom, though in the case of the shooting of the Burns' gang, the warehouse into which they retreat is also a prison from which they cannot escape, rather than a fortress. Here, Tom's penetration of their sanctuary involves a control of space that creates him as a heroic masculine figure, an effect that is reinforced, rather than questioned, when he re-appears staggering along the gutter only to collapse saying 'I ain't so tough'. This is an ambivalent statement that both questions Tom's masculinity but also affirms it in the context of what he has just done. Tom's audacity in going alone into a rival gang's headquarters signals the all or nothing philosophy of excess that has allowed him to take control of his environment but which also ultimately brings about his death. The energy and pleasure he has invested in his life of crime, however, is taken away from him once he has been shot and the scene in the hospital, which is also metaphorically a hideout, shows how restricted he is. The injuries and bandages are coded as curtailments of his freedom of movement and it is this that finally causes his death. He is unable to resist being kidnapped by the remainder of the Burns' gang and the final scene is of Tom, still just alive but unable to move, falling forward on to the floor with a look of horror in his eyes. He dies because he is no longer able to control his movements and is unable therefore to perform the acts of excess that his body allows him and which created him as a masculinised gangster. Cagney's body, its dynamic movement and controlled self-expression even in the acts of excess that Tom performs, has been the key reason for the success of Tom as a gangster and audience identification with him. This final scene, in which Tom is wrapped up like a mummy or a baby, represents a complete loss of power and dignity as Tom is utterly incapable of expressing the energy that has characterised his movement throughout the film.

The gangster and the gang

In *The Public Enemy* the gang becomes a metaphor for the opposition between modernity and residual ideology in its ability to offer the freedoms that the latter, in the form of the family, cannot. The gangster film, however, does not only map the relationship between system and individual in the gangster's relationship to the ideologies of official society, but also in his relation to the gang. As a gangster (an individual) he is represented floating free of social restrictions and expressing his desires amid the licence that modernity allows. The gang, however, relocates the gangster within a structure that controls his actions even while it gives him the power to express his desires. The gang can be a stifling power structure, as in the hideout where Tom finds it difficult to obey the gang chain of command with the result that he flees its restrictions, and there is an implication that the gangster escapes official systematisation in the Fordist workplace only to find it in the alternative economy of the gang and can only finally overcome it by taking control of the gang. The gang of the 1930s reflects the prevailing ideology of the

American Dream and its liberation of the individual, but removes it from being simply ideological and allows its enactment. The tension between freedom and control and individual and system return however, even in the gangster's success, because the gangster's desire for power is also an impulse towards rationalisation which causes him to rely on the gang structure he has created rather than on his own wits or power of will. The gangster requires an organisation to control this territory (to ensure his freedom of movement within this space), but finds that this both curtails freedom outside the territory and ensures the further dependency on structures of power that in the end confine him. The gang boss becomes so invested in the gang that he effectively becomes its system while the gang thus becomes a kind of fortress to protect the boss. The rise of the gangster is accompanied by an increasing prevalence of fortifications, an example of which occurs in *Scarface*. While he is just an ordinary gangster Tony Camonte is able to move around on his own with only his gun and his friend, Guino, for company. On becoming boss, however, he has to live in a fortified apartment or take his protection with him in the form of a steel body car with bulletproof glass for protection. His appearances in public are in the company of a phalanx of bodyguards, a mobile wall that acts metonymically as an image of fortification as, for example, when he is shot at in the night club scene where he takes Poppy away from Lovo.

The notion of control of territory is itself an important aspect of the classic gangster film. A twofold territorialisation develops in the classic gangster film, firstly the territorialisation of physical space (the city) and, secondly, of the screen. Battles for control not only take place in terms of how much territory the gangster controls and how easily he moves around in this space (and how many places are restricted because they are controlled by rival gangs), but also in how the gangster controls the screen. In the example of the night club scene from *Scarface*, given above, Tony takes control of space because he effectively territorialises the screen. This scene is a culmination of a battle for control over Poppy, who as the boss' girlfriend becomes the symbol or trophy to be possessed by the person who has the most power. Earlier in the film there is a scene when Tony, still a foot soldier, reports to Lovo in his apartment. The apartment has two rooms, one in the foreground – the main room where Tony and Lovo transact their business – and one in the background – an inner room separated off from the main room by an arch, in which Poppy is sitting at a dressing table making herself up. It is also the place where Lovo keeps his cash, thus associating Poppy with the money that power brings. The relations of power in this scene are represented by the fact that Lovo is able to enter the back room while Tony is not, so that the inner room also becomes coded as an inner sanctum of power, a territory that only the boss controls. Power is represented in terms of territorialisation of the screen which is further developed during an ensuing conversation in the outer room. At this point, Tony and Lovo are seated across from each other with Poppy in the background between them. Poppy is here represented at the centre of a tug of war, the trophy that the two are struggling to possess because Poppy is coded by the image as also representing control of the gang. That the two are seated opposite each other with Poppy in the centre also indicates that a turning point has been reached. Lovo is currently in charge but their equality in this scene in which neither are in control of the screen indicates that Tony has reached a point of equality with Lovo which will soon lead to his taking complete control. Poppy in the middle represents the trophy that will be won and which neither are fully in control of at this moment. In the nightclub scene, the ease with which Tony interposes himself between Lovo and Poppy when he sits at their table indicates how completely he is in control. He dominates the scene by his centrality (and by his extrovert nature) and completes the territorialisation of the screen that was begun earlier.

Scarface: everything to excess

Although *Scarface* (Howard Hawks, 1932) is part of the early gangster cycle it is more like *The Roaring Twenties* than *Little Caesar* and *The Public Enemy*, in that it is a summation of gangster concerns rather than a groundbreaking film. *Scarface* has everything that previous gangster movies has, but more of it. It is the epitome of excess even down to the number of people killed in the film, as Ben Hecht, the screenwriter, is reported to have said: 'In one [gangster] film, nine people were bumped off, so I went to Howard and said, We're going to kill 25 people' (Dargis, 1996: 16). The film also aroused particular concern from the Hays Office because of its excess and helped to bring the classic cycle to an end.[7] It also combines the family narrative, through the incestuous relationship between Tony Camonte (Paul Muni) and Cesca (Ann Dvorak), with the rise and fall narrative and includes virtually all the gangster tropes established in the earlier classic gangster films. Tony's rise to power is accompanied by more violence than Rico's rise, associated in the film with the use of Tommy guns, and his rise is both graphically symbolised and ironised by the Cook's tour sign: 'The World is Yours', under which he dies at the end in the same way that

Rico dies under the sign for Joe's movie. The film also has the gangster's long-time friend, 'Little Boy' Rinaldo (George Raft), whose romantic involvement with Cesca inadvertently brings about the downfall of Tony and whose coin-flipping introduced a much copied routine. There is even a policeman taking on the role of Nemesis, similar to Flaherty in *Little Caesar*.

The film begins in iconic style with the murder of Big Louie Costillo by Tony on Johnny Lovo's orders. The film is mainly about the rise and fall of Tony, but this scene shows that there are two rise and fall narratives in the film, already more of everything. Tony's rise and fall is preceded by Lovo's, a narrative structure that creates internal correspondences (and a sense of cyclical recurrence) which are also matched thematically as in the use of the air from *Lucia di Lammermoor* that Tony hums when he murders both Costillo and Lovo. *Scarface* also opens iconically with the image of Big Louie sitting among the detritus of a party he has just thrown telling his henchmen how he wants to hold another party next week to share the rewards of the rackets around, a party that will be bigger and have 'Much more everything'. The gangster life is immediately associated with an economy of excess, in this case pleasure, which, however, is replaced very soon after by an economy of violence. Violence is introduced in its most iconic form as the shadow of Tony Camonte, gun in hand, advances on Costillo while he makes a telephone call off-screen: shots are heard and then the thud of Costillo's body as he falls to the floor. This iconic portrayal of violence continues throughout the film, becoming ever more excessive. The violence is principally shown in montage form including sequences showing Tony the enforcer, roughing up saloon owners, undertaking a drive-by bombing, and taking part in a shoot-out at the Shamrock club. The montages are also associated with the Tommy gun which symbolises excess and violence in the film, firstly in a montage of a calendar changing dates to the sound of a Tommy gun and secondly in a montage of mobile violence, in which cars are used in a form of street tank warfare with machine gunners firing at random. The Tommy gun also has a metonymic value, being so closely associated with Tony that the sight of Tommy gun also suggests Tony's presence even if he is not seen, as with the St. Valentine's Day Massacre. Tony, thus, becomes a thing rather than a person, his drive for power a product of the objects he uses, and in this he is a summation or parody of the gangster figure, driven on unstoppably by a larger force which he also embodies. Excessive violence, however, is not just the domain of the gangster. The final scenes in which Tony and Cesca are trapped in Tony's fortified apartment show an excessive police presence with cars and officers swarming outside all to capture one man and his sister. The success that Tony achieves through excess becomes a model for society as a whole, therefore, and what was previously aberrant has by the end of the film become normalised.

Scarface can therefore be seen as a parody as well as a summation, gestured in the first scenes where Tommy guns are used. When Tony gets his first Tommy gun he reacts with joy because the Tommy gun will decide who gives the orders and he then leaves to 'write [his] name all over town with it'. There is a comic element to this which has been seen in the previous scene in which Tony and Poppy are under attack in a restaurant. Rather than hiding from the Tommy guns, a laughing Tony takes pleasure from their power and tries to peer over the window sill to see them in action instead of cowering under the table with the others. Technology also forms part of the parodic text in the film, not only in Tony's excessive embrace of the Tommy gun but also in the use of cars in the form of Tony's bullet-proof car. The love of technology entails an embrace of modernity but it is also a parody of the pleasures of modernity. This is compounded by the humour of the consumption scenes in *Scarface*, which offer an excessive version of the iconography of gangster consumption, going beyond just buying a sharp suit, as Munby notes (1999: 56). Once he has effectively displaced Lovo, Tony is shown winning Poppy's affections through his successful acts of consumption. In the first consumption scene Tony is seen in a new suit showing off his jewellery to Poppy as he describes his new car which has bullet proof glass and a steel body. Poppy describes Tony's new look as 'kinda effeminate' but this feminine form of consumption (the concern with looks and style) is juxtaposed to the ultra-masculine consumption signified by the new car, a boy's dream of a car.[8] In the second scene, which takes place in the fortified apartment, Tony in a dressing gown points, in the style of Gatsby, to a pile of shirts and says that he is only going to wear each shirt once. These are fantasies of consumption but, through Tony's gauche eagerness and his lack of awareness of the vulgarity of his desires, they are presented comically. Tony's acts of consumption also become metaphors for the collapse of value associated with modernity, of which Tony's lack of taste and his association of money with class are symptomatic. The collapse of value is further identified with excess, particularly the destructiveness of the excessive behaviour that modernity encourages. Tony's excessive behaviour is not confined to consumption but also includes violence and as such the embrace of modernity is represented as so full blown and exaggerated in the form of Tony that it not only becomes parodic but also dangerous. There is no restraint at all, and it is excess that in the end causes Tony's death. He is too ready to use his gun causing him to shoot Rinaldo without bothering to find out the truth of Rinaldo's relationship with Cesca (that they are married). This act causes his downfall and is symptomatic of his excessive desire: his desire for absolute obedience and control which is also an act of enforcing discipline on others.

Tony's desire for everything is also manifested in the gang wars that take place in the film, first of all with O'Hara and secondly with Gaffney (Boris Karloff). Lovo warns Tony not to enforce the gang's rule in O'Hara's territory, but Tony ignores him and takes 'business' into the Northside. This trespass has two effects. Firstly, it is an act of excess and lack of restraint that will cause a gang war and secondly it is a threat to Lovo's power as head of the gang. Tony has transgressed in two ways and threatened the stability of two power structures: the internal power structure of the gang and the spatial power structures of territory. In one act Tony has expressed his unlimited desire for more: more power, more violence, more territory. Tony's expansiveness is juxtaposed in the gang war with Gaffney's restrictedness. Although Gaffney is the first to use Tommy guns, he is fighting from a defensive position and this is indicated when he is first introduced. Whereas Tony is represented as having the freedom to move (not just in the city, but within the frame of the screen) Gaffney's first appearance is in a compacted crowded space. He is seen in a warehouse but despite the implied size of this space and despite his central position within the frame of the screen Gaffney, surrounded by henchmen, is both crowded out of the space of the screen and made to seem less central and less imposing. By the end of the gang war, however, Tony (as has been mentioned above) is as restricted in his movements as Gaffney. He is the one who is surrounded by henchmen at every turn and who is unable to move freely about the city, but here this restriction is self imposed and caused by his own excessive desires and actions rather than by someone else's.

The pervasiveness of excess in society is implied by the family sub-plot in which Tony's aberrance is highlighted by his incestuous desires for Cesca. The paradox of this relationship is that Tony also represents tradition in his disciplining of Cesca and his refusal to allow her the same pleasures of modern life that he experiences. Cesca's desire for these pleasures means that the family in *Scarface* does not have the same role as in *The Public Enemy*. Only Tony's mother acts as a voice of dissent against Tony's gangster life and she is ineffectual, with the result that the family becomes infiltrated by the violence and excess that the

Powers' family, in the form of Mike, manages to resist. Cesca and Tony are the same (as Cesca says 'You're me and I'm you') and although Hawks and Hecht saw the sub-plot as a rewriting of the Borgias, the sub-plot is more about the different desires and pleasures that Tony and Cesca have and the way that Rinaldo is destroyed because he is caught in the middle. Tony's desires are for violence while Cesca's are for sexual freedom, and in both cases they are excessive but where Tony's excess is represented by the Tommy gun Cesca's is represented by the sensual dance with which she seduces Rinaldo. Rinaldo, as Tony's friend and gangster-brother, is caught in the middle of their desires, split between loyalty to Tony and desire for Cesca. Indeed, Rinaldo is more of a trophy for both of them than Poppy is for Tony. Rinaldo is a sign of gang loyalty and therefore of Tony's status and power so when he kills Rinaldo this also signals his loss of control and soon after his loss of power and death. This final scene exemplifies the excess that characterises the film and which helped to end the early cycle. There is the obvious image of the carnage caused by police machine gun fire and the excessive spectacle of violence it represents. There is also, however, the image of the Cook's 'The World is Yours' sign which, like the film poster for *Tipsy Topsy Turvy* in *Little Caesar*, can be read as a ironic comment on Tony's failure, but also as a metaphor for the fracturing discourses and desires that modernity produces and which embody themselves in excesses of the gangster hero.

Repressing modernity: the studios and the Hays Office

The relationships between residual ideology and modernity, social restraint and desire, and discipline and excess do not only work at a narrative level but also ideologically and at the level of the production. One of the key articulations of these oppositions occurs in the restraints exercised on the gangster movie at the level of production in the form of censorship. Despite the presence of the family and the law, the gangster genre's representation of modernity is generally unproblematic in dramatising the excess and lack of restraint in modern urban culture. Religion, morality, and the work ethic are all absent from the gangster's life as he embraces violence, power, consumption, and technology without any check on his desires. The utter pleasure with which Tony Camonte embraces his first Tommy gun is a prime example of this. The gangster is in love with modernity and the possibilities it entails with the result that moral dilemmas, the narrative staple of Hollywood at the time, are virtually absent. The gangster does not ponder on the morality of what he is doing: he just does it. As such the element of controlled risk on which classical Hollywood is based and whose dominant narrative is described by John Ellis as one in which 'the disruptions are provided for a short while and then brought back in line' (Ellis, 1982: 68) does not apply to gangster movies where the disruptions are so excessive and even monstrous that they can only end with the extirpation of the gangster. This unfettered lifestyle is presented virtually as the norm and was unacceptable to the Hays Office which took a nostalgic and moral view in its desire to refuse modernity by censoring the perceived excess of violence and sexuality in the gangster film. *Scarface* particularly aroused the censor's attention, but also aroused concern in the industry itself when Howard Hughes announced that he was going to produce a gangster picture.[9] Put into production late in 1930 the film was not finally released until May 1932, partly as a result of haggling over the film's title but also because of demands by the Hays Office that changes be made to the film. Several scenes were cut, involving Tony hugging Cesca, Tony giving his mother presents, and another scene aboard a yacht which demonstrated the rewards of crime. More importantly scenes were inserted towards the end of the film showing a speech by the police chief vilifying Camonte and the cult of the gangster and another by a moralising newspaperman calling for new laws and 'martial law if necessary'. In effect, the Hays Office tried to insert its own sense of traditional values into the film as a way of policing culture and denying the freedoms, of consumption for example, made available by modernity.

In effect, what the Hays Office were concerned about was the gangster film's representational flexibility in its consideration of modernity. The gangster film dealt with the excesses that modern culture made possible, particularly in the realist mode of the early cycle which presented a problematic representation of the gangster world. Audiences were aware that many of the film gangsters were based on real gangsters, for example Al Capone in *Little Caesar* and *Scarface*, but principally paid money to watch the films as pleasurable fictions rather than documentary revelations of the horrors the gangster inflicted on innocent America. For audiences the violence was thrilling rather than horrific, the use of cars and guns a technological pleasure similar to computer generated dinosaurs in contemporary cinema, the star performances attractive in their vibrancy rather than repellent in their brutality, and the rewards of the gangster life a fantasy of consumption they could only hope for. Although the early gangster films were meant to realistically map the violence of gangster life as an apparent indictment of organised crime, the fact that 'Forewords' often had to be added to each of the films stating that they were indictments demonstrates that this is not how audiences consumed them. In the end, a moratorium on the gangster movie was declared in 1935 because the attempts to police the representations of the gangster world had led to audience pleasure rather than disapproval. It can be seen, then, that in the form of the gangster movie, cinema becomes part of the tensions experienced in modernity, rather than a means by which the excesses and flux of cultural and economic life can be controlled or policed, not least because of the gangster films' ability to reveal the contradictions of the existing social order even while it mapped its ideology. Despite the attempts of the studios and the Hays Office (later the Breen Office) to control the consumption of the gangster's articulation of modernity, he became an outlaw figure that was, for many in the audience, his main source of attraction. (Roddick, 1983: 99) The gangster confronted and challenged the ideological versions of society that circumscribed and limited the possibilities that modern life offered. The gangster achieved success and was able to earn money and engage in acts of consumption that the audience were mainly unable to fulfil. In effect the gangster existed outside moral categories for the audience despite the studios' attempt to direct attention to the immorality of the gangster in narrative and prefatory warnings. The response after the moratorium of 1935 was the creation of the good gangster – bad gangster formula (for example between Al Kruger and Bugs Fenner in *Bullets or Ballots*, Rocky Sullivan and Jim Frazier in *Angels with Dirty Faces* and Eddie Bartlett and George Hally in *The Roaring Twenties*) which is a recognition of the studios' and the Code's inability to control both the ideological divagations in the gangster film and its continued production and popularity. With the good – bad gangster formula, the studios created a fragile structure in which the gangster could both retain his authenticity (good gangster) while also articulate a condemnation of gangsterism as an unnatural evil that afflicted society (bad gangster).

2
The Post-Code Gangster: Ideology and Social Conscience

Chapter 1 discussed the significance of the 'classic' cycle of *Little Caesar, The Public Enemy,* and *Scarface* predominantly in terms of its articulation of the cultural tensions of the period of modernity within which it was produced. The intention behind this was to shift attention away from its critical position as a timeless embodiment of the conventions of the gangster genre in order to show that it is simply one variation within a mutable form while also highlighting the fact that it is an expression of specific historical social relations. When turning from the classic cycle to other 1930s manifestations of the gangster genre, the notion of genre as a mutable field of operations that articulates related but diverse forms becomes more obvious. The classic cycle is only one element within the early sound gangster movie. The racketeering film has already been discussed in relation to *Quick Millions* and *Doorway to Hell*, but other variations can also be seen, including the early social conscience gangster movie in the form of *Three on a Match* (1932), the urban tough variation in *Taxi!* (1932), the gangster-as-gambler in *Smart Money* (1931) and the female gangster movie in *Blondie Johnson* (1933). In many ways these films are as important as the classic cycle because they form models or sub-genres which are returned to, in modified form, in later years. The female gangster movie became popular in the early 1940s while the social conscience movie has arguably been as dominant in its creation of gangster thematics as the classic films themselves.[1] Another way of looking at the classic cycle is to see it not as a perfect manifestation of the gangster genre which exhausts its possibilities (Schatz, 1981:99),[2] but as a variation which, because of the attention it received from the Hays or Breen Office as a result of its excessive qualities, helped to curtail the development of other gangster forms and thus inadvertently guarantee its own canonical status. It is slightly speculative to say what would have happened had the Breen Office[3] not announced a moratorium on the gangster movie in 1935 following pressures from public interest groups such as the Legion of Decency,[4] but it is possible that the above mentioned variations might have developed their own momentum instead of being killed off. A study of the post-Code gangster film shows that they all re-appeared in one form or another over the course of 1930s and early 1940s.

The return of ideology: the G-Man and early post-moratorium variations

The first post-Code variation of the gangster genre occurs in what Schatz calls the Cain and Abel formula (1981:99–100), found in *Manhattan Melodrama*, which also forms the basic model for *Angels with Dirty Faces*. *Manhattan Melodrama* (W.S.Van Dyke, 1934) however, is more like a precursor for the gangster-as-cop narrative of the G-Man cycle for, although Blackie Gallagher (Clark Gable) remains a gangster throughout the film and dies for it, he is practically a member of the police force in the way in which he aids his childhood friend, Jim Wade (William Powell). The film is interesting as a variation of the gangster cycle because its gangster is a pro-social figure in direct opposition to the anti-social gangster of the classic cycle. In his representation as someone operating outside the law who does legitimate society's dirty work Blackie represents one of the first examples of the Production Code's impact on the gangster genre, taking on the role of gangster-as-policeman, a figure who re-appears in later films such as *Angels with Dirty Faces*, *Invisible Stripes*, *The Big Shot* and *Johnny Eager*. In representing the inability of the law to control crime without the help of the gangster, the film shows an unstable society, unable to guarantee its existence within the ideological parameters it has set itself. This has led Munby to argue that *Manhattan Melodrama* is paradigmatic of the gangster film's ability to 'consistently (and definitively) pose awkward questions about the terms and conditions of living in urban America' (1996:115). He argues that *Manhattan Melodrama* asks questions of society and ideology's ability to incorporate the ethnic urban dispossessed in its representation of the retention of power by the ruling class (in the form of Jim Wade) over the ethnic poor (Blackie). However, this is not the ostensible ideological message of the film which persistently represents Wade as having the moral and social high ground, to the extent that Blackie is always aware of his own illegitimate behaviour effectively becoming a cheerleader for Wade (and through him, for legitimate society) throughout the film, even cheering Jim on to arrest and convict him. During Blackie's trial, while Jim castigates him in public, Blackie fawns all over him ('Class, it's written all over him') while at the execution he 'looks lovingly at Powell from behind bars' (Clarens, 1980:124). This is a long way from the defiance that previous gangsters have shown and Blackie goes to the chair cheerfully, like a puppy that knows it has done wrong. Blackie knows he is a pariah and takes no pride in it but also knows that he cannot change, whereas the previous outlaw gangsters saw official society, in the form embodied by Jim Wade, as corrupt and illegitimate and did not want to change because the criminal world gave them more than official society and its work ethic ideology ever could.

As a gangster Blackie bears more resemblance to Sydney Carton than the urban tough of the classic cycle. Blackie is very restrained for a gangster and his main fault is poor timekeeping rather than bootlegging or violence. The acts of violence he does perform involve disciplining other criminals and preventing disruptions not only to gang society but also to the official society of Jim Wade. In the end, *Manhattan Melodrama* is a film in which tradition and ideology triumph over the gangster's embrace of modernity, represented by the fact that Blackie's girlfriend, Eleanor, leaves him for Jim because the latter represents the certainties of tradition ('oil lamps and horsecarts') whereas Blackie represents a shiftless transient modern world which is unproductive and purposeless. In *Manhattan Melodrama* law and ideology are never effectively threatened. Blackie lives the alternative criminal version of the American Dream, but this is always presented as illegitimate, as when Eleanor chastises Blackie for gaining a yacht through gambling rather than through work. This destroys the narrative dynamic of the classic gangster film and Blackie's actions are narratively determined by his support for Jim and the law rather than by transgression against them. The law has always already won in *Manhattan Melodrama*, a product of its Rooseveltian echoes and by the fact that Blackie is not really a gangster at all: he is simply Clark Gable being heroic and self-sacrificing. The film's main interest is that it was the film John Dillinger watched at the Biograph Theatre while the FBI led by Melvin Purvis waited outside to shoot him, a legally sanctioned assassination that rather problematises the film's conviction of the law's moral superiority.

Although *Manhattan Melodrama* is an early post-Code variation, it was not until the G-Man cycle beginning with *G-Men* in 1935 that the gangster movie was effectively revived. The G-Man narrative developed from the studios' need to retain the excesses of gangster life that had so attracted audiences but to place it within the Code's moral framework. The G-Man cycle creates a figure who uses gangster tactics as a way of disciplining the excesses of the gang in what Schatz calls the 'gangster-as-cop' narrative (1981:99) while also introducing a narrative trope that was to run through crime and gangster movies in the post-war *noir* period, the individual against a larger corrupt system, a feature seen, for example, in *The Big Heat*, *The Set Up*, and *Force of Evil*.[5] This is a development of the earlier gangster movies in which the gangster takes on society as a way of proving both his masculinity and the power of his individual will. In earlier films the gangster always had a gang behind him and although the law enforcers of the G-Man cycle have a larger 'gang' (the FBI or the police) to support them they very often act alone or as mavericks. This is significant in the genre's development because from *Dead End* onwards the gangster is often represented as a lone figure fighting against the odds, a paradigm of which is *The Last Gangster* (1937). Here, Joe Krozac (Edward G Robinson) is effectively pitted against the whole of society in his struggle with the prison system (legitimate society), the gangsters who have displaced him (criminal society), the wife who has disowned him (the family) and her news-paperman partner (the media) as he struggles to re-establish his power and regain the son who he wants to continue the family 'business'. Similar figures include Baby Face Martin in *Dead End* who is a solitary figure out of place in his old neighbourhood; Rocky Sullivan in *Angels with Dirty Faces* who may have the Dead End Kids on his side but is alone in his struggle against a corrupt alliance between gang and police; and Eddie Bartlett in *The Roaring Twenties* who struggles against history, the treacheries of 'bad gangster' George Hally, and his own integrity, repre-senting a gangster whose struggles take on Epic proportions because they are both internalised within his psyche and exteriorised in the domain of history.

The privileged position that the G-Man film gives to the individual is a product of the concern that in the classic cycle individuality had become the domain of the gangster and become coded as an aberrant ideology rather than the basis of legitimate society. In the pre-G-Man gangster film, signs of individuality, in action, thought or desire, were a reason to be punished by the State. The G-Man movie is an attempt to re-code individuality as acceptable behaviour and to ideologically recu-perate it. The G-Man film effectively offers a revenge narrative in which gangster society is punished for its excesses and very often extirpated. This is a double act of vengeance, not only within the film, in the punishment of criminality, but also within generic history, in the disciplining of the gangster for his pre-Code usurpation of individuality. The publicity for *G-Men* (William Keighley, 1935) explicitly sounded Warners' change of direction in the representation of crime, announcing that 'Hollywood's most famous bad man [Cagney] joins the G-Men and halts the march of crime' (Bergman, 1992:85). Warners were not only publicising the film here but also signalling to the Breen Office that they had disciplined themselves and were now following the line in their representation of crime. The narrative of *G-Men* not only involves the disciplining of gangsters but also entails a reprimanding of Cagney's screen persona, also represented within the film itself as he is tested and disciplined by an antagonistic FBI officer, Jeff McCord (Robert Armstrong), who subdues the gangster instincts that Cagney's character, Brick Davis, has learnt during his childhood in the slums.

The main focus of the film is the part Brick plays in disciplining the mob in a series of revenge narratives against the gang: revenge for the murder of his FBI friend, Buchanan (which also provides the motive for him to join the FBI), for the death of McKay (the gangster who has taken Brick from the streets and paid for his education), for the kidnapping of Kay (his sweetheart and daughter of his initially hostile boss), and for the death of Jean (his childhood sweetheart) – all at the hands of the same gang (the Leggett–Collins mob). Revenge, however, is constantly deferred, partly to provide yet more examples of the gang's evil nature[6] but partly also to extend the spectacle of violence in order to fulfill audience pleasure. Although Schatz calls this sub-genre the 'gangster-as-cop' film, it would be truer to describe it as the 'cop-as-gangster' narrative. In *G-Men* Brick and McCord are called upon to deal with the gangsters as if they were members of a 'fervid mob' themselves (Yaquinto, 1998:52), with the difference that their mob is the FBI. After early failures, the film shows a scene in which a spokesman demands that the FBI be given the same powers as the gangs (including the use of Tommy guns) and from this point on, the FBI begins what is effectively a legally sanctioned gang war against the mobsters with Brick and McCord becoming officialdom's 'gangsters'. After the arrest of Leggett, for example, Brick assaults him while McCord watches the fight with pleasure as if it were a boxing match. Like the gangsters before them the Federal Agents act outside the law and use any means to drive the gangs out of their territories in order to reconquer urban space for the government. When the mob flee to the Mid-West the film signals that the city and cultural modernity have been reterritorialised by the State and ideology and that an aberrant modernity, based on the release of desire, has been repressed.

The representation of the police as gangsters also has significance in terms of audience consumption, allowing the studios to show a spectacle of violence and excess within a framework of morality and discipline. There are several shoot-outs between the G-Men and the gangsters, more than in any gangster film up to this point other than *Scarface*. One shoot-out (when the gang frees Leggett) uses quick shots and cuts to give the sensation of action, excitement, and chaos while its excessive use of gunpowder smoke (compounded by the gangsters advancing in a line like soldiers), turns the action into a battle scene. A later shoot-out at the lodge where McKay is held hostage by the gang becomes a fireworks display in which people are relatively unimportant among the uncontrolled and undisciplined shooting, an image that is foregrounded when one the gangsters shouts: 'Give me noise, give me lots of noise.' The final punishment of Collins, the murderer of Buchanan, provides an iconic gangster killing, but this time performed by McCord who machine guns Collins' car and causes it to hurtle through a shop window. These are scenes of pure excess, performed as a cinematic spectacle for audiences who wanted to see what the death of a real gangster, like Dillinger, looked like. These scenes, however, sit uneasily in a film which also shows the realities of FBI detection and its concerns with forensic evidence. Laboratory scenes and examinations of account books are not things that make for action or sensation, unless, as in *G-Men*, they provide the basis for another raid and consequently another shoot-out. The shoot-out scenes serve another purpose in showing that the FBI agents are more masculine than the gangsters. Despite the excessive force the G-Men use, masculinity is a contradictory affair in *G-Men* because the film shows the need for a restrained masculinity on the part of the G-men in opposition to the gangsters' inauthenticity and excess. These are represented in terms of both violence and pleasure, the latter being displayed in a scene in Mac's club where extravagant Busby Berkeley dance scenes and glittery dresses made from artificial fabrics show not only the gangsters' penchant for excess in all forms but the inauthentic lives they lead. The G-Man is an 'authentic' man who doesn't just use a gun to express masculine power, but relies on his body, although the film fractures this view, and the ideology it expresses, in the fact that the FBI fail in their attempts to subjugate gangsterism until they are given Tommy guns, exteriorising their masculinity in the technology they use rather than placing it within the G-Man's body.

Bullets or Ballots (William Keighley, 1936) has a narrative as artificial as *G-Men* in its revenge tragedy form and undercover cop narrative, which follows the faked 'sacking' of Johnny Blake (Edward G Robinson) for corruption and his subsequent assault on the Police Commissioner at a boxing match. Blake is a similar character to Brick Davis in his mob contacts, being an old friend of Al Kruger's (Barton Maclane, this time playing the 'good' gangster rather than the 'bad' gangster role he had in *G-Men*), but also because he is represented as being tougher than the gangsters themselves. He also forms the model of the maverick cop who goes against the system while having official sanction for his behaviour, a variation that was to develop into the 'rogue cop' movie. The film has a revenge tragedy structure in which Bugs Fenner (Humphrey Bogart) plays a Machiavellian usurper who wants to dethrone Kruger but who is himself usurped by Blake (in his undercover gangster persona) as the latter searches for the secret cabal of businessmen who control the gang from behind their apparently honest front company, the Oceanic Bank and Trust Company. The film displays a Rooseveltian ideology, first by associating corruption and criminality with Big Business which is represented as working against the interests of both the nation and the little man and, secondly, by assuming that democracy will triumph against the gangs' tyranny, one of the first occasions that gangsterism is identified with Nazism. Gangsters are undemocratic, an idea shown in the opening scene in which a newsreel *exposé* of the gangs shows how they have become a nationwide menace who rule by 'the fear of their bullets' and who 'must be smashed by the power of your ballots'. The gangs in *Bullets or Ballots* are no longer the small scale city gangs of the earlier cycle but have developed into a 'crime combine' run on a national scale, a cinematic example of the gang as an Organisation and business enterprise. This is represented at several points, first in the newsreel *exposé* but in more detail after Blake has infiltrated the gang. Blake is effectively given a systems management job by Kruger which involves him scrutinising the whole set-up to find its weak spots. During his investigation, Blake discovers the gang's money laundering operation as they go through their accounts and report on the week's takings from their various rackets (loan sharking, pinball machines, jewellery fencing, and milk and fruit rackets), a structure based on corporate principles, with each gang boss having their own department administered by Kruger's CEO who then reports to the gang's 'shareholders', the bankers who control the gang.

Opposed to the discipline and restraint of the Organisation are Fenner and Blake, two old fashioned maverick figures who also embody the forces of excess in the film. Fenner's excess is represented by his murder of the newspaperman Bryant and by his desire for power in the manner of the classic gangster. He displays the same kind of unrestrained desire found in a figure like Tony Camonte as is shown when he takes over the numbers racket because of his desire for 'more', an act that also identifies him with the forces of unrestrained capitalism because it involves the corporate seizure of a small business rival, the numbers bank run by Lee Morgan (Joan Blondell). This produces a contradictory representation of crime in the film in which Lee's numbers racket is allowable because it is a small business while the corporate crime of the Organisation is illegitimate because it is a big business. Blake's excess is more contradictory. It is shown in his readiness to use his fists (for example, whe he puts Fenner in hospital), but it is also a controlled excess, performed in order to prove his allegiance to the gangsters. *Bullets or Ballots* is ultimately a film of contradictions. Its Rooseveltian ideology means that it tacitly supports the small business crime of Lee Morgan while condemning crime overall. It also has a paradoxical view of the gang because it is not a gang any more, just a collection of accountants run by bankers (who actually have no way of enforcing their power over the gang). The film can only express the aberrance of the gangster in its representation of Fenner as an old-fashioned gangster who opposes the corporate methods of the new gang and who therefore could be seen as the authentic Rooseveltian individual taking on the system in the same manner as Johnny Blake. In the end, Fenner and Blake are seen to be very alike and the latter only triumphs because not only is he more maverick than Fenner, but he is also a better gangster.

Overall, the G-Man cycle is a contradictory sub-genre. The studios needed to use the gangster, and the violence associated with him, to retain the genre's popularity but had to condemn the spectacle of violence they were presenting for public enjoyment. The G-Man cycle became ideologically problematic, not only because the law enforcement agencies had to be more violent than the gangsters to prove their abilities and to retain audience interest, but also because official tactics veered toward the fascism attributed to the gangs. A late G-Man film, *I Am The Law* (Alexander Hall, 1938), demonstrates the sub-genre's contradictions to the fullest. It has the same premise as *Bullets or Ballots*, focusing on a businessman who is secretly in charge of the rackets and whose son works for the Special Prosecutor, John Lindsay (Edward G Robinson). The film also explicitly aligns the gangs with Nazism by representing the gang as an anti-American mob, led by a charismatic patrician leader, and which forces its aberrant system on unwilling individuals through violence. In the end, however, it is not the gangsters who look like fascists but Lindsay and his private vigilante force.

Lindsay initially tries legal means to quell the gangs but when these fail he turns his investigation into a private organisation which uses extra-legal methods to deal with the gangs. In one scene, partly as a way of exercising his masculinity, Lindsay individually pummels three gang-sters into submission for a public audience in order to prove that they are not 'exceedingly tough *hombres*' but cowardly 'vermin' who hide behind guns. Ideologically, however, Lindsay is also proving that the gangs are the *untermenschen* of society (also seen in the images of 'rats', 'rodents', and 'maggots' that are used to describe the gangs) who need to be extirpated. The G-Man cycle is notable, however, for its representa-tion of gangs as rackets and it often blurs into the racketeering sub-genre, as in *Confidential* (1935) but more particularly in *Racket Busters* (1938) in which the individual taking on the mob is a private citizen working undercover for the special prosecutor. Perhaps the two most interesting features of the G-Man cycle are this blurring of boundaries and its re-definition of the existing formulae, aspects which already show that the gangster genre cannot be subjected to a totalising meta-narrative (such as a taxonomy based on the classic cycle). Instead, the gangster film's generic definitions are hazy and variable, either diver-ging from perceived norms or bringing together overlapping formulae like a Venn diagram. The new variation of the G-Man cycle is not, therefore, one of Schatz' 'derivative strains' that emphasises the status of the classic cycle (1981:99), but a different enunciation of the mutable conventions and iconographies that the gangster genre makes available. The gangster genre is, like any other genre, a domain of possibility that allows new narrative forms and variations of its iconographic codes to come into existence, as opposed to a restrictive and exclusive structure where the presence or absence of rigidly defined codes measures a text's successful articulation of conventions and its subsequent entry into the generic canon.

The social gangster

The G-Man sub-genre offers just such a variation within the genre's ideological codes in its concern with the two antithetical forms of socialisation present in capitalism and modernity: the ideological and the actual. The former entails learning the way of society (ideology) and focuses on how society imagines itself to be (the ideological fantasies of opportunity, enterprise, and success through work) and is associated with the law. The latter is the reverse and entails learning the way of the real world and how society actually works (the reality of the lack of opportunity in capitalism) and is invested in the gangster's knowledge that success is only possible through illegitimate means. The G-Man cycle attempted to destroy the distinction between these two types of socialisation by investing both in a G-Man figure, such as Brick Davis, who has a knowledge of how society works (his childhood poverty) but also lives by ideology (the force of the law). The post-G-Man social gangster movie creates a different articulation which problematises both forms of socialisation without ever finding a resolution of its own. *Dead End* sees the failure of the official ideology of success through work, but also sees only cynicism and futility in the knowledge that the gangster has of the world. This pessimism results from a new type of gangster figure as articulated in *The Petrified Forest* (Archie Mayo, 1936). The film metaphorically, through its gangster and poet characters, focuses on the individual's place in society. The film shows the now familiar scenario of a group of disparate people forced together in an isolated spot (an out of the way diner) and follows their discussions about the state of society. The main focus for discussion is the poet, Alan (Leslie Howard), and the gangster, Duke Mantee (Humphrey Bogart) and the oppositions they represent: contemplation and action, books and the world, idealism and pessimism, and possibility and reality. They are both, according to Alan, 'obsolete' and have no relevance in modern society, even though Duke, as a gangster, is 'the last great apostle of rugged individualism'. Society has no use for the individual and it is only in the wilderness of the Petrified Forest that his frontier spirit might have a place but, despite being on the frontier where he should be most at home, Duke is trapped and finally killed; destroyed because he represents an individuality that has no place in the machine age of modernity. Although the film is very static and has a stagy existential quality that doesn't fit well in the cinema its representation of the gangster as an icon of alienation and pessimistic negativity had a strong impact on the gangster movie with the coming of the new breed of post-G-Man gangsters who were 'low-key and moody loners who carried with them an aura rather than a milieu' (Clarens, 1980:145). The film's importance also lies in its use of the gangster as a sign of the failure of the ideology of success, showing Duke as a figure who is imprisoned by a society where even crime does not offer opportunity. Society is a place of entrapment and the only alternative is escape to its margins or beyond.

The gangster film becomes a way of placing the individual in a larger context in the late 1930s, either within a social background in *Dead End* or *Angels with Dirty Faces* or as part of a larger historical landscape in *The*

Roaring Twenties. As Roddick states: 'After the brief flurry of cop-centred movies in the middle of the decade, [Warners'] forays into the genre became almost uniformly dark, showing at best the individual provided with the opportunity to do the right thing at considerable cost, at worst the individual as an alienated victim of an uncaring society' (1983:117). The former approach is portrayed in *Marked Woman* (Lloyd Bacon, 1937) in which Mary Bryan (Bette Davis) fights gangsterism for revenge. Her sister, Betty, has become part of the gangster world of pleasure, as a gangster's moll, but this society is also one of violence that destroys her. The alternative gangster cultural economy is not a place of liberation, but a place of entrapment and death, an inversion of *The Petrified Forest*'s attribution of the same features to society, opposing the latter's pessimism with an optimistic pro-social recuperation of ideology and its institutions. A film that places itself between these two polarities is *Invisible Stripes* (1939) which also has a 'good gangster – bad gangster' formula. The film tells the story of an ex-convict trying to go straight but who is tempted back to crime out of necessity before he finally realises that the gang is a place of betrayal and not opportunity. He is punished by death for his criminality, but not before he has guaranteed the future happiness of his younger brother, receiving redemption for fulfilling his role as a father-figure, but also condemnation because he is a gangster who has illegitimately usurped ideological social structures in acting out the role of patriarch. The film therefore takes both the optimistic and pessimistic views, seeing both society and the gang as spaces of containment, but suggesting an optimistic view in individual acts of heroism, even if these are tainted by the touch of the gangster.[7]

Later gangster films of the 1930s consciously use the gangster as a paradigm of the individual – society relationship, focusing attention on the question of free will and the question of whether the actions of individuals are a product of choice or of socially determined necessity. Gangsters who enter crime out of choice are presented negatively because they have chosen alienation, whereas those who enter crime out of necessity (like Rocky Sullivan in *Angels with Dirty Faces*) are presented more ambiguously. They have alienation forced on them, but are 'good' people who have got in with the wrong crowd and are portrayed both positively (because as individuals they are inherently good) and negatively (because their actions are evil). There are, however, contradictions in these representations. Firstly, the gangster who enters crime out of necessity can never establish as full an individuality as the gangster who enters crime out of choice because he is represented as weak-willed. This weak will seemingly resolves a contradiction for the studios who can present honest citizens, such as Father Jerry in *Angels with Dirty Faces*, as the properly socialised individual, but leads to problems in the representation of the gangster who chooses crime out of free will, because he shares the same determination as the pro-social representative. Such a position allows the famous ending of *Angels with Dirty Faces* not only to take place but also to be convincing in its ideological interpretation: Rocky, the gangster who enters crime out of necessity, breaks down and has to be forced to go to the chair rather than going to his death as a defiant free-willed individual. This seems to prove the ideological view of gangsters as weak-willed cowards but is problematised both ideologically and narratively. Rocky's actions are ambiguous and there is a question over whether he has genuinely broken down or whether he has done it out of choice with the effect that 'although the slum kids on the screen (actors in a movie) believe in Cagney's cowardice, the audience (real slum kids among the people in it) views his death as a final, heroic gesture' (Schatz, 1981:100–1).

The second difficulty that the studios faced was with a representation of the causes of crime. They could only make the gangster positive if he was forced into crime by outside influences, but could not state that social conditions created the gangster. Such a view would imply the aberrance of society and that the gangster was simply an ordinary citizen rather than an untypical deviancy. The gangster is, therefore, most often represented as turning to crime by accident: Rocky Sullivan becomes a gangster because he cannot run as fast as Jerry, while Eddie Bartlett (*The Roaring Twenties*) turns to crime because he is convicted for unknowingly delivering alcohol to a speakeasy. Crime becomes a product of modern society without modern society actually being a cause of crime and that the studios have their ideological cake and eat it. They can be nostalgic for a pre-modern pre-crime society (most often presented in the idylls of bustling community life in the turn-of-the-century slums as in *Angels with Dirty Faces*), hopeful in looking forward to a new society that will eliminate the gangster (*Dead End*), and positive about society in the present by claiming that the causes of crime exist in the past (*The Roaring Twenties*), while also being able to present the gangster positively, because it is not choice or necessity that create him, just accident.

One of the first examples of the social gangster movie, *Dead End* (William Wyler, 1937), shares both *The Petrified Forest*'s compressed time scheme and its collection of disparate people – the rich, the poor, and the gangsters – as they interact in the course of one day. The action all takes place on one street in a slum neighbourhood, mainly at the dead end where the street meets the river and where the poor quarters of the city back on to the areas inhabited by the wealthy – who are able to appear in the poor areas because they must use the back entrance while the front of the house is being renovated. All of society meets in this one place and during the film various views of each group and of society as a whole are presented. The narrative develops the relationships between each group by focusing on the Dead End Kids and particularly their leader, Tommy Gordon, who in the course of the film is forced to make a choice about his future. He can choose to turn to crime like the gangster, Baby Face Martin (Humphrey Bogart) who represents a parasitic and destructive social force, or he can choose to be redeemed by his downtrodden sister, Drina (Sylvia Sidney), and thus learn to play a constructive role in society like Dave (Joel McCrea), an architect, whose job is used as a metaphor for a utopian vision of the creation of a new, more just, society. Drina and Dave are also faced with choices: Drina is torn between trying to escape to a better life with Tommy or staying and putting up with hardship; while Dave has to choose between taking the easy option by abandoning Drina and the poor and joining the society of the rich (through his relationship with the wealthy Kay) or staying with Drina and the life of work, using his skills to construct this new society. Like Martin he is an alienated figure but he also forms an opposition to the parasitism of the gangster and the wealthy elite who are aligned together, an identification signalled early in the film when Martin boasts to Dave of how he 'lives off the fat of the land' while showing off his $150 custom tailored suit and $20 silk shirt. Both the rich and the gangster represent easy money and both threaten to destroy society through their idleness and excess.

Baby Face Martin is the epitome of the moody loner that Clarens describes. He mooches around the neighbourhood and, like the rich, idly spends his time doing nothing, a representation that presents the two as socially irrelevant, but economically powerful. The film, however, ends by showing how unattractive the gangster life is by drawing attention to the fact that although it may involve pleasure and easy money it is also brutish. Dave tells Martin that if he doesn't leave the block, and take his malign influence over Tommy away, he will go to the police. Martin waits until Dave turns away from him, throws a knife into his back and with his henchman rolls him into the river. Dave survives and comes after Martin who is cornered by Dave and then finally killed by the police in an indiscriminate and excessive burst of fire. Martin's perfunctory violence against Dave and his death, like a cornered animal, show the gangster as a bestial creature who needs to be eliminated from society. With the death of Martin comes the climax of the choices each character has had to make: Dave decides to use his skills to re-build society, in the process persuading Drina to give up her dreams of escape, while Tommy decides on a path of honesty in his confession of having beaten up a rich boy. Work and honesty triumph over idleness, excess, and crime, but the film fails to resolve itself ideologically. Earlier in the film, when Tommy is first caught (and before he escapes) he is called 'a little gangster' by the rich boy's father who rather than offering forgiveness for his honesty in confessing threatens to send him to reform school. Drina replies that Tommy is not to blame because it is poverty that has caused his actions while also arguing that reform school will turn him from a tearaway into a fully fledged gangster. The film, at this point, sees social conditions as the cause of criminality, but by the end this view is contradicted and individual choice is seen to determine a person's honesty or criminality. The film further muddles its ideological position by showing that Dave is only able to make his choice because he receives a large reward for the capture of Martin, suggesting that it is not choice but accident and wealth that decide a person's future. Although Dave is presented as having 'earned' this money, it is effectively 'easy money' that a life of hard work cannot provide, but which the life of the gangster can.

Angels with Dirty Faces (Michael Curtiz, 1938) is another social gangster movie that follows a lone gangster as he returns to his old neighbourhood. Where Baby Face Martin in *Dead End* is presented as being out of place and powerless because he has no gang, Rocky Sullivan (James Cagney) is seen to be more powerful because his self-reliant individuality is complemented by several factors: his knowledge of the streets, the fact that his solo status means he has no ties and can thus move around at will, and because he has a surrogate gang in the neighbourhood people, particularly the Dead End Kids. Rocky is a new type of gangster, a loner who does not need a gang to assert his power and status. He outwits the organisation that has refused to pay its debts to him and which also attempts to betray him to get him out of the way. His self-reliance and quick wits make him more dangerous ideologically than Baby Face Martin, particularly as he is articulated as the 'good' gangster forced into crime by accident and necessity. An early montage not only expresses this, in showing Rocky's criminal career after having gone to reform school, but also articulates an ambivalent view of the gangster, because the montage is also intercut with images of night clubs and money. The montage sequence places a moral around Rocky's criminality by showing how he has no control over his descent into the underworld, but its main importance is in the way it shows the thrilling, pleasurable and glamorous lifestyle that the gangster leads, creating a conflicted image of the gangster as both a pariah and a role model to aspire to. The main conflict in the film, however, does not just focus on this dichotomy, but operates in an opposition between the lone gangster (and the street code he symbolises) and official ideology represented by Father Jerry (Pat O'Brien). The film superficially condones Jerry's moral position: that Rocky is not inherently bad because he is a product of the system but that he becomes a malign figure when his actions cause a new generation (the Dead End Kids) to mimic him. Jerry's role is to discipline both the Dead End Kids and Rocky to show that the rackets and the gangsters are not figures to emulate. Jerry also represents the voice of ideology in his view that society is not inherently corrupt but that it is aberrant people ('the rotten politicians' and the gangsters) who corrupt it. What this produces is a scapegoat narrative in which, once Rocky has done Jerry's work for him and destroyed Keefer and Frazier's organisation, Rocky can be sacrificed in order to show that corruption has been eliminated from society. Despite the film's attempts to make Jerry a likeable figure, he becomes the voice of hypocrisy. Jerry is never threatened by Rocky because of Rocky's loyalty to him and, in not only delivering Rocky to the police and the electric chair but also then using Rocky's friendship to make him feign cowardice for ideological and moral purposes, Jerry becomes a manipulative person who betrays Rocky's loyalty for his own ends. Jerry comes to resemble the 'bad' gangsters, Keefer (George Bancroft) and Frazier (Humphrey Bogart) who also betray Rocky and try to destroy him. The only difference is that Jerry succeeds.

In opposition to this, Rocky's street code is far more attractive, something that is compounded by the action scenes of the film and by a bravura performance by Cagney who fills Rocky not only with energy but an innocence and a high spirited good nature in the face of adversity that makes him an appealing figure. Unlike Baby Face Martin, Rocky is not an alienated gangster: he may not follow official ideology but this does not make him a bitter outsider. He has the support of the underclass to which he returns and, in this respect, the film is less about the gangster's lack of a place in society and more about his re-integration into an alternative society that official ideology (even in the form of Jerry) cannot understand. As a result, his death in the electric chair is less the death of the gangster and more the death of the underclass and its aspirations and if the film has a tragic quality it is not Rocky's self-sacrifice at the end, but an overwhelming impression that if someone as able as Rocky is destroyed by society then the rest of the underclass has little chance. In being positioned as one man against society Rocky is positioned as one of the dispossessed, but he shows a street knowledge and a facility for quick thought and action that allows him to outsmart everyone in the film (other than Jerry) and gain the support of the other members of the dispossessed. This, however, gives him an ability the gangs, despite their alliance with a corrupted official society, do not possess: control of the streets. Rocky's position as a lone gangster and his ability to rely on his own wits allows him to control both the gangs and the city space as when he is able to track down the Dead End Kids after they rob him because he knows the territory.

Rocky's ability to control space extends further than this. Although Rocky does not control a territory in the same way as Keefer and Frazier, he has physical control whereas theirs is theoretical. Rocky controls the space he occupies at a particular moment but his freedom of movement allow him a more effective territorialisation of the streets of the city. Rocky takes his control of space with him and in this it is the body and its movement through space that becomes more important than the invisible lines on a map that the gangs use to carve out their territories. In comparison to Rocky, whose freedom of movement is matched by his quickwittedness, Keefer and Frazier's mob are slow and ponderous. After Rocky has demanded both his money and to be cut into the organisa-tion Keefer and Frazier decide to have Rocky killed and send a hit squad to Rocky's neighbourhood to effect this. As Rocky walks down the street with Laury (Ann Sheridan) he notices he is being followed and uses his street-knowledge to help him escape. He pretends to have something in his eye and uses a mirror on a store to locate his tail and then ducks into a drugstore, not to escape his pursuer but to trap him. The mob telephone Rocky in the drugstore as a way of cornering him, but Rocky turns the tables so that when the mob arrive to kill him they shoot their own man while Rocky escapes through the back. Rocky's control of the streets, however, also signals a literalisation of his outsider status. While Keefer and Frazier are only ever seen indoors (in the night club or at Frazier's apartment), images that signal that they are on the inside of the power system of the gangs and the city government, Rocky is represented as being on the outside of power by only being at ease on the streets, an inverse of the classic cycle where control of the streets meant control of the city. Rocky's downfall occurs when he moves off the streets and into interior spaces of power which become prisons for him. In the final sequences he tries to take control of the gang in its headquarters, Keefer's office, but after he kills Keefer he becomes trapped in a space over which he has no control. Rocky's ease of move-ment allows him to escape but he is effectively in prison from this moment on, moving from one restricted space to another. These scenes show his loss of control of screen space and are complemented by the image of an army of policemen hunting him down, emphasising how disempowered he ultimately is. The excessive force that the State can call upon in capturing him also signals the impossibility of challenging existing power structures. Nevertheless, the apparent message that crim-inality is not only morally wrong, but ultimately pointless because of the power of society, is undercut by the film's ambiguous ending. Al-though Rocky goes to the chair appearing to be a coward, thereby setting a bad example for the Dead End Kids, it is not Rocky the gangster they reject, but Rocky the coward. In consequence, Rocky's criminal activities remain unchallenged and, although the film equates coward-ice with the gangster, this is revealed to be an obviously imposed mes-sage because it is the result of an act of blackmail on the part of Jerry, the voice of ideology in the film.

'He used to be a big shot': *The Roaring Twenties*, history, modernity, and the gangster

The final major film of the 1930s is *The Roaring Twenties* (Raoul Walsh, 1939) which, as a summation of previous gangster motifs and narratives, provides both an Epic and an elegaic full stop to the 1930's gangster film. The film has received surprisingly little critical attention consider-ing both its range and influence and the position it occupies in the transition of the gangster genre from the 1930s into the 1940s.[8] The film looks back to the classic rise and fall narrative and the good-gangster – bad gangster variant, while also placing itself within a social gangster context *and* looking forward to gangster *noir* and the 'death of the big shot' sub-genre.[9] There are two reasons why the film has often been ignored: firstly, its re-investigation of its generic history has led to a view that it is derivative (Yaquinto, 1998: 59); and, secondly, that its setting in a 'bygone era' makes it an irrelevant piece of retrospection (Munby, 1999:112). Its re-iteration of a multiplicity of gangster styles, both past and future, however, endows the film with an encyclopedic quality while its historical dimensions contribute to its Epic status. The film not only encapsulates the multiplicity and flexibility of the gang-ster genre more than any other film of the period, but also acts as a story of the individual within modernity and its fractured space while also, because of its nostalgic elements, identifying the fracturing of emergent

modern culture by residual ideologies. The film also enacts the displacement of the latter in its story of Eddie Bartlett (James Cagney) who is
transformed in the course of the film from ideologically enunciated
servant of the State (soldier) into an emblem of fractured modernity
(gangster) through a combination of historical accident *and* inevitability, before attempting to fight history by inventing himself as an 'individual' when he creates a city-wide racket. This, however, has the
opposite effect, first by recuperating him as a symbolic image of a new
systematised modernity (signified by the corporatised racket he sets up)
and then by re-inserting him into the system of history when his organisation (and his 'individuality') is destroyed by the Wall Street Crash.
The final result of this process is that Eddie is revealed to be what he
always was: a 'chump', as Panama Smith (Gladys George) describes him,
with no meaningful existence as a self-determined individual.

Exaggerating and re-defining the classic cycle's emblematic individual, *The Roaring Twenties* doesn't even show Eddie achieving the status of
'subject-outside-history', because he is always framed by the historical
timeline of the commentary and the chronological montages of social
change. Eddie is located within these social and historical processes with
the result that he is an Everyman figure who embodies the experience of
living inside history during a particular period of American culture. As
an Everyman figure, Eddie is always more of a 'chump' than a gangster,
someone who is defined and controlled by society, particularly the
ideologies of legitimate success and heterosexual fulfillment, which are
only ever simulated and distorted: in the 'taxi' company, which is a
front for Eddie's bootlegging business, and in his 'romance' with Jean
(Ann Sheridan), which is expressed predominantly through serial acts of
consumption which take on an obsessive fetishistic quality in his interpretation of the objects he buys for her not only as a sign of his love but
as a token of her love for him. Even as a gangster Eddie is a 'chump'
because of his belief that these facsimiles of success and romance can be
ideologically acceptable. The film makes a good deal of fakery, particularly the faking of quality alcohol (with salt stained casks and applejack
masquerading as champagne) associating the gangster with cheap inauthenticity. Eddie as a producer of this world embodies success through
fakery, but he is also destroyed by it. The loss of his fortune in the Wall
Street Crash identifies Eddie's control of society and space as a paper
empire worth nothing in itself. All his efforts result in a cyclical return to
his impoverished taxi driver status revealing his apparent power and
freedom of action to be simulations. Throughout his criminal career he
is shown to be increasingly in control of space, whether it is his easy

access to the backstage of the theatre, his boarding and capture of rival, Nick Brown's, liquor ship, the raid on the government warehouse, or his ability to make Henderson's night club his own territory simply by his presence. His rise to corporate racketeer (which is represented as a rise from a cottage industry where liquor is brewed in the bath to big business with gangsters taking orders as if they were sales reps) and extension of control across the city by his occupation of Brown's territory (symbolised by Eddie's successful invasion of the restaurant where Brown has his headquarters) also suggest extension of his individual will across economic and social space. All of this, however, is a product of Eddie's accidental entry into bootlegging after he is arrested for unknowingly delivering alcohol. He is not a self-determined willed individual, but a product of history like 'the thousands and thousands of other Eddies throughout America', as the film's commentary notes. He is never a producer of society but a product, something that also problematises the film's association of the fake with the gangster because Eddie is only ever an embodiment or symptom of an empty mass culture of consumerism, not its cause.

Eddie's death is symptomatic of this lack of control and he is revealed to have never individuated himself, even when he takes revenge on his gangster ex-partner, George Hally (Humphrey Bogart), for the latter's threats to Jean. This action is so counter his previous motivations, in its self-sacrificing qualities, that it implies self-definition against the historical forces he embodied as a gangster. That it is a self-sacrifice, and that its result is the perpetuation of the ideologies of the law, the family, and heterosexuality – as embodied in Jean and Lloyd – recuperates Eddie into the domain of official social forces, not only because he has transformed from gangster to society's policeman (in helping to guarantee ideology) but also because his death is represented in terms of redemption within ideology as he dies on the church steps. The final image shows a triptych of ideological forces (but also hints at their failure), as Eddie is shown lying dead in Panama's arms (a failed narrative of heterosexual romance), with a policeman standing over him (the failure of the law because it is Eddie who metes out justice to George) with the church he didn't quite reach in the background (the failure of religion and the narrative of redemption). The film thus becomes less of a psychological and moral study of the gangster than a study of social and historical forces and their contradictory success and failure. The failure and recuperation of ideology is part of the film's Rooseveltian ideology which locates America's failures in the *laissez-faire* capitalism of the 1920s and the nation's renewal in the responsible capitalism of the New Deal 1930s. *The Roaring Twenties*, however, also articulates a society in which ideology persists in the form of a 'grand narrative' designed to perpetuate itself as a simulation of social order without actually guaranteeing what it promises in the everyday life of culture. This is not to claim that the film is postmodern, as it can be characterised, in Baudrillard's theory of simulation, more in terms of the modern phase of the simulacrum before postmodernity which 'masks the *absence* of a basic reality' (1983:11). In this phase, the 'real' has disappeared, but there are attempts to conceal its loss by the creation of fake 'realities' (such as ideology) which are accepted as 'real' in order to maintain the façade of social cohesion and purpose. Similarly, even while analysis could, at a stretch, read the film's compendium of gang- ster styles and non-generic references to Eddie as a buccaneer or a gunslinger as a mapping of postmodern pastiche, *The Roaring Twenties* is more important in its mapping of the crisis of modernity that gangster *noir* more fully exemplifies, and thus it is not simply retrospection or replication of styles, but a reinvigoration of the genre in its creation of models that would develop into both *noir* and the 'death of the big shot' variations.

3
The Death of the Big Shot: the Gangster in the 1940s

With the exception of *High Sierra* the gangster movie of the early 1940s has received little attention. Like the films of the late 1930s it has either been ignored or seen as an interlude between the classic gangster movie of the 1930's and the development of *film noir* in the immediate post-war years. *High Sierra* has received a great deal of attention because it has been seen as a bridge between the 1930s and the gangster *noir* narratives of the 1940s, looking back to the former (in its representation of the tragic gangster) while preparing the way for *film noir* in its depiction of a new America of alienation (Shadoian, 1977: 59–66; Clarens, 1980: 168). While the gangster film of the early 1940s has been overshadowed by the rise of *film noir*, this period is nevertheless interesting for its creation of the 'death of the big shot' formula and for its other variations. The first wave of gangster cycles ended with the films that were in production at the time of the bombing of Pearl Harbor in December 1941 (*Johnny Eager* and *The Big Shot*). The gangster film was not a major genre during the War, as Schatz' outline of major trends in genre and production indicates in *Boom and Bust*[1] and tended toward the gangster-versus-Nazi variety, such as *Lucky Jordan* (1942) and *All Through the Night* (1942). Nevertheless, before the end of the gangster cycle in 1942, interesting developments had occurred in the gangster genre. Of particular interest is the fragmentation of the genre, no longer unified under a coherent set of iconographic features or narrative forms. This fragmentation was not new to the gangster genre as the late 1930s had also seen variants such as the social gangster film (*Dead End*), the Cain and Abel narrative (*Angels with Dirty Faces* and *Manhattan Melodrama*) and the cross-connection with melodrama in *Marked Woman*. The usual view of this process is that it marks the exhaustion of the genre after its early culmination in the classic cycle (Shadoian, 1977: 18; Schatz,

1981: 99–100).[2] Alternatively, the 1940s gangster film can be interpreted in terms of its variation of existing conventions or introduction of new cycles, a process that highlights its multiple and flexible form and which suggests that it may be better understood as a set of multiple overlapping *genres* rather than a singular entity. As well as the arrival of the 'death of the big shot' variant, the 1940s also saw the comedy gangster film (*Brother Orchid*); the bandit or 'twilight-of-the-gangster' narrative (*High Sierra* and *The Big Shot*); the female gangster film (*Lady Scarface* and *Lady Gangster*); the gangster-versus-Nazi formula; and the gangster as detective formula (*The Glass Key*).

This fragmentation has several implications. Even before war broke out the Hollywood studio system was uncertain about how to represent the gangster in the light of the Hays Office moratorium on the gangster movie in 1935. Many of the variations mentioned above do not explicitly represent the gangster hero as a gangster. *High Sierra* figures its hero, Roy 'Mad Dog' Earle, not as a traditional urban gangster bringing disruption to the heart of American society, but a figure who is as much in debt to nostalgic visions of the Western outlaw as he is to the rural Dillinger gangster. Similarly, *The Glass Key* presents its gangster hero as a detective searching for justice rather than someone trying to subvert the law. Even in *Johnny Eager*, which presents a familiar gang boss figure who murders to keep his power, the gangster-hero is more of a fraudster than a racketeer. The gangster-as-gambler or gangster-as-fraudster also became a popular device during this period and can be seen in films such as *Johnny Apollo*, *Lady Gangster* and *Johnny O'Clock*. In *The Big Sleep*, while the character of Eddie Mars is a murderer, he is principally present in the film as a blackmailer whose main crimes are gambling, fraud, and deception. What this development also suggests, however, is that a new set of codes was being developed in the gangster film in order to identify for the audience which characters were gangsters without actually saying that this was what they were. The gangster can be seen to go undercover from this time on, as an invisible presence who exists but cannot be named. The gangster becomes a more pervasive and insidious figure who inhabits the shadows of America and pulls strings in the background rather than overtly challenging law and society in a cops and robbers manner. Law and crime are also less distinct and the inception of the gangster-as-fraudster figure suggests that gangsterism is not a set of large organisations or rackets that can be eliminated one by one but a pervasive presence. Turning the gangster into a petty criminal neuters his threat, but also suggests that gangsterism has proliferated and that everyone now has a racket.

Early variations of the 1940s

The fragmentation of the gangster genre, however, can also be read as its exhaustion, something that can be seen in its subordination to the star persona as a vehicle by which an actor associated with the role of romantic hero (such as Tyrone Power or Robert Taylor) could also show that he had a 'tough' side. Examples of this type of movie include *Johnny Apollo* and *Johnny Eager*, both of which revisited existing gangster conventions but primarily as a framework within which the star's masculinity could be measured. In *Johnny Apollo* (Henry Hathaway, 1940) the eponymous hero, played by Tyrone Power, is not really a gangster at all because he doesn't commit any obvious gangster acts. Apollo is a cross between a fraudster and an undercover agent. He is in the world of the gangster (which acts simply as a code to signify that Power is in a world of danger) without ever being part of it. Apollo is effectively always part of official ideological society despite the gangster territory he occupies, as is evidenced by his attempts to get his father released from prison. This is made obvious by his view that he has simply put his 'soul in hock' to gangster society out of a sense of honour and family loyalty and thus can always reclaim his integrity. Apollo plays at being a gangster without ever really being one, signified by the fact that he retains his original name (Bob Cain) as well as having an adopted gangster persona. What is interesting about the *Johnny Apollo* is that, like the prison drama *Each Dawn I Die*, it suggests that the law cannot provide justice and is part of a new gangster variant that represents the gangster as society's policeman, guaranteeing and usurping the law in the face of the failure of the official system. *Brother Orchid* (Lloyd Bacon, 1940) is a variant on this narrative, though it is also as much a comedy as it is a gangster film. At the opening of the film, Little John (Edward G Robinson) retires from his life of crime, but runs out of money and tries to return to his old mob. Rebuffed by the new boss Little John starts up a new gang which invokes retaliation from the old mob, leaving Little John to flee to a monastery. From his new headquarters he takes on the mob and wins but not before he has learnt the true values of life from the monks, finding redemption by closing down the mob he has won back. Unlike Johnny Apollo Little John is a gangster, but again because of the triviality of his criminal acts (which are mainly acts of fraud and deception) he is as much a simulation of a gangster as Apollo. Also like Johnny Apollo he has two personae: Little John the gangster and Brother Orchid the kind monk. As well as varying the Cain and Abel format (by locating both law and crime in one figure) this also introduces a Jekyll and Hyde aspect to the gangster genre in an attempt to modify its formula by utilising elements from other genres.

These early examples from the 1940s suggest a genre reaching the end of its existing possibilities and narratives in its need to borrow from other genres in order to create new forms. This sense of exhaustion is also suggested in other variants of the early 1940s, for example, the female gangster cycle which seemed to offer a new perspective, but whose offerings, *Lady Scarface* (1941) and *Lady Gangster* (1942) were both fairly anaemic. *Lady Scarface* is more of a G-man movie focusing on the police's efforts to track down the female gangster rather than directing attention to her criminal activities and psychology. *Lady Gangster* offers a female gangster who is more a liar or trickster than a gangster and the film is quite muddled about her motivations. It constantly returns to the theme of her potential redemption by expressing the view that she is really 'a lone helpless little girl' caught up in the gangster world, but her impulse to redemption is muted as she continues to commit criminal acts until she is finally redeemed by 'love'. Another cycle, instigated by the United States' entry into the war, was the gangsters-versus-Nazis variant. *Lucky Jordan* (1942) has Alan Ladd giving up his gangster life to go undercover in order to infiltrate a Nazi spy ring while *All Through the Night* (1942) is a more obvious gangsters-versus-Nazis film which actually went into production in July 1941, before Pearl Harbour. Despite its comic basis and its incongruous representation of gangsters defending the American way of life the film does nevertheless offer an interesting variation on the cops-and-robbers formula. The comic elements, however, draw attention to the absurdity of gangsters defending America and emphasise that gangsters are more suited as opposition to American ideals than as supporters despite the film's message that the Nazis are the real gangsters, 'part of a mob that makes you and me look like Little Bo Peep'.

High Sierra: re-visiting and renewing the genre

1941 also saw the release of *High Sierra* (John Huston), the last major gangster movie released before Pearl Harbor and the one that effectively brought the gangster cycle to a temporary end, something that muted its influence in the short term, but amplified its importance when the gangster film was revived at the end of the war. The film has often been regarded as fundamental to the later development of *film noir* (Krutnik, 1991: 200; Yaquinto, 1998: 68) because of its focus on the romantic alienation of the individual as it is refracted through the gangster hero. Shadoian, for example, pinpoints Bogart's portrayal of Roy 'Mad Dog' Earle as the focalisation for these concerns, noting the romantic qualities in Earle's ennobled folk hero persona and his sentimental idealism as represented by his desire to live by the values of the dispossessed rural family (the Goodhues) that he becomes involved with (1977: 69, 72). Above all, for Shadoian, Earle's importance is as a representation of a new kind of gangster figure, one who is a 'value center, a man of honor, integrity, and feeling in a world shown as mean and humanly defective' (79). This sense of an ennobled but alienated gangster is also shared by other critics such as Clarens (1980: 169) and Krutnik. The latter, however, still locates Earle's persona in the antisocial tendencies of the gangster genre, pointing out that the film's 'fantasy of alienation validates the individual at the expense of society', but he also notes that, unlike the classic gangster's outwardly directed masculine energy, Earle represents a narcissistic defensive 'ego in retreat' (1991: 199–200). Criticism has also focused on the new formula that *High Sierra* generates for the gangster genre in its use of the bandit narrative (Schatz, 1981: 103), but the film is perhaps as important for its establishment of the 'death of the big shot' formula and its use of a compressed narrative that was to become common in the gangster film. The action takes place over a short time, charting the gangster's life over a period of days rather than narrating the rise and fall of gangster over the course of months or years. In its focus on the final days of a 'big shot' the film also suggests doom right from the start and the opening shot of the Sierra Mountains over the credits already shows the inevitability of Roy's death at the end of the film.

High Sierra is also imbued with nostalgia and Roy's representation as a Dillinger figure or as a western 'bandit' implies that he is a man out of his time, an anachronism with no place in the modern world. This is emphasised by Roy's association with Pa Goodhue (who refers to the Roy and himself as 'old timers') and by his relationship with the dying gang boss, Big Mac, with whom he has a pre-heist conversation where the talk is characterised by nostalgia for the old days and by a sense of loss at the death of all the 'A1 guys' who have been replaced by a new gangster generation of 'jitterbugs, 'screwballs', 'young twerps', and 'soda-jerkers'. Several important issues about society and about the gangster system are raised in this discussion. First, there is a sense that the old gangster culture was a world of certainties where the individual gangster could rely on the loyalty of gang and not be betrayed, as is the case with the current generation of gangsters. Mac and Roy see the present as a place of wildness and uncertainty, dominated by individual desire in the form of the 'jitterbugs' who have no sense of loyalty to anything other than themselves. The conversation also, however, implies the pervasiveness of the gangster and his individualist ethos throughout society in the rise of this 'jitterbug' generation because everyone either is or wants to be a gangster (Babe, Red and Mendoza) or they are on the make like Velma (who wants something for nothing) and her lover, Lon Preiser.

What is significant about this is a general sense of upheaval and fluidity in society as a whole where, as Shadoian points out, an old time gangster like Roy is the last bastion of honour, morals and loyalty (1977: 69). Ideological and moral structures are inverted and official society turned inside out to become its 'other' by transforming itself into what it sought to repress: the society of the illegitimate gang culture of the 1930s gangster film. Society has become a chaotic unstructured space of disruption which is represented by the social upheaval the film shows in the Goodhues' uprooting from Ohio and in their unconventional family structure. Old structures and certainties have disappeared in society and it is only in the honourable gangster figure that the old values reside. Roy is represented as a chivalric figure on whom society relies in order to function even as it outlaws the same figure and implicitly outlaws his value system. In helping Velma, Roy effectively stands in for the State which has abandoned her and left her to survive as best she can. Roy stands as an isolated father figure suggesting the persistence of patriarchal structures, but also highlighting the death of social paternalism in favour of a chaotic and fluid society which Velma's self interested attitude symbolises. Roy's attempts to be a father are, however, confused in relation to Velma because although he acts like a father he also desires to be her romantic partner. He is thus unable to impose patriarchal control and can only discipline her selfishness though displacement when he punches her boyfriend. The theme of ineffectual patriarchs is a main concern of the film, from Pa Goodhue's inability to quiet the noise of Lon and Velma listening to dance music to Mac the dying patriarch. The film shows a fatherless society with no adequate controls or structures of discipline with the gang itself an example of this process. The gang seems to offer more structure than society because of its national organisation (as shown when Larry from Kansas City seamlessly takes charge when Mac dies), but it is also merely an empty structure, one that serves itself rather than its members. There is no real gang boss or patriach controlling the gang which leads to internal disruption where loyalty is replaced by individual desire.

The gang itself is the site of a conflicting representation in *High Sierra*. On the one hand there is a sense of its pervasiveness throughout the nation, but on the other hand there is also a nomadic quality with the gangsters represented as free-floating individuals roaming the country rather than being tied to a particular city or territory. The gang is not focused on territory any more but centres itself around money which is where power now resides. The plan for the raid in California implies this nomadic quality for the gangster and suggests two levels of gang organisation, an upper administrative level (represented by Big Mac and his assistant Kranmer) and a lower operational level of the individual gangster who moves from place to place as and when the gang bosses choose. As part of the operational gang, Roy has no control over his destiny because his actions and decisions are determined for him by the gang's administrative structures. The gang is therefore both more reified and more fluid. Reification is indicated by the fact that Mac remains in charge even while he is dying because the structures of the gang keep him in power but there is also instability because the free floating nature of the gang at the operational level of Roy's foot soldier means that the gang is endemically divided and disrupted by disloyalty, as is represented in Kranmer's treachery. The gang's fragmentation is highlighted by the fact that Roy has to perpetually impose his authority over Babe and Red who are not the loyal henchman of old, but are driven by their own self-serving desires. The gang is a fractured entity, paradigmatic of an unstable society represented in the culture of travel that forms the setting for the film, whether this is the Goodhues' migration from Ohio to California or the culture of motels and auto courts that the mobile gangster of the 1940s inhabits.

This fragmentation and uncertainty extends to the unreliability of the new breed of criminal who only plays at being a gangster without having either the self-reliance or loyalty of the 'old-timer'. Kranmer, Babe and Red simply mimic old style gangsters in their actions while Mendoza copies the gangster's ostentatious style of dress and the film presents an opposition between Roy's authentic gangster and the new inauthentic gangsters who simply look like tough guys. Roy, for example, is in charge simply through his presence and does not need to simulate power through the spectacle of being a gangster or by shouting at or hitting women (as is the case with Babe and Kranmer). The film suggests that these actions are symptomatic of a feminised masculinity against which Roy's authentic masculinity is measured. Roy, for example, doesn't use a gun except when necessary and is unlike the undisciplined younger gangsters – as well as the 1930's gangster – who wave their guns around. Roy is represented as entirely self reliant because it is his body and will that give him his power, not the gun – whereas Babe and Red think it is the gun that makes them gangsters and makes them important. Marie (Ida Lupino) becomes a better gang member than any of others because she shows exactly the same characteristics as Roy in that she is loyal, reliable and obedient and is therefore more like an old-time gangster and a better 'man' than either Babe or Red. Marie and Roy are shown, however, to be untypical or even aberrant in contemporary society and, in the case of Roy, represented as out of place everywhere in this new world whether it is the city or the countryside where his historic values have their roots. Indeed, it is on the top of a mountain, in the middle of the wilderness that Roy feels is his true home, where he is cornered and killed, his dislocation represented by the way his black suit jars with the whiteness of the mountain's background. Roy's death is seen by the film as 'crashing out', an escape from the false society he inhabits, but it is not a true release because it is not an act of transcendence, simply an end to a life of alienation.

The Big Shot (1942) is often seen as an 'inferior remake' of *High Sierra* (Clarens, 1980: 178), but has interest within the 1940s gangster cycle because of its *noir* elements, such as its *femme fatale*, flashback structure, and narrative of double-cross and betrayal. Like other early 1940s gangster films it is a hybrid that experiments with the genre while also using old formulae, being part gangster, part noir, part heist and part prison drama. Like *High Sierra* it shows an old time gangster returning for one last job while also evoking the same bandit spirit through Duke Berne's black suited appearance. The film differs, however, in its predominantly urban setting and by representing Duke (Humphrey Bogart) as a criminal trying to go straight who is only forced back into crime by circumstance. The film also differs narratively in the fact that Duke does not go through with the heist which goes badly wrong without his involvement. It is here that the film enters the domain of *film noir*. Duke is persuaded against joining the heist by Lorna (Irene Manning), an old flame who is now married to Martin Fleming, a corrupt lawyer who is the secret and apparently reputable controller of the gang. From here on, the film becomes a *noir*-ish narrative of betrayal orchestrated by Fleming while also introducing Lorna as an interesting variation of the *femme fatale* who causes Duke's downfall, but doing so unwittingly rather than out of malice. Although the trope of the man of reputation as gang boss was already a stock device in the gangster genre, the narrative of concealment and double-cross was a new idea. Most previous gangster films such as *I Am the Law* had adopted a detective formula that used the revelation of the boss' identity as the denouement of the film. In *The Big Shot* the narrative focuses on Fleming's control of the gang from the beginning and suggests that it is official society which generates and controls gangster criminality.

The film, however, goes further than simply drawing attention to official corruption. During the scene when Lorna persuades Duke not to get involved in the heist, she comments on the distinction between the respectable and apparently safe gang bosses like her husband and the gangsters lower down the order who do all the work and get paid little for it, 'the little guys like you [who] get shot at, pushed around, sent to jails, to hospitals, to the morgue'. This offers a vision of a criminal class system with a gangster upper class (the officials within society) and a gangster proletariat (those who perform the crimes), generating a structure that replicates the same power structures and lack of opportunity found in legitimate capitalist society. The class distinctions in the gangster world are made evident when Duke is crossed by Fleming, who has learned of Lorna's renewed involvement with Duke, and who deliberately sabotages Duke's defence in court by drawing attention to the flaws in the evidence of his alibi, George Anderson, the honest little guy who also goes to prison. The legitimate capitalist and gangster class systems are indistinguishable with the result that innocent 'little guys' on both sides of the law suffer while the powerful are invulnerable. There is an implied critique of capitalist society here, but presented in terms of nostalgia for the founding ideals of America. The criticism of American society is thus more concerned with how contemporary America has perverted ideals of opportunity and freedom by forcing Duke back into crime and by causing George to turn to dishonesty in giving Duke a false alibi so that he can earn money to advance himself.

The Big Shot also has interest in its nostalgic revisiting of the bandit theme of *High Sierra* after Duke and Lorna escape to their hideout in a wilderness cabin after the prison break. Here Duke finds the domestic frontiersman life that Roy wanted in *High Sierra*, but the scenes of Duke stirring batter and talking of his satisfaction at 'just rockin' and a'settin'' create him as a feminised man as opposed to Roy's alienated self-reliant masculinity. The film suggests that this domestication is a failure of masculinity because it is both a selfish realisation of desires and a retreat from the duties of being a man who owes responsibilities to others. Duke owes an obligation to prove George innocent and he only becomes a man again when he gives up the satisfaction of his own desires and selflessly directs himself toward this cause. The film, however, has already suggested that Duke is a passive feminised figure because he has followed Lorna's advice to choose inaction during the heist. Duke's entrapment by Fleming's upper class gangster, therefore, can be seen not as a result of Duke being a 'little guy', but of being a 'woman'. He can only become a man by becoming active in his pursuit of justice for George, an act that is symbolic of Duke becoming a father to George and fulfilling his obligation to his surrogate son. The end of the film sees the death of Lorna, which is also the symbolic death of the feminising influence of women, followed by the death of Duke. In the final scenes, Duke re-enacts Roy Earle's position as a father in a fatherless society, firstly by bringing Fleming to justice and secondly, with his death-bed confession, by guaranteeing the success of George's romantic relationship with his girlfriend, Ruth. Duke becomes the patriarchal guarantor of legitimate society reestablishing the effectiveness of the law and ensuring the perpetuation of the family so that in the process he becomes the necessary but unwanted keystone of social ideology.

Revisiting the family plot

This concern with the question of the father and the implied death of the social patriarch was a common theme in the early 1940s gangster film. The death of the father was not new to the gangster film and had been important in films such as *Scarface* and *The Public Enemy*, although here a surrogate father had always existed in the form of society and its ideological institutions. In the 1940s gangster film, society does not have this role and is presented as fatherless with the patriarch absent or ineffective, such as Big Mac in *High Sierra*, Ralph Henry in *The Glass Key* or Farrell in *Johnny Eager*. The 1940s gangster film has as an important feature the revisiting of the family narrative, but this return entails an ideological reversal in that the gangster does not reject the family, whether this is his own or the larger social family body, but tries to enter the officially sanctioned world of the family as a way of gaining legitimacy and official power. Two films released in 1942, *The Glass Key* and *Johnny Eager* both deal with the relationship between gangster and the family.[3] Of the two, *The Glass Key* is the most important because, like the contemporary hard boiled novel (such as Chandler's *The Big Sleep*) it locates corruption in society as a whole and maps this by tracing the interconnectedness of gangsters and wealthy families. In the hard boiled genre this connection is usually made through an errant child such as Carmen Sternwood's links to the blackmailer Geiger and the gangster Eddie Mars in Chandler's *The Big Sleep* or in the case of *The Glass Key*,

Taylor Henry.[4] These narratives also have as an absent centre an impotent father, very literally in *The Big Sleep* in the form of General Sternwood who is confined to wheelchair and who is hardly alive. There is more at stake in *The Glass Key* because the patriarch is a powerful figure in politics, but his inability to control his own family indicates his lack of real effectiveness. Henry is a Reform candidate up for election whose policy is based on cleaning out the gangsters from his city but his lack of power over his son's involvement with gangsters indicates he cannot take on the gangs.

This impotence is compounded in the film by a narrative that focuses initially on the gang boss Paul Madvig's political courting of Henry and his romantic wooing of Henry's daughter, Janet (Veronica Lake), which would sanction, by marriage, the entry of the gangster into the family and legitimate society. *The Glass Key* implies that the relationship between legitimate society and gangster society is in place from the outset, however, and that the intended political and romantic union between the Henry family and Madvig's gang is simply a form of official recognition. The opening sequence establishes the blurred status of the gangster as it shows Madvig entering his campaign headquarters in business attire and having his photograph taken as if he is an important public figure. He is, however, flanked by a corps of bodyguards in the recognisable and iconic gangster attire of pinstripe suits and snap brimmed fedoras. As the camera tracks beside Madvig as he moves through the foyer it also tracks along various conversations in the background in which various people discuss his status with one person refering to him as the Head of the Voter's League, while another calls him 'the biggest crook in the State'. The sequence enacts the blurring of official and illegitimate social hierarchies suggesting that it is now the gangster who is the law and shows Madvig as someone who is both respectable and illegitimate. The appearance of Janet Henry during this sequence, while apparently drawing attention to Madvig's illegality, actually highlights the way in which the distinction between official power groups and the gangs has disappeared so that the two are now coterminous. Janet launches into a diatribe against Madvig in which she defends the virtue of official society and expresses her desire to reform Madvig 'right out of existence', an image intended to re-establish the divisions between virtuous official society and gangster criminality. Madvig replies by referring to her brother Taylor's gambling activities, undermining Janet's speech and suggesting instead that the distinction between the family or official society and the gangs is fluid. The narrative of the film, which focuses on the investigation by Beamont (Alan

Ladd) into the death of Taylor, reveals further connections between official society and the gangs, most obviously in its denouement with the discovery that it was the father who killed his own son in order to prevent his involvement with the gangs, a revelation that shows the apparently legitimate family to be as criminal as the gang. The pervasion of gangsters through society is also suggested in that unlike the 1930s gangster film, *The Glass Key* never dispels the gangster world nor brings it to justice; Madvig is not incriminated for anything, while the romantic attachment between Beaumont and Janet at the end also literalises the connection between gangster world and official society.

The pervasiveness of the gangster is comparable to the earlier gang-ster's acceptance into high society, in his literalised entry into the territory of the home. When Madvig is seen at the Henrys' house he is not simply accepted by them, but is in control of their territory as shown by the fact that it is he who invites Beaumont to enter the house not Ralph Henry. The family home becomes a spatial literalisation of power in the city and the ease of access and sense of ownership on the part of the gangsters suggests that gangster territory is not confined to working class or public space but now extends across all of the city and into both legitimate society and the private world of the home. A similar mapping of screen territory with wider social and city territory occurs shortly after when Beaumont gives instructions to the DA in his office, Beaumont also being placed centrally within the image and sitting on a desk looking down on the DA (who is framed toward the edge of the screen), suggesting that the gangsters are the real power in the city, both legally and territorially. The fluid boundaries do not just exist between legitim-ate society and the gangs, but also within the organisation of the gangs themselves. The gang structure has its own class system, though this is expressed more as a feudal arrangement of power with Madvig as the overall city boss with other gangsters under him as city barons. The overall tone of the film is of the gangsters as medieval barons plotting the overthrow of the 'king' and constantly having to be disciplined. As well as Beaumont's detective narrative into official cor-ruption the film is therefore also a more traditional film about gang rivalries but this is placed within the context of official society's rela-tionship to the gangster world. The film presents a hierarchy in flux where official society is no longer the bastion of legitimacy and stability it once was. The gangster of honour, represented by Beaumont and, in part, by Madvig, come to be the figures of law and legitimacy, as shown in the fact that it is Beaumont who uncovers the criminals and Madvig who enforces justice. Nevertheless, in the context of the ideology of the

Hollywood system of the period, the gangster cannot be shown to be entirely reputable. Thus, as a counterpart to Madvig and Beaumont, there are Madvig's rival and underling, Varna, and his thuggish henchman Jeff (William Bendix).

The figuring of Beaumont, however, does cause some ambiguity in the film (as it does with the similar figure of Tom in the Coen Brothers' remake of *The Glass Key*, *Miller's Crossing*) as it is often suggested that although Madvig enforces the organisation it is Beaumont, as the 'cerebral gangster', who holds the real power. It is Beaumont who ultimately re-imposes the power of Madvig's gang on the city through the utilisation of his intellect to solve the murder of Taylor Henry. There is therefore a sense in which *The Glass Key* shifts the emphasis away from the body of the gangster and the physicality of gangster violence to the notion of the 'cerebral gangster'. Despite Beaumont suffering torture and assault by Jeff when he is imprisoned by Varna (in an image that also invokes the feudal relationships of the film, suggesting as it does imprisonment in the torture chamber of a medieval baron's castle), this is only the temporary triumph of the body over the mind. Despite being a passive figure bounced off the walls like a 'rubber ball', Beaumont outsmarts Jeff and ultimately tricks him into a confession that returns Madvig to power. Although Madvig is still boss, Beaumont is confirmed as the real power, as is seen by the fact that it is he who is romantically united with Janet Henry and not Paul. There is thus a shift from the power of the body to the privileging of the mind in which the 'cerebral gangster' triumphs by intellect rather than imposing his will on the city through violence.

The post-war big shot

By the end of the war, the big shot narrative had mainly fallen out of vogue, as Sklar notes: '[t]he old-fashioned underworld had fallen (temporarily) out of cinematic favor, except as an atavistic threat to a better postwar social order' (1992: 254). As will be discussed in the next two chapters, the inception of gangster *noir*, syndicate, and heist narratives led to a focus on the foot soldier, henchman, or little man, often in opposition to the gang or gang boss. The post-war years do, however, begin with the return of the 'big shot' in *Dillinger* (Max Nosseck, 1945) which Munby sees as a re-awakening of the controversial aspects of the gangster film that the studios and the Breen Office had attempted to suppress in the 1930s (1999: 151–6). As Clarens notes, the film 'took no sides' (1980: 190), offering a dispassionate, if mainly fictive version, of Dillinger's life with an emphasis on the spectacle of violence itself rather than on the psychology or social reality inhabited by the protagonist. *Dillinger* located the gangster back in his brutal and violent milieu and moved him away from the experiment of the 'cerebral gangster' found in *The Glass Key* and *Johnny Eager*. Although the 'cerebral gangster' was present in *noir* variations of the genre, the big shot narratives, in the fashion of *Dillinger*, saw a return to the violent bodily gangster reliant on his strength and willpower, representing the big shot as either intensely brutal (Rocco in *Key Largo*) or psychopathic (Cody Jarrett in *White Heat*).[5] Unlike the big shot of the 1930s, however, the 1940s big shot is marginal to society. He is not a big urban gang boss who dominates and threatens society and nor does he represent the dangers of a corrupt capitalism or uncontrolled modernity. He is often simply a minor pimple to be eradicated after a brief but intense crime spree, but is important because he represents a return of a repressed form of gang-sterism (and this cycle might be termed the 'return of the big shot' rather than the 'death of the big shot') which is ideologically presented as insignificant or aberrational in the context of a positive representa-tion of booming post-war America.

Key Largo (John Huston, 1948) is a paradoxical film in terms of this return of the big shot narrative as well as in terms of gangster control of America. The film is ostensibly about the return of a once important gangster to America. However, Rocco (Edward G Robinson) is not plan-ning to return to America as Clarens and Munby suggest (Clarens, 1980: 224; Munby, 1999: 132), but is simply bringing counterfeit money into the country before returning to his exile in Cuba. He is simply a go-between, holing up in an isolated hotel (whose owners and occupants he keeps hostage during a tornado) and although he has a gang and was once a big shot his power is diminished because he is a courier not a major player. This suggests not a return of criminality and corruption to the United States, but an ambiguous position as regards the return of the gangster because although the film represents the gangster as all perva-sive, there is also a focus on his powerlessness and irrelevance. The narrative as a whole suggests this, not only because it ends with his defeat, but because the film's principal focus is not Rocco's downfall, but the moral dilemma faced by the anti-hero figure Frank MacCloud (Humphrey Bogart) as he decides whether or not post-war society is important enough to defend against the threat of gangsters like Rocco. Rocco is simply an emblem of post-war America's potential corruption and Frank must decide whether there is enough of value within it for him to oppose Rocco or whether to simply leave it to its own devices and withdraw into the alienation of the self. Nevertheless, Rocco does represent a pervasion of society by the gangster who has extended his power beyond the city to occupy the margins of America (Key Largo). This control of society is symbolised by the take-over of the Temples' hotel , an act that prompts Rocco to say to Mr Temple that 'you're going to be my guest for a while'. Rocco's occupation of the hotel suggests an inversion of traditional notions of ownership and territory. Control of space is not about legal ownership, but the occupation of the space (and the film makes much of war metaphors of occupying territory) extending the notion of the territorialisation of space by gangsters: they do not have permanent urban territorial bases any more but have become more mobile and are therefore able to occupy and control any space in America just by their presence.

There are nevertheless as many images of the gangster's powerlessness within the film as there are of his pervasiveness. When Rocco is first introduced, for example, he is in the bath hidden initially by the bars of a chair to imply his criminality and then by a fan with a newspaper in front of his face. This image clearly signifies the shadowy nature of gangsters, but also suggests that Rocco is not really present. Because he is hidden from view, he is absent from the shot and there are implications in this of his impotence, that he is an isolated figure outside of society, killing time while the action takes place elsewhere. The fragile power of the gangster is represented best by the figure of Toots, however, who despite his brutal exterior and propensity for violence displays a threatened masculinity that is emblematic of the powerlessness of the gangster. At one point, the invalid Temple jeers at Toots from his wheelchair, laughing at the thought of Toots posing with his gun in the mirror, an image that carries implications of Toots being a boy rather than a 'man'. Toots cannot reassert his masculinity except by referring to his beating of the policeman Sawyer which, however, is presented as empty bravado because Sawyer was tied up at the time. In order to protect the image of the masculine power of the gangster Rocco has to intervene by stepping forward to reassert Toots' control which is done in a quite literal way as Rocco moves into centre-screen from behind Toots. This actually has the effect of undermining Toots who is pushed off screen by this act and who is suggested therefore to be irrelevant. In the same way that Toots' masculinity is only guaranteed by the gang, Rocco's ability to impose gangster masculinity is only possible by the power of the gun. This is made clear when he plays a trick on Frank by offering him an unloaded gun and apparently giving him a chance to rid the world of the gangster corruption he despises, but dying in the process by a bullet from the loaded gun that Rocco aims at him. This is apparently a test of will and masculinity which Frank fails by throwing the gun away, showing himself to be unwilling to die for the values of honour and decency he espouses. What the scene also shows, in the fact that Rocco's gun is loaded while Frank's is not, however, is that masculinity and power are not intrinsic, but exist as externalised masculinities dependent on either an outside structure (the gang) or technology (the gun) to generate them. This is very different from the masculinity ultimately shown by Frank which the film privileges and which is located within the self. Although he initially fails the test when he refuses to shoot Rocco knowing that he will die as well, his self-reliant masculinity is gradually developed first by giving Gay a drink when Rocco has refused her one, then by supporting Temple when Rocco pulls a gun on him and finally in his triumph over the gang on the trip to Cuba when he turns from being a victimised hostage to an American hero, using his wits to overcome an apparently overwhelming force.

These images suggest that the gangster is an illusory and powerless presence in America, not a real threat. However on another level the film also suggests that gangsters are no longer as open in their activities as in the pre-war period. They are just as pervasive, but they have gone underground or into the shadows, as witnessed by the use of an isolated hotel as scene of criminal activity. This also implies that gangsters have created an inverted image of America, moving from the corrupt city to the purity of rural America and thereby infecting the 'home' of American values. The fact that Frank returns 'home' from war to a place which is actually the home of his dead best friend and to the sweetheart (Nora, played by Lauren Bacall) who is his best friend's wife, suggests this problematised vision of America. Post-war America, the film implies, has lost touch with its true values and traditions, turning honest and honourable people such as Frank into drifters who feel they have no place in society any more whereas it is the gangsters who are entrenched within society. However, the images of the true American hero and the gangster are unstable and this is most obviously seen through the way in which the film configures its ideology of the 'hero' in the form of Frank who is not a hero who goes up against the mob head on, a role taken on by Sawyer the policeman who dies for his trouble. Over the course of the film Frank is transformed from war hero to nobody to post-war anti-hero. This problematised notion of the traditional American hero, alongside the ambiguous representation of the gangsters, suggests an unstable society. This is figured most obviously in the symbolic levels of the film with the metaphor of the storm and the washing out of the roads. Nothing is fixed or permanent in post-war society which induces a nostalgia for older times where a lost cultural coherence seems to be possible. Both official society and the gangsters are nostalgic, but for different things. Temple and Frank are nostalgic for an innocence that at least Frank knows never existed, but which is the endless hope of an American ideology of virgin America. Rocco is nostalgic for the 'big time' of the pre-war gangster period when there were stable structures to the gang and people did what they were told, such as corrupt officials. Rocco's nostalgia, however, is contradictory because he still has hopes for the future, based on his individual desires, best expressed by his statement (which almost sums up the gangster philosophy) that 'I want more'. This desire is an image both of the excessive quality of gangsters (their unfulfillable desires and the sense of endless destructiveness in going after 'more'), but also of the social instability they create. Nothing is sacred and all structures of society are under threat from gangster desire. In *Key Largo*, the gangster becomes an image of the unleashing of uncontrollable individual desire on society, a desire that will disrupt all social relationships.

This sense of disruption and displacement is also presented in other early post-war gangster and big shot films. Munby argues that films such as *Nobody Lives Forever*, *I Walk Alone* and *The Gangster* 'feature the problems of old-styled "ethical" gangsters failing to adjust to the new order' of the syndicate (1999: 130). It is not just society that is unstable in these films, but the gang structure itself, even while the rise of the syndicate suggests a new more organised system being imposed on the fluidity of the gangs. Both *Nobody Lives Forever* and *I Walk Alone* focus on a returning gangster (one from the war, the other from prison) who find that they are effectively displaced persons. In *Nobody Lives Forever*, Nick Blake (John Garfield) returns to find he is no longer in control of the gambling operation he has helped to create while in *I Walk Alone* Frankie Madison (Burt Lancaster) comes out of prison to discover that his partner, Noll Turner (Kirk Douglas), has built up a corporation using the proceeds from their earlier nightclub operation. Turner refuses to allow Madison any part of the corporation he has developed and offers Madison only a share of the money from the sale of the nightclub. Blake and Madison are both one time big shots who have no place or 'home' in the contemporary world and no power. A similar narrative is mapped in *The Gangster* where a gang boss, Shubunka (Barry Sullivan), finds that his territory is being taken over by a new syndicate. At first he is unconcerned because they are just small-time hoods, but once he realises that they are part of a larger operation he finds he is unable to take any action to prevent their take over and is gradually stripped of everything he once controlled (his territory, his gang, the loyalty of his partner, and his girl). However, the film also questions his notion of ownership. His territory is legally owned by his partner for whom he acts principally as an enforcer and his gang is a notional collection of hired hands. The same is also the case with the rival syndicate who hire people as they are needed and these mercenaries feel no loyalty to the gang, willing to sell themselves to Shubunka for a higher price. Gang structures are represented here as taking on new and paradoxical forms. The film shows a contradictory gangster society of both fluid gangs and more organised structures of the syndicate. In this world the individualistic big shot either recognises he is just another hired hand (as Shubunka refuses to do when the syndicate offer him the job of enforcer) or he is a nobody, just another 'citizen' to be ignored, controlled, or killed, as happens to Shubunka at the end of the film.

Munby has argued that many gangster films of the immediate post-war years (particularly the syndicate film) represent a concern with the loss of individual male agency (1999: 132). Not all films of the period displayed this tendency, however, and there were still two examples of the driven excessive free willed gangster in the 'death of the big shot' style, the most notable of which was *White Heat* (Raoul Walsh, 1949). Many critics have commented on James Cagney's personification of Cody Jarrett whether this is his 'gruesome exaggerations' of individuality (Yaquinto, 1998: 85) or his anti-social aggression (Shadoian, 1977: 198). Such manifestations of the individual will are represented as aberrations and point to a failure of masculine socialisation as a way of representing the illegitimacy of gangster criminality in opposition to the properly ideological male of official society (represented in *White Heat* by the figure of Hank Fallon, played by Edmond O'Brien). Cody Jarrett represents an abnormal masculinity rather than a typical maleness as is shown through his mother fixation which highlights the fact that he has been insufficiently socialised in terms of the Oedipal drama, as Clarens notes when he implies that Cody is a 'mother's boy' who hasn't matured (1980: 225). Cody is presented as not just deranged but isolated therefore in the film: he is 'other' to society's notion of the individual as represented by Fallon's anonymous corporate man who subordinates his self to the needs of the legal organisation of the Treasury Department.[6] In effect, the Treasury Department is an equivalent of the syndicate or corporation and one of the problems that the film has, even while it attempts to show that crime is illegitimate, is that Cagney's performance of Cody Jarrett still makes crime look more attractive than the law (Sklar, 1992: 255). Fallon himself is a grey figure who despite showing the nimble-mindedness of the traditional American individual, has his identity subsumed into the Treasury Department and effectively becomes an organisation man. This is represented by his undercover alias, 'Vic Pardo', who has the identity that 'Fallon' lacks, his selfhood overshadowed by the procedural elements of the plot and by the representation of technology in the film.[7] While Fallon commits the death blow to Cody, the successful destruction of the gangster is not the result of individual detection and skill (the ideological myth of the detective genius), but more a product of police procedure and the technology the Treasury Department uses (spectographs, psychological profiling, oscilloscope and radar tracking), a dehumanising scientific system which can in some respects be seen to create what it seeks to control.

In this case, the law (and its system) creates Cody as its inhuman and chaotic other, but Cody is outside of the T-Man's notion of acceptable individual agency and the film represents his version of individuality as something that is illegitimate and destructive. Cody's unrestrained will is chaotic and excessive, manifested in the psychotic acts of violence which occur at random or very casually, as when he shoots another criminal in the boot of his car while eating a chicken leg. Shadoian describes him as 'energy itself, a force unleashed upon the world' (1977: 199) suggesting that Cody's individual will is expressed as inhuman. Cody's disloyal moll, Verna (Virginia Mayo), says to Big Ed (her new lover and previously one of Cody's underlings) as they prepare for him to take his revenge on them: 'Cody ain't human. Fill him full of lead and he'll still come at you' while at the end of the film after he has been shot several times, Fallon asks: 'What's holding him up'. There is a sense of inhuman will about Cody, which is able to overcome the fragility of the body, something which manifests itself in an impossible control over self and body. The mess hall scene, after Cody has heard of his mother's death, also references this in the way that despite the fact that Cody is struck repeatedly by the prison guards he keeps on going. The resolution and determination represented here suggest superhuman qualities rather than inhumanity. Nevertheless, this drive and exaggerated individual will is shown to be meaningless as Cody is gradually stripped of his free will when the law, in the shape of its technology and procedural system, entrap and finally destroy him. It is implied that criminal detection is itself inhuman, reducing everything to a system, resulting in the dehumanisation of its subjects, not only the criminals it punishes such as Cody, but also the people who work within its system such as Fallon. Cody's death, however, is represented as a triumphant excess and has implications of apocalypse for the social systems that bring about his downfall. He dies on top of a gas tank in the midst of a dehumanised industrial complex which is allied in the film with the industrial techniques utilised by the government to bring him to justice. His death, while it is an act of self-consumption, can also be seen to offer a critique of the industrial machine systems upon which official society bases itself. The film identifies with the gangster's excess in this act and with the sheer scale of the destruction he has wreaked taking a position in opposition to Fallon's epitaph that Cody 'finally got to the top of the world and it blew right up in his face' which comes as a weak ideological footnote to Cody's gleeful 'Made it ma. Top of the world.'

Cagney reprised his aberrant gangster role in *Kiss Tomorrow Goodbye* (Gordon Douglas, 1950) which, like *The Big Shot*, is often seen as an inferior version of the film that preceded it. The film nevertheless has interest because Cagney's gangster, Ralph Cotter, is even more exaggerated in his excessive behaviour than Cody Jarrett and the narrative even more based on a logic of action and movement than *White Heat*. The narrative momentum never lets up as one crime follows another in quick succession. For example, as soon as Cotter is out of prison he is back to business, robbing a supermarket and bludgeoning the manager to the floor. While Jarrett was a murderer and a robber, Cotter is these and more: he is a blackmailer, petty crook, fraudster, and shakedown artist. Cotter like Cody Jarrett is a creature of excess who is willing to go one better than anyone else in the film. For example, when Margaret Dobson, the daughter of a wealthy industrialist tries to scare Cotter by driving along tight roads very fast, he moves his foot across to the accelerator so that it goes even faster. Cotter is an elemental creature who overwhelms everyone he comes across by the force of his will, whether it is Holiday, the sister of his dead accomplice, who becomes his lover, or the corrupt cops who are soon in his pocket. As Krutnik comments, Cotter 'achieves immense sexual and political power' and becomes 'an object of fascination for the other characters in the film, and for the spectator' (1991: 200). Meeting him is presented as on a par with meeting the devil as he corrupts and taints at will and seems to be a force that cannot be contained. The corrupt cops who try to control him find that he soon has evidence with which he can blackmail them and the scene where the tables are turned is lit so that Cagney's eyes seem to be burning with a diabolic glint. His derangement and satanic qualities are most evident in his relationship with Holiday which is principally represented in terms of violence and hatred. They become lovers after Holiday throws a knife at Cotter and he has whipped her to hysteria with a towel. Similarly when she learns of his affair with Margaret she responds by throwing a pot of coffee at him. Rather than striking back he laughingly eggs her on by saying he likes cream and sugar with his coffee which results in a jug and sugar pot coming his way, both of which he ducks under. Here Cotter takes pleasure in Holiday's release of emotions and relishes her anger because it makes her like him, a figure of unrestrained desire. He is both inhuman and superhuman, but he is also like an automaton gone out of control, going further and further to excess. As a result he causes panic in everyone he comes across and becomes a force of chaos and disruption because he is an absolute and seemingly unstoppable threat to the stability of society. Indeed, the opening court scene already suggests that he has destabilised society with its shots of a row of corrupt officials and a litany of their crimes. Ultimately he is contained, but not by the ineffectual forces of the law. Cotter is killed by Holiday when she discovers that it was Cotter who killed her brother in the prison break. His death is a testimony to the difficulty of containing his diabolic spirit. Holiday shoots him, but he gets up with an inhuman grin on his face and a broken bottle in his hand and it takes a second shot to finally destroy him. Cotter is effectively the last of the individualistic gangsters because big shot gangsters like Cody Jarrett and Cotter are aberrations in terms of other gangster movies of the period which principally focus on death of individual agency and subjectivity.

4
Outside Society, Outside the Gang: the Alienated *Noir* Gangster

Post-war transitions: *film noir*'s cultural and cinematic context

The period of the 1940s and 1950s is testimony to fact that the gangster genre cannot be understood solely in terms of either a stable set of generic conventions or a fixed iconography as these are represented by the classic gangster narrative and its persistence as a generic narrative dominant.[1] Even in the 'death of the big shot' variation, which is closest to the classic cycle of the early 1930s, there are too many variations to be able to understand this genre solely as a product of the genre's earlier conventions. The 'death of the big shot' cycle, most notably, does not follow the classic rise and fall of the gangster because it only shows his fall, nor do the films in this cycle share the same tragic scope that Warshow (1977: 127–33) attributes to the gangster genre not least because the gangster has already lost his 'big shot' status at the start. It is when turning to the variations outside the 'death of the big shot' formula, however, that the flexibility and mutability of the genre becomes clear and its reduction to the conventions and iconography established in the classic cycle becomes untenable. This is obvious, first of all, by the range of gangster sub-genres that came into existence in this period including gangster *noir*, the syndicate film, the heist narrative, the rogue cop, the development of the undercover and G-Man formulae, the *exposé*, and the one-man-against-the-mob narrative. Equally, the fact that many of the films in this period do not reside in any single sub-genre indicates a cross-fertilisation and innovation within the gangster genre. *The Big Combo*, for example, has been placed in the next chapter in the section on the syndicate film, but could just as easily have been considered in terms of gangster *noir*, rogue cop, *exposé*, or one-man-against-the-mob narratives.

One key difference between the 'death of the big shot' formula and other gangster films of the early post-war years is a very different approach to the issue of male individuality. The former generates a nostalgic evocation of the free willed gangster individual that other gangster narratives of the 1940s and 1950s find impossible to even remember. Each of the new sub-genres of this period however offers a different response to individuality and masculinity. *Noir* and syndicate variations, for example, map the loss of individuality through their representation of a new relationship of the individual gangster to the gang, which becomes a structure of entrapment rather than a source of power because its system of rules and conventions smothers individuality. The *noir* gangster is alienated from the gang as well as from society, cut adrift from any sense of social or communal coherence or identity. On the other hand the heist sub-genre maps the fragmentation of individuality by placing the gangster in a society with no system or order. The gangster becomes a mobile figure allied loosely to a gang which is now more a system of contracts and temporary alliances. The heist gangster is a development of the gangster *flaneur* of the classic narrative but extends the principle of mobility across the nation rather than placing it solely within the city. A further difference is that this mobility does not necessarily bring freedom, but instead brings fragmentation and a sense of loss as there are no structures to organise identity any more. Two things need to be noted in this concern with individuality; first, it is specifically a loss of *male* subjectivity and identity and, secondly, that the loss of male individuality in this period is as much a myth as a reality. Post-war gangster films do not necessarily reflect a culture of the loss of individuality and the attenuated male, as Reid and Walker point out in relation to *film noir*, noting that American culture in the years after the war can be seen, rather, as a renewal of masculinity and the recuperation of a 'phallic regime' (1993: 65).

This construction of a new vision of society is mapped in the figuration of the gangster. Where the classic gangster film represented the gangster straining against social restrictions and finding that individuality was only possible outside official society in the world of criminality, the films of the early post-war years represent new power alignments where the individual gangster is often straining to assert his desires against the limits imposed by the gang. The gang as a structure is no longer in opposition to society because increasingly it is identified as being synonymous with ideology. The individual gangster is still seen in opposition to official ideology, but the gangster film starts to adopt the view offered by *The Roaring Twenties* that the gangster is now typical of the experience of male individuality as a whole and he becomes an Everyman figure to be identified with rather than to be condemned. This can be seen in the ways that the gang as a structure develops its own alternative economy to official society but also that this 'black market' economy runs parallel with and even displaces the official ideological economy. The key 'racket' in the post-war period is thus not the distribution of illicit substances such as alcohol or drugs, but the numbers racket which is used, on the surface, to differentiate the gangster economy from official capitalist production but also to show that official and unofficial economies are indistinguishable. The 'numbers' racket can be seen as a distillation of the circulation of capital because it involves not only the pure flow of money, but also because there is no product being bought or sold except money itself. The numbers economy as a paper economy mirrors capitalist production: the issue of paper (bank notes, cheques and notes of credit) in order to facilitate the acquisition of more paper (notes of ownership, bonds, and share certificates). Moreover, *noir* and syndicate films in particular suggest that the gangster economy is not simply a monetary system, but that it is also coterminous with the ideological economy of corporatisation and its application of industrial or machine systems to cultural and social production. The gangster exists in opposition to both the alternative and official corporate ideological economies and his aberrance is measured by the fact that he has no place in either.

Film noir and its discourses

As Neale has noted, it is usual to begin any discussion of *film noir* by commenting on the heterogeneity of the films designated as such (Neale, 2000: 152) as, for example, Walker does when he says that *film noir* is 'too diverse a group [of films] to be constituted with any precision as a generic category' (1992: 8). This is not the place for a full account of *film noir*, but in order to consider the *noir* variation of the gangster genre, some consideration of *film noir* as a whole is needed. There are many accounts of *film noir*, including a number of essay collections, all of which stress the diversity of *film noir* and take divergent positions (Kaplan, 1978; Hirsch, 1981; Telotte, 1989; Krutnik, 1991; Silver and Ward, 1992; Cameron, 1992; Copjec, 1993; Palmer, 1994; Silver and Ursini, 1996; Christopher, 1997; Naremore, 1998).[2] Dominant tendencies in the study of *noir* have, however, focused on the detective hard boiled versions of *noir* found in film adaptations of works by Hammett, Chandler, or Woolrich or identifed *noir* with the suspense thriller in the mould of *Double Indemnity* (Walker, 1992: 9–16). A further dominant thematic identified with *noir* is its focus on the diversion of desire into female criminality and male entrapment by it (Telotte, 1989).[3] Finally, criticism of *noir* has focused on its transgressive qualities (Telotte, 1989: 2) and the way in which it offers a critique of an affluent post-war capitalist economy. While it is not possible to classify the whole of *film noir* in such a way, one area that does offer a critique of society is gangster *noir* with its concerns with power and money, the capitalist economy and the development of new engines of oppression in the form of the corporatisation of society. This does not necessarily mean that gangster *noir* offers a left critique of capitalism because many gangster *noir* films place themselves within a distinctly American ideological economy. It is the death of the American dream and its implications for individual success and achievement that is bemoaned in *noir*, not the ideology of the American dream itself.[4]

This tendency in *noir* to identify the failures of American ideology without actually criticising the ideology itself, or offering any solutions, can be seen as one of its most important elements. One way of describing *noir* is to see it as an articulation of a crisis in modernity and its ideologies and economic systems, but one that is less a reflection of an actual crisis in modernity than a construction of it.[5] *Noir* is a refraction of cultural concerns through the lens of the text, responding to cultural phenomena but exaggerating or re-focusing them textually. *Noir* is not necessarily a result of specific aspects of 1940s society, but more a response to larger cultural movements such as the Depression, and extensions of consumer society, as Reid and Walker have argued (1993: 63–6). For example, modernity's development of a culture of the commodity and the exteriorisation of the self through the commodification of identity can be identified in the figure of the *femme fatale* whose concern with money and objects of value creates her as an objectified embodiment of the cultural pervasion of the commodity. It is also implied in *film noir* that masculine integrity is under threat from the commodity, or that it has been perverted in some way as is the case with Mike Hammer in *Kiss Me Deadly*. Hammer is effectively an empty self and his identity is constructed through its externalisation in terms of the spaces the body occupies and the objects that surround it, whether this is Hammer's clothes, his apartment or his car. The sense of this as a perversion stems from the way in which commodification is linked to Hammer's brutality, solipsism, and narcissism in what might be seen as an early version of Jameson's postmodern 'waning of affect' (1984: 61–2; 1991: 10–12) in which the private self of emotion and intellect is displaced by an exteriorised identity that is more concerned with spectacle and display than with psychological, moral or emotional responses to, and relationships with, society.

In this respect, *noir* can be seen as an extension of modernism's critique of mass culture and the melting of selfhood in the face of commodities because identity no longer resides solely in the body. *Film noir* can also be seen to position itself within the discourses of modernism in its representation of femininity and, in its demonisation of women in the figure of the *femme fatale*, shares the same approach to modernism's vision of a feminine mass culture.[6] *Film noir* also offers a parallel fetishisation of the male body, particularly through the broad shouldered double breasted jacket, as a way of emphasising the maleness of the body. In focusing on the angular lines of the shoulders, the *noir* double breasted jacket draws attention to its masculine shape while also emphasising the male body's solidity and its ability to occupy and dominate both physical space and the image space of the cinema screen. However, this kind of overdetermined masculinity only resides in the jacket which is itself part of the same culture of commodity represented by the *femme fatale*. The double breasted jacket also draws attention to the fact that maleness is not intrinsic to the male body or intellect any more, but is dependent on external accessories. There is an emptying out of male identity as the masculine self becomes externalised, dissipated into the clothes the male body wears and the commodities it utilises, much like the figure of the *femme fatale* whose identity is created by the objects that adorn and surround her. In this respect, the double breasted jacket becomes almost as iconic and significant as the *femme fatale*'s fur coat and emphasises not the re-masculinisation of the male but his feminisation.

Film noir can in many ways be seen to share the same tension as modernism's relationship to industrial and urban culture. McArthur notes *film noir*'s fears over the dissolution of traditional structures and certainties which gives rise to a 'general mood of malaise, [a] loneliness and *angst*, and [a] general lack of clarity about the characters' motives' (1972: 67), a description that could fit most modernist novels. It is the *noir* city that has particular resonance for this collapse of structure and the entry into a fluid and unstable cultural milieu that is 'a realm in which all that seemed solid melts into the shadows, and where the traumas and disjunctions experienced by individuals hint at a broader crisis of cultural self-figuration engendered by urban America' (Krutnik, 1997: 99).[7] The *noir* city is not the city of modernist architectural visions of order and system (Heynen, 1999), often demonised by postmodernist critics such as Jencks (1989), but a fluid feminised space of commodities, signs and images. The *noir* city is a trap, not a place of freedom and mobility, and the image most often associated with the *noir* city is the labyrinth. Thus, in *film noir* it is not just women who seem to ensnare the male hero but the whole of contemporary urban society. There are, however, two distinct types of configuration of the city in *film noir* and it is possible to distinguish two modes of city representations that can be identified as cultural discourses associated with the East Coast and the West Coast. Pre-war gangster films tended to focus on East Coast cities because they were historically the places with a large proportion of immigrants but also because they were the most violent and chaotic in terms of gang wars.[8] As large industrial cities, they represented places of opportunity and were particularly associated with the flow and acquisition of capital. In the *noir* period, there is a tendency to see the West Coast replacing the East so that, as Munby notes, Los Angeles replaces New York and Chicago as a cultural dominant (1999: 137). In the postwar period the two modes can also, however, be seen to be informed by the Western genre's opposition of East with West, where the East represents system, government and lack of freedom while the West is a place of freedom, though in the context of *noir* this is refigured as fragmentation and an excess of individual desire that creates chaos instead of engendering liberation and mobility. While *film noir* generally adopts the West Coast discourses of the city, gangster *noir* tends to the East Coast vision of society, reformulating the pre-war gangster city of opportunity as a space of systematisation and oppression so that, whereas the classic gangster film utilises the skyscraper as a symbol of achievement and individual success, in gangster *noir* skyscrapers become looming monoliths that surround the hero like bars of a prison as in *Force of Evil*.

Gangsters and *film noir*

The issue of space is a key concern in gangster *noir*, particularly as the films in general can be characterised by a transformation of the significations attached to urban space. The classic gangster can be seen as part of a process of territorialisation (both of space and of the screen), a figure who takes control of space, by the literal acquisition of territory for example, but who is also able to occupy any space simply by his presence. The gangster *noir* hero, on the other hand, is part of a process of deterritorialisation in which his identity is not expressed through the extension across space, but dissipated by it, existing in 'liminal

uncertainty' (Dargis, 1996: 16). Gangster *noir* has several different tendencies in relation to this, one of which is to see the gangster hero lose
all control of space whatsoever except for a minimal personal space as is
the case with The Swede, in *The Killers*, who ultimately controls only the
bed on which he lies waiting for his death. Another version of this
deterritorialisation occurs in the loss of identity when the hero becomes
part of a wider cultural space, as with Charlie Davis in *Body and Soul*, for
example, who is turned into a public spectacle not only as an image of
success, but also because his identity becomes expressed in his consumption of money and commodities. A further kind of loss of identity
involves the extension of the self into the gang system, a process developed most obviously in the later syndicate movies in which personal
identity is surrendered for the purposes of power, creating the self as a
corporate or syndicate automaton with no private selfhood. This is the
situation of Joe Morse in *Force of Evil* who desires to express his personal
identity by helping his brother but is unable to effect this because the
gang system does not allow him to do so until he steps outside their
domain. The replacement of identity with power is linked to deterritorialisation because the gang system of gangster *noir* is more fluid than the
pre-war gang. The gang of the gangster *noir* sub-genre is more invested
within the system and the national structures of the gang itself, so that
the occupation of a literal territory is no longer important. The gang of
gangster *noir* finds power by owning and controlling money rather than
space and because money is fluid and moveable the gang becomes
paradoxically more fluid as it becomes more systematised. With his
investment of identity in the gang the gangster *noir* hero thus finds
that he is dissipated rather than empowered by the new systems of
operation.

Although it has a consistent focus on the death of the individual
gangster *noir* is imprecise as a description of a distinct sub-genre. It
takes in films that could be included in other sub-genres such as racketeering films like *Force of Evil* and *The Big Combo*, undercover narratives
such as *T-Men* and *The Street with No Name*, Cain and Abel stories such as
Cry of the City, as well as films that focus on the lone man taking on the
mob, whether this is a law official (as in the undercover narrative), a
criminal as in *Kiss of Death*, or a boxer as in *Body and Soul*. It is difficult to
sustain consistency in the iconography, narrative structures and cultural
thematics of gangster *noir*, not simply because it is part of *film noir* but
also because it partakes of the same flexibility and diversity that the
gangster genre displays. Gangster *noir* films, however, do share a tendency to focus on the wider sphere of the rackets, on how society

becomes pervaded by the illegitimate gangster economy, and on how it becomes impossible for the individual to escape the embrace of a pervasive gangster society. As McArthur points out, gangster *noir* is often concerned with one man's relationship with the world of crime as in *Kiss of Death* and *Force of Evil* (1972: 49) as a way of articulating the tension between self and society as a whole, but such films also entail the increasing sense that gangster values and the gangster economy have not only infiltrated official society but usurped it so that the gangster world is no longer an unofficial or illegitimate economy, but has become the dominant or 'legitimate' economy.

The emasculated male in early gangster *noir*

The Killers (Robert Siodmak, 1946) is a useful film with which to begin a discussion of gangster *noir* because it exemplifies this generic flexibility. The film is placed by Krutnik in the tough investigative thriller sub-genre of *noir* and he interprets it principally in terms of the fracturing and entrapment of post-war masculinity by the *femme fatale* (1991: 114–24). Shadoian places the film in the gangster genre, but admits that the gangster figure is no different from the other urban heroes of *noir*, 'cops, private eyes, murderers, John Does displaced from their daylight world into nightmares of criminal violence, psychopaths, and other lone-wolf variants' (1977: 62). In *The Killers* the gangster becomes just another marginalised male trying to survive, not someone seeking to stamp their mark on society as in the classic gangster film. The narrative concerns the apparently meaningless and unmotivated killing of the Swede, also known as Ole Anderson and Pete Lunn (Burt Lancaster), and the attempts of an insurance investigator, Reardon (Edmond O'Brien), to discover both the reasons and history behind this criminal assassination. The film is principally narrated in flashback by various characters as they tell their stories about the Swede, detailing how he developed from has-been boxer to gang fall-guy in the double-cross engendered by the heist gang-boss, Colfax, and his lover (and later his wife), Kitty (Ava Gardner), who have actually made it look as if it was The Swede who crossed the gang. The Swede is murdered by Colfax's killers because Clofax has accidentally driven through the town where the Swede now works in a gas station and fears that other members of the gang will also happen across the Swede and learn the real story. Much is made of fate and accident in the film, particularly the accident that the Swede's gas station is part of a larger chain insured by Reardon's company. Reardon's investigation itself, although apparently a linear ordering of events, is generated predominantly by chance encounters and revelations, the symbol of which is his piecing together of the fragments of Blinky Franklin's confession to create order and meaning out of apparent randomness. In the narrative present, Blinky's confession is just fragmentary ravings, but when enacted in flashback these are ordered into a consistent narrative. Reardon himself is a contradictory figure because his investigation apparently creates him as a purposeful controlling linear figure in the mould of the hard-boiled detective, but his inquiries are also principally controlled by chance. Because his actions are determined by arbitrary events, Reardon becomes as marginal and controlled a figure as the Swede even though he apparently represents masculine normalcy and provides an alternative legitimate centre for the film's events as part of an attempt to extirpate the inverted sado-masochistic masculinity represented by the Swede's relationship with Kitty. Discovering the motives for the killing of the Swede and how he metamorphosed from the masculine icon of the boxer to a duped masochist is for Reardon therefore an attempt to rescue and recuperate official masculinity and to give himself purpose at the same time.

The specific gangster aspects of the film are provided by the Swede's involvement with the heist gang, but he is never anything more than a hired heavy or foot soldier. He also tends to be fairly marginal as a gangster figure because his criminal life is motivated by his desires for the monetary success that will attract Kitty rather than the personal glory money brings in itself. His criminality almost seems incidental and the Swede is more of an accidental gangster, both in his entry into the criminal underworld and in his attempts to usurp the existing gang boss, Colfax, which is done at the instigation of Kitty as part of the double cross created by Colfax himself. Neither is the gang of *The Killers* a gang in the traditional sense. It is much more fluid than the classic gangster hierarchy, with its different ranks to be negotiated in the rise to gang boss, and there is the implication that Colfax's gang is simply a collection of free floating individuals which makes no demands on the individual gangster's allegiance and loyalty. Nor is Colfax a traditional gang boss, but simply a big wheel in the underworld who has the power to make plans for robberies and to collect together people to fulfil the plan. There is no organisation or racket as there is, for example, in *Force of Evil* or in the syndicate films of the 1950s, more a fluid transnational network of connections and operations. *The Killers* thus both suggests the pervasiveness of gangsterism but also represents the gangster as a marginal or even ghostly figure because there is no centralised criminal underworld. The Swede is a symbol of this as an invisible presence in the film, an effect compounded by the flashback structure which contributes to the fragmented quality of his identity.

In this, the film is also part of a wider representation of the gangster in the 1940s focusing on the death of the gangster personality. There are effectively no more big shots and it is in gangster *noir* that the final death of the big shot can be seen. The Swede is a minimal or attenuated gangster and his representation helps to engender a new variation of the gangster film which concentrates on gangsters who are not really gangsters, but whose gangster identity is utilised to represent the death of individuality or masculinity, of which the Swede's infatuation with, and entrapment by, Kitty is the symbol. *The Killers* has a fatalistic quality to it (Shadoian, 1977: 109) and the film makes much of the fact that its hero is already dead, as when the Swede in his final fight is knocked unconscious on his feet and is described as having 'dead man's legs'. However, this is only the case for the individual gangster. The criminal or illegitimate gangster economy is shown to be flourishing in the film and society is seen to be pervaded by violent criminality, as when the killers take over the diner in the opening scenes and openly admit that they are there to kill the Swede. Their openness suggests that they effectively administer the law of society, something which their attitude and apparel compounds as they could as easily be police detectives as gangsters. Their ability to both occupy and control the space of the diner (to territorialise it, even if only temporarily) also suggests that ordinary honest people are not only no longer the centre of society, but also have no impact on the ideological landscape of a gangster controlled culture. The townsfolk are turned into meaningless pawns or spectators, represented as useless people without any power.

The Killers is a crime film in which the gangster and the gangster milieu are simultaneously both fundamental and incidental to its main concerns. A similar situation is mapped in *Out of the Past*, aka *Build My Gallows High* (Jacques Tourneur, 1947), which shares similar concerns with both the social pervasion by the gangster and the entrapment of a male hero by a *femme fatale*. Unlike *The Killers*, however, the attempts to normalise masculinity by understanding an inverted feminised masculinity are less evident. In *The Killers*, although the normalisation of masculinity in the figure of Reardon becomes ambiguous, it is implied that he manages to stabilise and reverse the loss of male power by bringing Kitty to justice and therefore helping to prevent the further spread of passive masculinity. In *Out of the Past*, the situation is more complex with both the normalised masculinity and inverted masculinity existing simultaneously in the same person, Jeff Bailey (Robert

Mitchum), who is represented both in terms of an obvious masculinity in the narrative present (as signified by his pioneer-hunter's clothing), but who has a past as a passive male (principally shown in flashback). The main focus of the narrative concerns Jeff's loss of masculinity during his attempts to discover the whereabouts of Kathie Moffett (Jane Greer) and the $40,000 she has stolen from her gangster lover, Whit Sterling (Kirk Douglas), because in finding Kathie, which seems to be an apparent triumph of the self-reliant detective masculinity, Jeff is entrapped by her (Krutnik, 1991: 103–12; Grist, 1992: 207–8). Krutnik locates the imagery of entrapment in the luminescent quality that surrounds Kathie, particularly in the scene in the Acapulco cantina when Kathie first appears surrounded by a halo of light. Jeff is represented as a moth circling a bright light and his active persona is displaced by a passive masochistic demeanour as he lets Kathie 'determine when they shall meet' (Krutnik, 1991: 107). Although Jeff and Kathie decide to flee Whit together, Jeff is ultimately betrayed by both his partner, Jack Fisher, and by Kathie who, as Jeff is later to discover, goes back to Whit leaving him to clean up after her murder of Fisher.

Jeff, like the Swede, is accidentally discovered in hiding some time later by one of Whit's hoods, Joe Stephanos, and taken back to Whit apparently to atone for his betrayal, but actually to act as the fall guy (a persona which would re-establish his irrelevance and feminisation as an object to be used) for the murder of Whit's attorney, Leonard Eels. Jeff realises he is in the frame for Eels' murder, however, resulting in his attempt to take control of events as a way of making his own personal amends for the way he ceded control to Kathie earlier in the film. In order to achieve this, he takes possession of the tax files which will allow him control over another man (Whit), an act of attempted domination which he also believes will allow him to dominate Kathie who he thinks is submissive to Whit. This assertion of masculinity is represented in the scene in which Jeff takes possession of the tax files, entering one of Whit's clubs like a gangster figure of old, and assaulting the manager, an image of the invasion of Whit's territory that in the classic gangster film is a symbol of the invading gangster's superiority over his enemy. Although Jeff is later forced to go back to the club, the scene in which he, Kathie and Whit's henchmen discuss what is to be done represents Jeff apparently in a position of power, seated centrally behind the manager's desk as if he were in control of the space that the others move around in. This, however, is an ambiguous situation as is shown by the fact that the other figures surround him suggesting that he is being closed in on, as ultimately occurs narratively when the police discover

Eels' body sooner than expected. This results in Kathie taking the initiative from him by killing Whit and as a result leaving Jeff with some meaningless evidence over a dead man's tax evasion while also leaving him in the frame for the killing of Eels. He decides, however, to take control one last time, albeit an act of resolve that is self-destructive (suggesting that assertion of individuality and masculinity is itself self-consuming), by guiding Kathie to a police roadblock where she kills Jeff for betraying her before she herself is punished by being shot.

Although *Out of the Past* suggests that loss of masculinity occurs as a result of the release of female desire into society (represented by Kathie's self-interested articulation of desire), Jeff's predicament is also represented against a background of a society pervaded by gangsters. Like *The Killers*, the film uses gangster society as a symbol for the loss of control of society by the male individual because, although the gang is represented by a single individual (Whit), it is also represented as a more structured and larger scale operation than in *The Killers*. The gang world cannot be escaped no matter where Jeff runs, something that is underscored by the fact that the film opens with his discovery by Whit's mob. The gangster world is however itself contradictory in its images of male power. Early in the film when Jeff is taking the investigation job from Whit, he is represented as lying back in his chair virtually horizontal. This can be interpreted as an image of his own certainty and potency, but it also suggests feminised passivity in the face of gangster power. The film, however, problematises gangster masculinity by giving Jeff an erotic charge in relation to Whit and Joe which is illustrated when Kathie says that Whit wants revenge on Jeff because he hates him in the same way that he loved and hated her. There is an implication that Whit and Joe are both attracted to Jeff, something heightened by the style in which Jeff wears his trench coat which flares out at the bottom as if he were wearing a dress. The gangster world is represented as a homo-erotic feminised space, not least because it is revealed that the machinations Jeff is trapped in in are directed as much by Kathie as by Whit. At the end of the film, the feminisation of the gang is compounded when after killing Whit, Kathie announces that she is now running the show, leaving Jeff at her mercy because without Whit's power to make people do things Jeff cannot guarantee his own safety. Kathie thus emasculates the gangster by destroying the gangster law of the enforcer (the male power system). In some respects it is Kathie who is the most important gangster figure in the film (and her character might be read in terms of the rise and fall narrative) something that is particularly evident in her death when, on realising that Jeff has betrayed her she uses the language of the gangster in calling him a 'dirty double crossing rat' before dying in traditional gangster style in a hail of bullets. Ultimately, Kathie's aberrance is represented in her attempt to take on the role of gangster boss, a role usually reserved for the male patriarch. She is no longer the traditional *femme fatale* of *film noir*, an uncentred woman following money around from one man to another, but is simply doing what the classic gangster did: centering herself by taking control of the 'show' and manipulating the money that will give her power. This is no more aberrant than traditional gangster criminality, but *film noir* sees this not as an act of empowerment but a threat to masculine dominance. In the end, Kathie is destroyed not for her criminality but for being a woman.

Kiss of Death (Henry Hathaway, 1947) also uses the gangster genre to investigate the issue of the feminised male, but takes a more positive position in its representation of Nick Bianco (Victor Mature) and normalises the domesticated masculinity he comes to symbolise. The film follows the narrative of Nick from a small time gangster to member of legitimate society after he has turned informer because his gang have failed in their promise to support his family. In the course of this narrative he is drawn into an undercover operation which is intended to ensnare a psychopathic gangster, Tom Udo (Richard Widmark), that ultimately leads to a *High Noon* style showdown between Nick and Udo. The film thus varies the G-Man style narrative, firstly by utilising an undercover variant, but also by using a criminal as the operative who takes on the mob. Unlike the Swede, Nick Bianco strays from legality and becomes a gangster out of necessity, but unlike *The Roaring Twenties* the film does not legitimise the representation of the creation of the gangster out of social environment. This is principally because Nick is an unusual gangster who has a strict code of morals that is untypical of the gangster world he inhabits and which is seen as better represented by the figure of Udo who is shown as a born psychopath. Nevertheless, this apparent binary opposition of 'good' and 'bad' gangster is undermined by the film's uncertain view of criminality. Nick's experience hints at a critique of social conditions, but the film draws back from this not only in its representation of Udo as a born thug but also because Nick is able to overcome deprivation and enter official society of the family and labour as a way out of the gang world and as a way of finding a legitimate domesticated masculinity in opposition to the aberrant masculinity of Udo's gangster. Nick is a feminised male, but the film does not see this as illegitimate, partly because this masculinity is ideologically sanctioned by society, but also because the absolute alterity of

Udo's selfish desiring masculinity has the effect of highlighting Nick's code of honour as expressed in both his unwillingness to turn informer and in the selflessness with which he sacrifices himself to bring Udo to justice.

The code of the gangster that Nick adopts is, however, represented as a somewhat empty system which at times seems more like an attitude, a mode of dress, or a form of behaviour rather than any deep sense of kinship. For example, when Nick is offered the chance of parole in exchange for information, he is represented as an iconic gangster tough guy draped over a chair with a sneer on his face, an attitude that is very similar to the self-conscious bravado shown by Udo on the train to the prison. Nevertheless, while Udo plays at being a gangster (as he does in the night club after Nick's release in the almost parodic excess of his brutal treatment of his moll), Nick's posturing is caused by his sense of loyalty and is a product of the gang system within which he has invested his identity and desire. Udo on the other hand is presented as having little loyalty beyond himself. He is a psychopathic gangster cut free from any social values or wider structure of belonging. Udo is will personified and in his first appearance, on the journey to prison, he is suggested as being beyond good and evil in his view that his crime of slicing the ears off a man is 'traffic ticket stuff'. Udo is a nomadic thug, floating aimlessly through the film and the city he occupies. He is a development of the gangster as *flaneur* of the classic gangster narrative, but he is all *flaneur* and in this respect can be seen to be the first incarnation of the purposeless gangster that has become popular in contemporary gangster films such as *Mean Streets*, *Goodfellas*, and *Pulp Fiction*. He is also a creature of randomness, his violence coming on suddenly, as in his murder of Rizzo's mother, who he kills by pushing her wheelchair down the stairs. Udo thus symbolises a desiring but affectless gangster masculinity which is seemingly immune to the feminisation of the male because his identity is engendered by the immediate gratification of his masculine desires without thought or reflection. It is this which causes Udo's downfall as his inability to live outside the present causes him to succumb to Nick's taunts and respond by shooting him just as the police arrive to witness the event and to arrest him. The final scene of the film represents the opposition between the gangster world at its most irredeemable (Udo) and an ideological vision of society's ability to reform the gangster by directing his loyalty away from the gang and toward the family (Nick). Nick's willingness to sacrifice himself in order to incriminate Udo is the result of his desire to protect his family and the style that is adopted in the restaurant and on the street is very resonant of the later *High Noon*, which similarly focuses on the defence of family and civic community, and also includes the clock on the wall that, in *Kiss of Death*, tells Nick how long it is before the police will arrive to witness Udo's crime against him. In this final scene, the film also re-defines what it is to be a masculine hero. For Udo, the world is split between people who are 'big men' (those who follow the gangster code) and 'squirts' (those who live outside this code who it is implied are weak feminised men). In the restaurant, Nick finally antagonises Udo enough to shoot him by calling him a 'squirt', reversing Udo's categorisations of masculinity and attributing a failed masculinity to Udo, which the film also adopts, thus legitimating the domesticated maleness that Nick has adopted.

While Udo embodies the loss of moral certainties that envelops the world of gangster *noir*, he can also be seen as a Nietzchean gangster who lives beyond the moral categories of good and evil. Martin Rome (Richard Conte) in *Cry of the City* (Robert Siodmak, 1948) in a similar vein could be described as a Schopenhauerian gangster. His representation extends the tragic elements that attach to the gangster by re-inscribing him as a fatalistic figure who while he is a willed subject is also driven by something beyond himself. The narrative of the film follows Rome's escape from justice and his movements across the city as he seeks to evade his nemesis, Lieutenant Candella (Victor Mature). His will seems to be embodied by a larger abstract principle which means that even though throughout the film he is constantly trying to impose his will on the world, it is fate and not individual desire that determines his actions and motives. Much is made, for example, of religious imagery and improbable blind chance (Rome's accidental shooting of a corrupt lawyer's secretary) to suggest that this is a depersonalised world where individuals simply act out the will of some higher transcendent force and Rome's path around the city seems to develop an inevitable and circular path that leads him back to where he began. The film similarly presents Candella as a driven character obsessively pursuing Rome to prevent him from becoming a hero (particularly in the eyes of Rome's younger brother), which is a condition of individuality toward which Rome strives. Ideologically, *Cry of the City* resists this movement and seeks to bring Rome down to the level of the human so that Rome is not an embodiment of a larger principle, but just a minor and insignificant hoodlum. In doing this Candella himself comes to embody an abstract principle of justice and becomes an archetypal 'nemesis' figure rather than an embodied individual. There is also a further contradiction that stems from the Cain and Abel narrative of the film, as Langman and Finn point out (1995b: 62), because although the choice between law and crime is a product of individual will it also commits the two characters to a particular path from which there is no going back with the result that they have no control over subsequent events. There is a sense of inevitability about the characters' actions, but it is not social or historical forces driving the individual, but a transcendent force over which humans have no control. It is no accident that the film starts in a religious hospital and ends outside a church, but it is also no accident that the final actions do not take place within the church. Ostensibly this is to deny Rome redemption, but the movement back on to the streets brings actions down to an individual and human level, as does Rome's drawing of a flick knife, although as Clarens points out this is also an instinctual act that Rome cannot avoid (1980: 217). In the end, as the title of the film implies, it is the city which seems to have most personality and, in *noir* terms, it is perhaps the urban landscape that provides the motivating cause for the characters' actions. Rome is driven as much by the city itself and becomes a symbol of urban movement in his inability to find a resting place (at one point, for example, a doctor operates on his wounds in the back of car). He can also be seen as an embodiment of generic conventions, a lone gangster cut adrift from society with no-one to trust and nowhere to settle, both territorialised by the city because it entirely determines his identity, but also deterritorialised by it, because he comes to embody its alienation and momentum, and it is in this embodiment of the depersonalised space of the city that at the same time that it fills his identity also empties it out in its exteriorisation.

From small gangs to big business

The films discussed so far still loosely retain the gang structure of the classic gangster narrative but are filtered through gangster *noir* re-definitions of the gangster hero who is now an attenuated figure, melting into the background, rather than transcending social convention. The gang is also re-formulated so that it is a much more fluid entity, though it still has its codes of loyalty and its modes of behaviour. Nevertheless, it is now an empty system of conventions rather than a place of real belonging for the alienated male. As gangster *noir* developed, an element of systematisation displaced the loose network becoming ever more dominant until it led into the syndicate movie of the 1950s. Early examples of the gang as a system rather than a network or community can be found in *noir* undercover films such as *T-Men* (Anthony Mann, 1947) and *The Street with No Name* (William Keighley,

1948), though the former adopts an ambiguous position because the gangs are both independent units and part of larger nexus. These undercover narratives follow the cops-and-robbers format, but with the difference that not only do they entail undercover operations, but also work against the opposition of master detective and charismatic villain found in early cops-and-robbers films, such as Lewis Milestone's *The Racket* (1928). There are very few charismatic individuals in *noir* undercover films and the emphasis tends to be on the erasure of identity rather than its expression. This stems primarily from the police procedural aspects of the films which play on the virtues of system and scientific technique which demand that undercover operatives undergo a process of depersonalisation. In *T-Men* the two treasury agents, Genaro (Alfred Ryder) and O'Brien (Dennis O'Keefe) are shown painstakingly transforming themselves into criminals called 'Galvani' and 'Harrigan' with criminal records, new clothes, and most importantly, a new set of memories (of criminal acquaintances, contacts, previous crimes and a detailed knowledge of mob history). Effectively, this new set of knowledges can be seen as a kind of implanted memory that effectively displaces their old identities and creates for them a new subjectivity. In some ways, it actually creates subjectivity for them for the first time, as they only begin to have personalities when they become criminals, something which is particularly evident with Gene Cordell (Mark Stevens) in *The Street with No Name*.

Undercover films therefore seem to imply that the ideological identities provided by legitimate society (the police) create corporatised men and suggest that individuality is only possible within the criminal fraternity. This does not mean that the films valorise the gangster world because in both *T-Men* and *The Street with No Name* the gangs use exactly the same scientific methods as the police and expect their own 'operatives' to fit into a mechanical structure. Legitimate society and gangster society are represented as indistinguishable as is also mapped in their overall structures. Both the Treasury Department and the counterfeit gang that Genaro and O'Brien infiltrate are represented as having a national domain but organised along the lines of a cell structure with local 'outlets' or offices. The gang consciously mimics the style of government agencies so that it is both centralised (in terms of its overall structure) and decentralised. The gang also mimics the government in that individual power is generated by the gang in much the same way that the law officer's power is signified by the badge that identifies he is acting on behalf of government. This is represented in *T-Men* after O'Brien has infiltrated the inner circles of the gang, when he is given permission by the local gang boss, Triano, to exact revenge on one of the gang's enforcers, Moxie, who has interrogated and tortured him. While this is also a reassertion of the masculinity that O'Brien has lost to Moxie, it also signifies that acceptance within the gang gives him a protected status, not only in terms of society as a whole, but also in terms of the hierarchical assertion of power. He hits Moxie without any retribution being taken, suggesting that the gang has become like a legal authority which grants its 'agents' the licence to act on its behalf; in this case disciplining Moxie for the excess of his actions against someone who has now become a trusted agent of the gang. This is a development that is extended in the syndicate movie where it is the gang that is the guarantor of individual power not the will or strength of the individual as in the classic gangster film.

Nor does occupation of territories matter any more. While the gang control space, it is a notional control because the power lies in the ability of the gang to impose itself at any time rather than to have to constantly enforce its control. Such a transformation can be characterised in terms of the move to a capitalist mode of production from the predominantly feudal or Renaissance hierarchies of the classic gangster film gang and can be seen in terms of Deleuze and Guattari's interpretation of capitalism as a deterritorialising principle in which territory is no longer needed because all value is subject to the deterritorialised flows of capital in which capitalist societies are 'defined by the process of decoding and deterritorialization' (Deleuze and Guattari, 1984: 257). Nevertheless, capitalism also reterritorialises at the same time and creates 'neoterritorialities' though these are often more arrangements of power that allow control of society rather than literal control of space. In this sense, the gang of *T-Men* and other *noir* gangs become extraterritorial entities more concerned with wielding economic or social control than territorial control. It is no accident that in *T-Men* the gang's racket is counterfeiting, while in many other gangster *noir* films, the main operation is 'numbers' which is entirely based around the generation of capital and has no 'product' that is being sold. The 'neoterritorialities' that *noir* and syndicate gang call into being can be seen in their fetishisation of system which is what now gives them their power rather than occupation of territory. *The Street with No Name* differs this format slightly because the gang in this film does not have a national scope. In some respects, the gang is almost nostalgic for the classic gang in that it has an obvious headquarters (a gymnasium), a defined urban territory, and a clear gang boss, Alec Stiles (Richard Widmark). The film does, however, attach the same value to system that is found in *T-Men* and the undercover agent, Gene Cordell, finds that moving from the government to the gang entails moving from one organisation where he has no identity to another where he has no identity.

The Street with No Name can be seen to operate within a framework of political paranoia about communism where any system not attached to the government is suspected of Un-American activity. *Force of Evil* (Abraham Polonsky, 1948), on the other hand, distances itself from this vision of contemporary cultural paranoias and instead offers a critique of society that refuses to legitimate capitalism and its new corporate structures. *Force of Evil* is a new variation of the gangster genre and one of its seminal movies because it introduces the rackets as a fully integrated and dominant power group in society. Rackets had been shown before but there had been a tendency to see them as having a very specific operation, as in *Racket Busters* (the trucking industry) and *Boss of Big Town* (city markets). A more contemporary film, *Thieves' Highway* (1949), shares the same local concern with the racketeering as it operates in the fruit markets of San Francisco but has a main criminal who is more fraudster than racketeer. In *Force of Evil*, however, although there is a specific racket (numbers) it has a much wider significance because the effects of the racket pervade society and, as Munby and May have argued, it is used to present a critique of capitalist economics (Munby, 1999: 127–30; May, 2000: 226). The film tells the story of Joe Morse (John Garfield), a lawyer for the rackets, who is administering the amalgamation of the numbers racket for his boss, Ben Tucker, through the manipulation of the system so that the small numbers 'banks' will either be bankrupted or forced into a merger with Tucker. One of these small 'banks' is run by Joe's brother, Leo (Thomas Gomez), who Joe tries to persuade into the organisation. Leo initially joins but gradually becomes less willing to co-operate with the result that he is killed by the mob leaving Joe to exact revenge on Tucker and a rival boss who has joined the syndicate.

The film traces the process of corporatisation of the rackets (into Tucker Enterprises Inc.) and enacts the triumph and legitimisation of the gangster system. The institutionalisation of the mob is not simply represented as a way of commenting on the pervasion of criminality, however, but to analyse the ruthless logic of capitalist society in its new corporatised mode. The gangster syndicate is identified with economic determinism in its capitalist forms and its simultaneous ideological control of subjectivity which turns the individual (Joe) against himself (in his creation of the syndicate that ultimately oppresses him) as well as society. The film is less radical than has been claimed, however, because it does not oppose capitalism in all its forms, only in its corporatised monopoly form. *Force of Evil* offers a quite clear distinction between big business (Tucker's syndicate) and small business (Leo's bank) and places value in the latter by showing Leo as a caring employer not a rapacious shark like Tucker (Munby, 1999: 129). Joe's choice therefore is between different types of capitalism, an uncaring depersonalised version represented by the syndicate and a paternalistic one represented by Leo, something that is made clearer by the fact that the film views this as an opposition between the mob and the family in which Leo acts as a surrogate (if failed) father for Joe. Throughout the film, Joe is offered the choice between family and mob, nearly always choosing the syndicate as when Leo has been arrested and Joe symbolically abandons him by walking over to Tucker and his henchmen. Although this opposition seems to offer a reversion to the classic narrative, the film does not represent the gang as a substitute family, but it does exaggerate the classic opposition by making the gang (or symbolically capitalism) actively hostile to the family and seeking to pervert it. When Leo becomes part of the combine he is no longer a father figure to Joe or his employees, but instead turned into an enforcer or minor gang baron. Like Joe, he is shown as sacrificing his values for money, but unlike Joe he feels remorse.

Force of Evil does ultimately show Joe's redemption but it is empty of meaning, because Joe is left with nothing. His redemption stems partly from the influence of Doris, one of Leo's employees, who Joe becomes romantically involved with and who acts as a Chorus figure commenting on Joe's self-deceptions.[9] Joe develops a conscience because he sees the depersonalised nature of the rackets, which is symbolised by their treatment of one of Leo's ex-employees, Bower, but also by the entry of rival gang boss, Ficco, into the syndicate which arouses Joe's concern over his methods because they hark back to the brutal enforcer gangsters of the pre-war years. Tucker himself initially wants to use force to take control of the city until persuaded otherwise by Joe, suggesting not only that Joe becomes complicit in his own oppression, but that he actually creates it by originating the corporatisation of the gangs himself. The gang, in *Force of Evil*, may be represented as a syndicate but it still uses the old techniques which Joe wishes to strip away in order to make it legitimate. Joe, in some respects, represents the ideal corporate gangster and arguably with Tucker's return to the ways of the enforcer it is not corporate gangsterism or its legitimisation, or even capitalism itself that is being opposed, but the classic violent gangster who can never enter legitimate society. Joe's narrative ultimately follows the one-man-against-the mob formula that was to become popular in the 1950s with the difference that he is trying to escape what he has created. Arguably, this completely empties him of identity when he transforms and reaches redemption, rather than creating him as a willed individual outside the deterministic system of the syndicate. In either case he is without identity because he is either part of a process (the capitalist legitimisation of the gangster) that subsumes his desires and feelings (for Leo) into business operations or else completely isolated, outside any structure or community. By the end of the film, he has lost his place in the syndicate and the family (with the death of Leo) and has no place left within society. As he says, when he goes searching for his brother's body by the river, he just keeps on going ever further down. In the form of Joe, the *noir* gangster is not someone liberated and empowered by his rise to success, but someone who is increasingly trapped until the whole world becomes a prison, not just the organisation he has created. Ultimately, this is the point of the film; that even when Joe has escaped the numbers syndicate he has not escaped the capitalist system that engendered both the racket and Joe himself. His only future is to continue to be complicit in his own oppression by working for the legitimate syndicate which is capitalism itself.

Although released a year later, *Force of Evil* is often taken as a pair with the gangster boxing film, *Body and Soul* (Robert Rossen, 1947), partly because many of the same figures were involved in both films,[10] but also because the two share a similar vision of the rackets as a capitalist enterprise and have a similar focus on an individual enmeshed in the mobs. Narratively *Body and Soul* has other similarities with *Force of Evil*, including the good woman who redeems the hero (Peg) and the small business figure who is destroyed by the racket, this time a friend (Shortie) rather than a brother. Boxing films had often been used in the past to represent alternative routes to success for both immigrants and the working class, an example of which is *City for Conquest* where Jimmy Cagney sacrifices himself and loses his sight in order to allow his younger brother to escape from the tenements and rise out of his class. Such films were also often set against a background of gangster corruption and manipulation as in *Kid Galahad* which acts as an ideological alternative to the classic gangster film by showing how the individual is entrapped by gangsterism rather than liberated by it. *Body and Soul* offers a different perspective because, unlike Kid Galahad, Charlie Davis (John Garfield) is aware of gangster racketeering and even seems to sense its apparent necessity, but believes that he will be able to retain his integrity.[11] He deceives himself into believing that he is still outside the system of corruption and part of legitimate capitalist enterprise as an embodiment of the ideal of opportunity, though as the film makes clear, there is no outside because capitalism and the boxing racket operate under the same system. In this respect Charlie is very similar to Joe Morse in that both misrecognise themselves as individuals rather than as ideological subjects controlled and exploited by the rackets and, by extension, the capitalist economic system, which is more overtly criticised in this film in its representation of Charlie, as a boxer, selling his body for the acquisition of money. Charlie does not understand this, however, and believes that he is in control of both his body and the money it earns him, at one point saying of money that 'it's not like people, it don't think'. He believes that money is just a tool that provides benefits rather than a force that drives society and desire. The film, however, offers a different view, particularly focusing its comments through Shortie, Charlie's friend who directly links gangsters to capitalism when he comments on how Roberts, the racketeering promoter, has turned Charlie into a 'money machine', like a gold mine or an oil well, and later that Charlie's 'not just a kid who can fight, he's money.'

Unlike earlier boxing films, *Body and Soul* does not follow Charlie's gradual entrapment by the mob (although the chronological plot does) because much of it is told in flashback. Charlie looks back on his life already in a position of loss, not just as someone who is already entrapped, but as someone who always was despite his earlier belief in his ability to control his body and thus his identity. The flashback structure represents an attempt to put things into order and to provide meaning, but also, however, acts as an emblem of a self that is fragmented and controlled because looking back over the past doesn't resolve Charlie's present predicament, it simply highlights his entrapment. The moment before the flashback, Charlie's thoughts are heard in voice-over saying 'All gone down the drain' and the fact that he is in the stadium changing room stripped waiting for a fight he has agreed to lose highlights the fact that he has already been stripped of everything (his dignity, power and money) except his body even though he is the champion. Charlie is reduced to a puppet controlled by the racketeer Roberts and only one amongst many as the narrative of the previous champion, Ben, who has been exploited and sold out by Roberts, makes clear. The film represents the rackets as a symbol of un-American values because they not only exploit the American Dream of the individual success of the boxer in the pursuit of money, but also because they stand in the way of its achievement (a boxer does not win the title on his own merits, but only because the racket decide that he is a profitable venture).

The racket is the social reality that stands in the way of individual dreams and aspirations, acting as a force for stagnation and representing the reality of exploitation in America because it undermines the ideological myth of individual opportunity. The boxing ring, as Munby argues, thus 'assume[s] the space once occupied by the gangster's speakeasy as a privileged site for the dramatization of social oppression' (1999: 160). The ring is, however, a paradoxical space as it also represents both the commodification of the body (and almost becomes like a commodities trading floor with people buying and selling wagers around it), but is also the only space where Charlie is free, despite the fix he has agreed to. It is in the ring that Charlie thwarts and defeats the racket once he has realised they have double-crossed him and the place where he re-assumes control of his body and his individuality. However, this is a temporary reassertion of control, because he must once more leave the ring and re-enter society where his body belongs to the racket who plan to take control of it again, it is implied, by killing Charlie.

Late gangster *noir*: the triumph of technology

At end of the 1940s the gangster genre re-invented itself again with the development of the heist or caper movie and then the syndicate film. Gangster *noir* persisted, but either shifted into different thematic areas or exaggerated the ideology of the powerlessness of both human and individual endeavour. Against a backdrop of nuclear systems and communist paranoia the survival of the American ideology of the individual seemed impossible so that in *Nightfall* (Jacques Tourneur, 1956) the hero is not simply entrapped by gangsters but actively hunted down by them. *Kiss Me Deadly* (Robert Aldrich, 1955) has in Mike Hammer someone who seems to be a fully fledged self-reliant individual (a hard and callous detective who cares for no-one but himself) but the film demystifies Hammer's self-reliance by showing how, in the face of the new warfare of nuclear weapons, his individuality is meaningless. Hammer is represented more as an inward looking narcissist, rather than an active agent. He actually does very little detection of his own and is dependent on his secretary Velda to uncover the connections and information that is the staple of detective work. For most of the film, Hammer is more like a gangster than a detective and acts as an enforcer who beats information out of people. The development of gangster *noir* into the syndicate film exacerbated this sense of a waning of individuality in the era of nuclear and communist paranoias, though syndicate films also still strive (in the figure of the single man taking on the mob) to re-affirm the continued validity of individual action. The development of gangster *noir* in the 1950s was not always overtly concerned with gangsters, but with the pervasion of gangster ethos so that in *Kiss Me Deadly* it is not the detective who is entrapped by the gangster, as in *Out of Past*, but the detective who becomes the gangster. The film is not a traditional gangster movie but an abstraction of the gangster genre in terms of its post nuclear context, replacing racketeering and heists with a 'violent rush into pure jagged paranoia' and extending the genre 'by straining it' (Hardy, 1998b: 164). The gangsters are presented as meaningless in the context of the evil of nuclear armageddon and their irrelevance is indicated by the fact that Hammer is more ruthless and sadistic. This also implies that official society now fully mimics gangster society and is better at it so that Hammer is able to invert the usual gangster occupation of official society's space by invading and controlling the space of the gangster Evello's home. Hammer's power and apparent individuality are also, however, shown to be both meaningless and destructive. Hammer almost becomes an embodiment of the nuclear destruction that infuses the film and he is very often linked to technology and the destructiveness of the atom bomb as in signalled by Nick the mechanic's comment on his car ('Va-va-voom. Pretty Pow') which links Hammer's individual violence to nuclear violence. Similarly, Hammer refers to a bomb under his car as a 'torpedo' but this also seems to refer to the car itself, suggesting that machines and technology as a whole are products of violence and destructiveness. Hammer's love of this technology thus locates him as an agent of destruction (which is also linked to Hammer's consumption of consumer products) and part of the masculine violence that the film critiques.

Nightfall also links technology with violence to articulate the vision of gangs as machines that have gone out of control, but also attempts to rescue individuality from mechanist social structures. The film follows the story of James Vanning (Aldo Ray) who is being pursued by two gangsters for a bag of money he has unwittingly taken from them. In *Nightfall* the gangsters are emblems of a society governed by machines or systems in a triumph of the modernist nightmare. The two gangsters, John and Red, are represented as relentless in their pursuit, calmly hunting Vanning down with slow moving menace as they follow him in a robotic fashion. Much is made of machine imagery in the film, particularly machines which seem to have a life of their own and act as automata, such as the nodding donkey oil rig with which the gangsters threaten Vanning and the snow plough which continues on its path even without a driver. The gangsters are not individuals and although they have distinct personalities they are both 'types': Red the sadistic psychopath and John the icy enforcer. That they have no surnames suggests that they have no identity as distinct individuals, but are simply representatives of a larger gangster system. Red and John are no longer people and there is a particular emphasis on the guns they carry which implies that they themselves have become machines with one function: to point guns at people. Nevertheless, *Nightfall* attempts to salvage individual agency through the figure of Vanning who finally manages to convince others of his story with the result that he is re-invested with a history and an identity which allows him to triumph over the gangsters. This is represented in his taking control of the runaway snow plough at the end of the film, an act that shows individuals mastering machines and implying that the social machine principle can be inverted and 'individuals' can once more take control of their destiny. There is a final irony, however, in the last shot of the film which shows the bag of money sitting alone in the snow. The shot emphasises the real principle underlying the *noir* world: the abstraction of money that drives the machine systems and actions not only of the gangsters but of society as a whole and it remains an abstraction outside individual agency even though the characters decide to go and 'keep it company'.

5
Order and Chaos, Syndicates and Heists

Gangster *noir* reached its apotheosis in the mid-fifties, by which time two other gangster cycles had appeared: the heist (or caper) movie and the syndicate film. These two gangster 'sub-genres' highlight the flexibility of the genre as a whole, because the two have so many differences from the classic conventions that they are almost two distinct and entirely different genres.[1] They still deal with the individual's relationship with society and share iconographic similarities (sharp suits, guns, and fast cars) with previous gangster films, but their emphasis is on the meaninglessness of individuality and the code of the gangster as these are subsumed into a rationalised society or gangster system. The heist genre began with *The Asphalt Jungle* in 1950 which, although it had a short life-span, was to intermittently re-appear over the next few decades, as it mutated into more obvious 'caper' style associated with films such as *Kaleidoscope* (1966) and *The Heist* (1971). The following year saw the release of *The Enforcer*, aka *Murder Inc.*, in which can be found the beginnings of the syndicate movie that developed in response to the Kefauver hearings into organised crime and which also led to the pseudo-gangster sub-genre, the *exposé* film, examples of which included *The Captive City* (1952), *The Phenix City Story* (1955), and *New York Confidential* (1955). The heist and syndicate sub-genres in the 1950s both re-define the gangster genre because they emphasise the 'gang' rather than the gangster, to the extent that they are 'gang' films rather than 'gangster' movies. They retain an interest in the gangster, but the focus is on the role the gang plays in society and how it both metonymically displaces and metaphorically stands for legitimate society. It is now the gang that threatens official ideology and its operations, posing a greater threat because, as an organisation, it is both less easy to extirpate than an individual gangster and more likely to rival and supplant official institutions. This is most evident in the syndicate film where the rackets dominate society and more effectively negate the individual gangster than was ever the case in the classic period of the genre. The heist gang also marginalises the gangster, even while the narrative is focalised through him, by providing a rationalised structure that creates him as an industrialised unit of production during the heist before casting him adrift into an atomised society when he has no further use. The gangster's experience of society is either absolute system in the gang or fragmented emptiness outside its confines.

Heists: rationalised gangs and fragmented individuals

Heist and syndicate movies represent two antithetical visions of society with the former dramatising a society of marginality and apparent chaos while the latter movie enacts an increased fear of systematisation in the rise of the corporate ethos. This is also represented as an opposition between a focus on individual desire in the heist film, which often causes the gang to fragment, despite the attempt to impose regimentation, and the gangs as totalitarian organisations in the syndicate film.[2] Heist films suggest a release of unrestrained male desire in the manner of *femme fatale*'s release of female desire into society in *film noir*. The heist sub-genre 'others' masculinity in its dispersal across society, represented by disempowered men chasing after money, thereby producing an uncentred masculinity determined by the flows of capital. It is often the case that the heist itself, as in *The Killing*, is referred to as the 'big one', a term that articulates an unconscious desire for the heist to be an act that will re-embody male sexuality and allow the male to regain the phallus through the achieval of monetary fulfillment. The investment of masculinity in the heist, however, implies the failure of male sexuality because male potency is not located inside the male body but in the money after which the gangster chases. The heist gangster consequently has a fluid identity, matched by the fragmented underworld of free floating dispossessed individuals he inhabits, representing a more thorough deterritorialisation of the gangster than even gangster *noir* envisaged. In opposition, the heist gang often forms a system within which the gangster can find meaning to compensate for the fragmentation experienced in society, a simulation of structure that offers a 'false community' for its outcast members (Munby, 1999: 138). Marginalisation, nevertheless, still attaches itself to the heist gangster as is the case with Earl, in *Odds Against Tomorrow*, who is a feminised male, doing household chores while his wife works, but who seeks to counter this impotence through violence and through the seduction of a neighbour. The heist offers a release from this fragmented masculinity with crime becoming a way of escaping society. The heist film represents crime therefore as a strategy of evasion rather than an attempt to control society in its offer of a fantasy of life outside society because life within it is impossible (Rafter, 2000:58).

The gangster, in the heist gang, is a contradictory individual who is both selfless and selfish, desiring and desireless, a person and a cog in the machine. The gang in the heist movie is a paradoxical place split between individual desire and the gang structure which demands the subsumption of the self into the gang. The gang members have their identity and desires stripped from them as they become simply functional units in the gang in an industrialising process, based on the Fordist division of labour, with each gangster assigned a specific task or role from which they cannot stray (getaway driver, strongarm man, safe-cracker). The heist gangster is just a hired hand, as alienated from gang labour as he is from social labour and the gang is no longer a substitute family that allows the gangster to escape from social alienation. The heist gang industrialises and corporatises the gangster, becoming a corporation in miniature. Individual desire, however, reasserts itself as soon as the heist is over and heist films end with the fragmentation of the gang and with their failure to hang on to the money, implying an inability to retain identity or phallic power in the re-entry into society. When Johnny Clay, in *The Killing*, watches the money being scattered to the air at the end of the film he is also watching the scattering of himself now that the heist is over. Fragmentation is already implicit in the heist itself because the rationalised structure of the gang cannot effectively strip away the individual desire that led the gangster into the gang in the first place with the result that heist gang is often the site of internalised conflict. The genre in its representation of the gang – gangster relationship follows a trajectory of gang against society and gang against gang in the 1930s to gangster against gangster in the 1950s, symbolising a vision of a thoroughly atomised society. In *Odds Against Tomorrow*, after the heist has failed, two of the gangsters instantly fall upon each other to settle their scores and engage in a running shoot out as they chase each other through the streets.

The Asphalt Jungle is often referred to as the first proper heist movie, but *Armored Car Robbery* (Richard Fleischer, 1950) also shares the honour, being released on exactly the same date (Hardy, 1998b:134). *Armored Car Robbery* is perhaps the most typical film of the heist subgenre and despite its lower production values looks more modern than the nostalgic romaticism of *The Asphalt Jungle*. The film focuses on the gang's fetishisation of planning, opening with a scene in which the gang boss, Dave, is shown with a stopwatch gauging police response times to a faked alarm. The planning scenes also highlight the systematisation that is the basis of the heist gang and Dave constantly insists on the need to practice, telling the gang they have to study the routine 'until it comes out of your eyes'. There is a precision to the planning that makes it look like an army operation, a militarisation of gang life in which the heist gang is shown as if it were a commando unit committed to discipline. The individual gangsters are trained and beaten into shape with the concomitant sacrifice of individual desire. However, the gang is also shown to be fractured by the desires of its members, particularly Dave, who shoots his partner Benny when the latter is injured, ostensibly to ensure the success of the heist, but in reality to take his share of the money. The rationalisation of the gang is revealed to be a simulation of structure that cannot enforce loyalty or community, in part because the apparent patriarch figure plans to double cross his gang 'sons' (as is also the case in *The Asphalt Jungle*), but also because of the ephemeral nature of the gang. The gang is a temporary structure in a decentralised world, based on movement (signified by Dave's constant changes of address), a representation which implies that the gangster is a mobile agent and the gang a deterritorialised unit. The heist gang is not based on the occupation of space or territory, as in the classic formula, but is founded on movement and dispersal across space.

Although *Armored Car Robbery* configures a world of social fragmentation it is principally an action film whereas *The Asphalt Jungle* (John Huston, 1950) uses the heist to comment on contemporary alienation and corporatisation. The film opens with images of bars and nets, showing the main character, Dix (Sterling Hayden), hiding from the police behind the pillars of an arcade as the police drive by beneath a net of telephone lines. This is an image of Dix's criminality, but it also directs reference to the notion of society as a trap, particularly the prison of corporatisation, as Munby has argued (1999:135). Images of corporate activity pervade the film as in the planning sequence involving Emmerich, the respectable gang boss in need of money, and Doc Riedenschneider, the brains behind the operation. The two discuss the personnel required for the heist, as if they were appointing for corporate positions, including tack of the 'wages' each gangster will earn and the possibility of having fences tendering offers for a contract to deal in the stolen merchandise. What the scene emphasises is that the gang does not exist until the plan comes into being, but is a notional gang that is controlled by the plan for the heist rather than having any investment in a larger organisation and its operations. As in *Armored Car Robbery*, the gang members are controlled by an abstract system in which they fulfill a functional purpose with individual desire being discouraged.[3] The organisation of the gang also maps on to class distinctions: Emmerich is a patrician executive while the gang are proletarian hands, an opposition symbolised by the two planning sequences. The corporate planning meeting takes place in a well lit room that looks like a gentleman's club with stable camera angles to suggest solidity and respectability. The scene involving the gang is shot in a dark smoky room with more variety of camera angles (including a cut across the 180 degree rule). Where the former scene establishes the centrality of Emmerich, the *mise-en-scène* of the latter expresses both the gang's marginality and, in the instability of camera angles, creates narrative misinformation to suggest that the problems with the heist will originate within the gang rather than with Emmerich.

Despite the corporate imagery, the gang members are more serfs than workers, emphasised by the representation of Dix as a hobo with battered hat. Despite Munby's view of the gang as a 'false community' there is still an opposition between their sense of community (particularly in the loyalties established between Dix, Doc, and Gus) and Emmerich's distant aristocratic employer. These loyalties between outcasts persist after the heist (and are thereby taken out into society as a whole) and are symbolised by the appearance of Doll, a middle aged alcoholic, who becomes Dix's lover and who displays a loyalty to him that Emmerich does not show. The film is nostalgic for community and belonging which it temporarily locates within the gang, but which unravels because modern society does not allow such communities to exist. Outside the gang, life is purposeless, most obviously shown in the figure of Dix who drifts from one place to another clinging to his outmoded code of honour and his nostalgic memories of a rural childhood outside urban industrialised society. These exist only in fantasy rather than in reality and Dix's final flight to his childhood home ends with his death in one of the fields with his home in the distance, emphasising the impossibility of achieving individual desire in contemporary society. The film, however, does locate Dix as its centre of identification, endorsing his vision and indulging in the same nostalgic fantasy of the individual which it valorises in representing him as a quick on the draw gunslinger in his shoot-out with Brannon. The film also opposes Dix's loyalty to Emmerich's betrayal of the gang from outside and thereby locates authenticity and integrity in the gangster and treachery in 'respectable' legitimate society which becomes 'other' to itself in the process.

The Killing (Stanley Kubrick, 1956) presents fragmentation and failure not as a result of external betrayal (although it plays with this narrative in the attempts by George's wife, Sherry, to sell the gang out to her lover) but shows fragmentation as inherent within both the heist and the gang. The film has a crime procedural quality similar to that of *Armored Car Robbery* with a voice-over, like that of a police procedural film, explaining the gang activities and including precise times for events. Despite the sense of structure that this gives the film, the narrative emphasises fragmentation because it does not follow events chronologically. Instead, the narrative cuts from one character to another and follows his movements for a period before cutting to a new character, so that action and scenes overlap and footage is repeated, though from a different perspective. The fragmentation of the gang is embedded in this structure which, however, also draws attention, in cutting from one character to another, to the fact that each gang member is a cog in the machine. Most of gang have one very small role to play but their function is pivotal to the success of the heist; for example, George's role is simply to open a door to let Johnny into the back offices, but if he doesn't do it at the right time the heist fails. Absolute precision is required, but that it is so absolute implies that the heist is always on the verge of failure and that the gang cohesion is itself just as fragile. This instability is portrayed when Sherry turns up at one of the planning sessions and George is instantly suspected of betraying the gang, while Johnny's late arrival after the heist leads the other gangsters to voice suspicions over his loyalty.

The absence of social cohesiveness outside the gang is also implied and the heist operates as a metaphor for society, rather than having the function of creating temporary order in a fragmented world. Nevertheless, as in *The Asphalt Jungle*, there is a sense of belonging within the criminal underworld, shown in a scene where Johnny hires a room at motel owned by a fellow convict's father who has no interest in why Johnny wants the room, but offers him trust despite not having any direct relationship with him. This does, however, contribute to an overall sense of fragmentation in that gangs are now loose sets of connections not cohesive units and the individual gangster is nomadic and isolated, only able to make temporary connections in an atomistic society. There is no centre of identification within the film, as there is with the figure of Dix in *The Asphalt Jungle*. This lack of a centre is generated by the narrative structure which, in cutting from one character to another, doesn't fully centre itself on one figure until the moment of the heist itself when it locates itself with Johnny. Johnny, however, is a slightly empty figure overall. He evokes affection from other characters, including Maurice, who speaks of him as the last of the individuals, and Fay who is devoted to him even though he is just out of prison and already planning a heist, while another member of the gang, Marv, sees him as a surrogate son (though this also blurs into a homo-erotic attachment on the part of Marv). He is the focus of other characters' attention, but their divergent aspirations and desires make him a contradictory decentred figure. Johnny himself seems something of a vacuum in terms of identity because he becomes so obsessed with the plan that his selfhood is subsumed by it and he appears as a cold affectless figure rather than a paradigm of individuality. At the end of the film, when the money has been lost, Johnny walks like a dead man to suggest either the death of individuality or that his individuality was a myth all along. The dispersal of selfhood is symbolised by the dispersal of the money, an image that is repeated several times but is most significant when the suitcase bursts open and scatters money across the airport runway at the end of the film. This image implies that the money is meaningless and empty of value and that Johnny's investment of his identity in the desire to gain the money is equally as empty. In opposition, although George is presented as a feminised male, his final act in gunning down Sherry's lover and his partner as they seek to take the money from the gang seems more of an affirmation of masculinity and individuality. There is also a negation of self in this scene, however, because when Val enters he notices George isn't present and asks 'Where's the jerk?'. George appears from the kitchen, shooting, and replies memorably with 'The jerk's right here', his action implying affirmation of masculinity, but in an act that is ironised into a negation of self with the admission that he is a 'jerk'. This is compunded by the fact that although he kills Val and his partner, he is fatally wounded and the camera pans round to reveal that the rest of the heist gang are also dead.

Odds Against Tomorrow (Robert Wise, 1959) places itself interestingly within these concerns of masculinity and individuality but, where *The Killing* focused on the loss of maleness and the self in isolation from wider social contexts, *Odds Against Tomorrow* (written by Abraham Polonsky under the pseudonym John O Killens) uses the heist scenario as a means to explore social and cultural issues. The film is particularly concerned with issues of ethnicity, but also focuses on the disempowerment and feminisation of Earl (Robert Ryan) and his attempts to regain masculinity through random violence and racism, which allow him a control over both other people and objects (as with his exhilaration at accelerating the getaway car up to a hundred before the heist) as a substitute for social usefulness. Earl is a redundant male taking out his frustrations at a personal rather than social level. One key focus of the film is Johnny Ingram (Harry Belafonte) and his disempowerment through ethnicity. For example, the gang boss, Dave Burke, who appears early on to be a caring father figure, uses his position of power to effectively force Johnny into the heist by persuading underworld gangster king, Bacco, to call in Johnny's debts. The heist thus becomes a way for the characters to escape disempowerment but it is suggested that although it resolves present problems it does not remove the root problems of marginality. Dave says, at one point, that the heist will 'let us live again', implying a re-birth as new selves, but whether the heist will ever entail real escape or just a fantasy of escape that leaves gang members still trapped in society is open to question. Before the heist itself, there are long scenes showing the gang members waiting aimlessly until the time of the operation suggesting that their lives are on hold, but the images also portray their overall purposelessness and inertia. Although the heist forms the basic narrative of film, this wider implication of social disempowerment and individual irrelevance directs more attention to the relationship between Earl and Johnny. The emphasis on Earl's racism, as part of a wider sense of control by virtue of ethnicity (as with Bacco's control of Johnny), raises issues of power and ethnicity that the film suggests will be ever-present. Earl can only 'prove' his masculinity through his condescending treatment of Johnny, as with his dismissal of Johnny in the discussion over how to solve the problem of the chain on the bank door – which Johnny ultimately solves. The social pervasiveness of racism and the subordination of African-Americans is shown most obviously in the argument between Earl and Johnny before the heist and in its continuation afterwards. The final scenes of the film show a running shoot out between Earl and Johnny which results in a suicidal gunfight on top of a gas tank that utterly destroys both characters, implying that racism and the oppression of African-Americans is destructive and meaningless.

The 1940s and 1950s also produced other examples of the heist movie, but these often had a different emphasis. *The Big Steal* and *Kansas City Confidential* both focus on an honest man trying to prove his innocence after he has been implicated in a heist operation. They thus concern themselves with the retention of individuality in the face of a threat to it by gangster society and more clearly articulate an ideology that identifies gangsters as a threat to American values. *The Big Steal* was actually released prior to the heist movies discussed above (1949) and is more a suspense caper in the tradition of Hitchcock movies in its vision of an innocent victim caught between the law and the criminal world. *Kansas City Confidential* is similar, but where *The Big Steal* has a light hearted and self-parodic tone, *Kansas City Confidential* has a darker vision in its focus on entrapment of individual. *Criss Cross* (Robert Siodmak, 1949) shares similar thematic concerns, but locates itself within a *film noir* social vision in its representation of the entrapment of Steve Thompson (Burt Lancaster) by Anna (Yvonne de Carlo), the wife of the gang boss. The film also has a more convoluted *noir* style because of its focus on multiple forms of deception, whether this is deceiving the police with an elaborately staged 'fight' to show tensions within the gang or the deceptions on the part of the gang members. The ultimate deception is the double-cross within the heist itself with Steve turning from gang member to honest citizen when the gang try to kill him. The *noir* aesthetic is emphasised when the gang take revenge on Steve for attempting to save himself from their double-cross, resulting in his inevitable death.

Syndicates and rogue cops: un-American visions

Syndicate movies offer both a parallel and an antithesis to heist films. Where heists have temporary deterritorialised gangs, the gangs in syndicate films are so organised that they become totalitarian structures. The treatment of the gangster also differs because where heist films have apparently mobile nomadic individuals, the syndicate doesn't seem to recognise individuality as a meaningful notion. Gangsters are effectively things and any show of individuality is seen as aberrant behaviour to be punished. Syndicate films developed as a response to the Kefauver hearings and offered a vision of gangs in America where there is only one gang organisation with different branches in different cities. The particular concern of the Kefauver hearings however – the apparent pervasion of the United States by gangs – becomes in syndicate films a concern with wider issues because the syndicate film uses the notion of the organisation of the 'combine' metaphorically to make links to both the rise of corporations and cultural Cold War paranoia. Although the psychopathic gangster film exaggerated the gangster as an individual during the same period, the syndicate film represents the gangster as a man trapped in the gang, someone who, in the vacuum of a contemporary society of commodities and corporations, has no identity except within the systems he inhabits.

Although syndicate films always have a top gangster, the usual representation of the gangster is of the foot soldier, someone obeying the commands of the system he works for. Even the head of the syndicate is a controlled foot soldier in some ways as he too must bow to the system he apparently controls, a situation represented in *The Racket*, in the figure of Nick Scanlon, an old-time big shot about to be replaced by the syndicate. In a metaphor on corporate capitalism, he is shown to be under the control of outside shareholders, the mysterious figures from out of town who give the syndicate boss his orders. The syndicate film represents the absolute loss of individuality and envisages a society where there is nothing left but oppressive system, one of the syndicate movie's un-American visions of America.

This un-American-ness is coded in terms of the conspiratorial nature of the syndicate and taps into Cold War concerns over Communist conspiracies in America. The syndicate movie is interesting in terms of generic conventions because, although it utilises the gangster style, it also has aspects of the espionage suspense thriller, mapped in the secrecy of gangs and their infiltration into society. Critics have pointed to the importance of the Kefauver hearings for the syndicate film (Yaquinto, 1998:93–4) and the McCarthy hearings for *film noir* (Naremore, 1998:127–8), but arguably HUAC is as important for syndicate movies because of its representation of cultural paranoia over mobs destroying American values. As Shadoian points out: '[i]n the fifties the tensions of the cold war are evident. Crime, like communism, is against the American way of life. The evils of these poisonous systems are analogous' (1977:210). In seeking to root out un-American corruptions and in their narratives of infiltration into secret organisations, syndicate films are as much espionage or suspense films as gangster movies. While the films' concern with individuality relates to an anxiety over corporatisation and the death of individual (Munby, 1999:133–4), it also corresponds with the paranoid espionage film's concern with the rescue of individuality from the threat of destruction by an alien 'other' and the rescuing of American values in the form of the self-reliant individual. *The Enforcer* and *The Big Heat*, for example, have men fulfilling themselves as individuals in order to establish the persistence of American ideologies, although in the latter case, as will be seen, the individual, as manifested in Dave Bannion, is an Un-American version of the individual who uses criminal techniques to combat an Un-American system.

The mapping of concerns over freedom can be seen in relation to the different representations of individuality in heist and syndicate films.

Despite their implications of the emptiness of individuality heist films still retain a nostalgic fantasy of individuality that syndicates do not admit to being possible, seeing a reality of social disempowerment instead. The heist also retains a fantasy of escape to a freedom outside society, whereas the syndicate film relentlessly insists that there is no outside and that everyone is trapped in the system of reified social structures of both the syndicate and society. This stems from the syndicate movie's basis in the idea that gangs extend across the nation, even into rural America, as in *Hoodlum Empire*, where the hero seeks escape from the gangs in a small town, but discovers gang agents installing slot machines in diners and bars even here. *Exposé* films, such as *The Phenix City Story* and *The Captive City* are emblematic of this re-territorialisation by the gangs, as opposed to heist deterritorialisation, because they represent small towns being taken over by gangs and imply the absolute pervasion of America, and the concomitant displacement of American values, by gangster values of criminality, corruption and authoritarianism. The heist film's fantasy of escape and mobility is exactly that and everybody knows it with the result that there is a sense of a crushing weight of oppression in syndicate America. Lack of freedom in syndicate films is often referenced in terms of the representation of the gang boss who was always someone who held court, surrounded by minions, but who, in syndicates, becomes more overtly mapped as a feudal figure to suggest the permanence or institutionalisation of gangster power structures. The big shot narratives of the 1930s represent the paradox of the gang (a system) being a means by which the individual gangster can establish himself as an individual who is able to control society, even in foot soldier narratives like *The Public Enemy*. In the syndicate film this is still possible, but only for the head gangster who is a feudal 'king' while the remaining gangsters act as serfs, a representation most evident in *The Big Combo*.

Although the pre-Kefauver *The Black Hand* (1949) includes elements of the syndicate film with its sense of a hidden remorseless organisation, *The Enforcer* (Bretaigne Windust, 1951, but also substantially shot by an uncredited Raoul Walsh) is generally regarded as the first syndicate film (Clarens, 1980:235). The story is narrated through a multiple and layered flashback structure as the hero, District Attorney Ferguson (Humphrey Bogart), tries to piece together a case against Mendoza, the gang boss of 'Murder Inc', and to uncover the operations of a national organisation whose 'racket' is assassination. In a flashback late in the film (focalised through Mendoza's lieutenant, Rico) Mendoza describes assassination as the perfect racket because the murders are performed by killers without motive and who are thus able to maintain their anonymity. Secrecy is paramount within the organisation which is represented as a shadowy operation with its own secret language of 'hits', 'contracts', 'fingermen' and 'undertakers'. The gradual piecing together of the racket's operation is principally shown in flashback, as Ferguson chases after people who disappear or die suddenly and horribly (one character is burned in a furnace). The structure also suggests he is chasing ghosts, giving a sense of the intangibility of the gang which, however, is a paradoxical entity because it is both highly structured, in its national scope, and very fluid, in the mobility of the assassins themselves. The assassination racket has local 'branches', but the killers always operate at a distance from the home branch, something that conveys the apparent invulnerability of gang in that they are present and absent at the same time. They thus take on a ghostly quality (Mendoza, for example, is an absent presence for most of the film and is not actually seen until near the end) whose operatives appear and disappear without leaving any traces. Despite this fluidity, the gang is also run on rational lines. When Rico is introduced, the local headquarters of Murder Inc. is shown as if it were an employment agency with Rico wearing a businessman's suit. The assassins themselves are also treated as functional, like corporate drones who are expendable – in the clean-up operation, for example, they are just evidence to be disposed of. Nevertheless, despite this rationalised system, the failure of Murder Inc. is caused by the intervention of individual desire, when one of killers, Duke, falls for his victim, Nina Lombardo, who the gang mistake for Angela Vetto, a witness to Mendoza's first and only killing and who is the cause of Mendoza being finally brought to justice. Although it is not until later that both Mendoza and Ferguson realise the gang killed the wrong girl, it is Duke's distraught confession to the police that 'they made me kill my girl' that begins the unravelling of the racket. Murder Inc is designed to erase desire, and concomitantly erase selfhood, from the operation, but fails because of its re-emergence. Unlike the classic gangster, who is a creature of desire and excess and who creates himself as a subject through their expression, Murder Inc removes desire and turns individuals into machines who kill, to the extent that the only form of identity the killers have is the ice pick that they carry to perform the murders.

Because of its business of death, the racket in *The Enforcer* is represented as an inversion of American values and the gang is represented as something that cannot be comprehended because it is apparently beyond moral categories. For example, when Ferguson, asks two of his subordinates whether it is possible for an organisation like Murder Inc.

to exist, one answers 'Yes' and the other 'No'. Murder Inc. has a quality that cannot be apprehended because it contradicts the values and rules of society so utterly but at the same time is entirely believable because it is based on making money, the prime determinant of American society.[4] Paralleling Murder Inc.'s shadowy operation is the implication that it is an ineffable and even unpresentable entity because it turns the world upside down. The police, for example, are constantly saying that they don't understand things or that the whole murder operation is just 'Nuts' because of the absolute inversion that the murder racket implies. Mendoza himself is represented almost in terms of a gangster sublime, as a godlike figure, partly because of his invisible presence, but also because of the fear he inspires. When Rico is taken into custody, for example, he is constantly looking at doors and windows fearful of what might come through them. There is an implication that Mendoza and the gang are omniscient and omnipotent, able to invade any space, even the heavily fortified jail where Rico is held. This sense of omniscience is also suggested by the representation of Mendoza who is off camera for most of film. He is 'shown' usually by a shot of his cell door, a motif which suggests that although he is confined he is still free. The inversions, however, also work in reverse in the way in which the film implies that the police are an official Murder Inc. This is made most obvious through the image of Ferguson gunning down a gangster at the end, but there are also a number of times when the film draws attention to the connection between the operation of justice and death, as when Ferguson tells Rico that Mendoza is going to the chair and that 'you're going to help kill him' or when he says that the jail is quiet 'like a cemetery'. The law becomes an official version of the un-American racket it despises and by adopting Murder Inc.'s methods becomes an un-American version of itself.

Other early examples of the syndicate formula include rather programmatic films such as *The Mob* (Robert Parrish, 1951) and *Hoodlum Empire* (Joseph Kane, 1952), though both of these are part of the *exposé* genre in that they have an 'exploitational logic' and are more concerned with the 'cataloguing of vice' (Straw, 1997:118, 111). Like *exposé* films, with titles such as *New York Confidential* or *The Phenix City Story*, where it is the town or city that is the main character rather than the gangster, films like *The Mob* or *Hoodlum Empire* suggest by their title a de-individuation of the gangster, representing the transformation of gangsterism into an abstract social process rather than a product of individual action and desire. *The Mob* follows an investigation narrative, but does so as an undercover plot which links it to espionage conventions. Its hero, Damico (Broderick Crawford), infiltrates a conspiratorial racket in search of a mysterious criminal mastermind after he has inadvertently let him escape. He is given a chance to atone for his mistake by going undercover to discover the real identity of the racket boss and, after proving himself a worthy addition to the mob, he is finally led to the big boss who turns out, in a fairly standard espionage convention, to be the first person Damico met after going undercover. *Hoodlum Empire* has a more standard approach to the syndicate *exposé* as it follows a Senate Crime Committee's investigations into the mob. The narrative follows the story of a mobster, Joe Gray, who learns new values while in the army and decides to leave the rackets for a new domesticated life (signalled by his changing from smoking cigarettes to smoking a pipe) in a small town running a gas station. As the narrative develops, however, it is revealed that he has been set up by the mob who are acting in his name so that the Committee, headed by his ex-army captain, are led to believe he is the big boss of the syndicate. The story ultimately therefore resolves into his attempt to prove his innocence without going back on his pledge not to squeal on the rackets. The film is most interesting for showing the syndicate as a national operation with legitimate front organisations and regular board meetings. It also portrays the gang's perversion of America with its entry into the smalltown, the heartland of American ideology and the family values it represents. This places it in the context of family or community in peril narratives such as the *Out of the Fog* which places the threat to family or community in an urban setting and looks forward to *The Desperate Hours*, where the threat takes place in suburbs of a smalltown, and *He Ran All the Way* where the gangster threat to American family values occurs in the literal occupation of an American home.

Despite their anatomy of a new pervasive criminal society, *The Mob* and *Hoodlum Empire* still express a confidence in the triumph of the law. *The Racket* (John Cromwell, 1951) is much more ambiguous. The film is a remake of Lewis Milestone's 1928 film of the same name, re-focused, in the context of the Kefauver hearings, on the establishment of gangs as a syndicate. The film retains the narrative structure of the earlier film in focusing on McQuigg's vendetta against the gangster Nick Scanlon (Scarsi in the original), and uses this to reflect on the changing nature not only of the gangster but also of the police. The film sets up several relationships focusing around McQuigg (Robert Mitchum) and Scanlon (Robert Ryan), particularly the opposition between McQuigg's old style police integrity and Scanlon's criminal gang lord. This relationship also places the two in opposition to new forms of policing and gangsterism, which are identified with gangster pervasion of the police force and the rise of the combine, respectively, using both to create a dichotomy between individual action and the 'system'. Like a lot of syndicate films, *The Racket* suggests that the values of the gangster are no longer part of an alternative ideological economy which runs parallel with official society, as in the gangster *noir*, but that the gangster economy now works inside official society and, indeed, is identical with it. Aberrance and anti-social behaviour are not measured, in the film, in terms of gangster opposition to society but by opposition to the gangs (McQuigg to all forms of gangsterism, Scanlon to the syndicate), to the extent that honesty itself becomes aberrant. In the opening scene, a group of law officials draw attention to the way in which McQuigg is treated as an 'enemy' by both the gangsters and their corrupt agents in the upper echelons of the police force. This is also reflected in the use of the idealistic but doomed rookie cop, Johnson, who shares McQuigg's integrity, but who is ultimately killed in a pointless showdown with Scanlon. This contributes to the impression that the individual acts of Johnson and MQuigg are irrelevant and that, in going after Scanlon, they are mistaking the nature of contemporary crime by personalising it and directing their attention to the wrong quarters, because Scanlon is also an old fashioned irrelevance in the age of the syndicate.

McQuigg's honesty and non-conformist defiance of the new syndicate economy register him as archaic. Scanlon, at one point, says to him that he is 'two administrations behind' and that he is 'standing in the way of progress', but although Scanlon sees this negatively, the film uses McQuigg to embody American values in opposition to the un-American quality of the syndicate's monopoly. This is also referenced early in the film when a group of policemen are talking about McQuigg's methods. Johnson praises his approach to policework but is opposed by others who think of their work as just a job, setting up an opposition between old style civic duty and the alienated labour of the post-war corporate world where to be a police officer is to be a wage slave. Nevertheless, McQuigg is an ambiguous representative of American values, as also is his protégé Johnson, both of them working outside the legal process in order to get results. At one point, McQuigg tears up a writ of Habeas Corpus and then falsely books a bailbondsman on a drunk and disorderly charge. McQuigg's unorthodoxy is also shown when he bursts in on Scanlon, in a reverse mimicry of the classic gangster's invasion of official space, and shows a similar lack of respect for Scanlon's possessions by pushing things off a table in order to sit down. Johnson similarly uses questionable techniques when he gets a journalist friend,

Dave, to highlight his name in a news report so that he can act as bait and become a focus for the gangsters' revenge. This is apparently part of an old style self sacrifice, but is designed to allow Johnson to set a trap for the gangsters so that when they arrive at his home, he can use Dave as a decoy in order to ambush the hoods and effectively commit judicial murder. Not only does this suggest that gangster corruption has affected honest cops, but also that, in resisting the gangster, legitimate society has 'othered' itself and become what it opposes. Scanlon, however, is also outmoded because he too represents a defiant individuality that does not correspond with the syndicate's de-individuated corruption in which people become things or commodities that have a price. Although Scanlon is still ostensibly in charge of criminal operations, he is simply a figurehead for the new syndicate. The film suggests that, like McQuigg, Scanlon operates outside the law and that in the same way that McQuigg is a 'rogue cop', Nick is a 'rogue gangster', operating outside the law of the syndicate, which is the real law of America. Nick's methods are presented as old fashioned and amateurish, however, and the film opposes his 'Hoosier stuff' with the professionalism of syndicate. Nick prefers irrelevant strong-arm violence which not only mires him deeper in trouble, but also makes him impotent. Towards the end, Johnson mistakes him for a 'cheap hood', implying that he has been reduced to a meaningless foot-soldier as opposed to the gang boss he is meant to be.

A similarly problematic masculinity is figured in *The Big Heat* (Fritz Lang, 1953), but where McQuigg's version of masculinity is validated in *The Racket*, despite the impression it is a nostalgic anachronism, there do not seem to be any positive versions of masculinity in *The Big Heat*. The film is driven by the representation of the inadequacies of masculinity in its representation of both the syndicate and its 'other', the rogue cop, Bannion. The film is more a study of the masculinities that are found in the legal and criminal worlds rather than a definitive syndicate film, although it does clearly concern itself with gangster issues and the conventions attached to syndicate film, not least in its one-man-against-the-mob format. The film also assumes that the syndicate is already a fact of life, unlike other Kefauver syndicate films, with the racket having established itself not only through its occupation and territorialisation of the city, but also in its acceptance into the ranks of the police. Honest police officers and official society are isolated within small enclaves, something that is shown toward the end of the film in the image of the upstairs apartment where Bannion's daughter is being kept in safety, protected by vigilantes, which is one small citadel resisting the power of the syndicate. The film also differs from earlier syndicate films in that Bannion's crusade against the mob is motivated not by a desire to cleanse America of corruption, but as revenge for the death of his wife. It is revealed half way through film that Bannion, like everyone else, has known about the syndicate's rule of the city for years and has accommodated himself to it, so his fight against the racket is not motivated by civic duty or integrity, like McQuigg in *The Racket*, but generated by the mob's intervention into his own life. In this he is very similar to Diamond in *The Big Combo* whose obsession is as much filled by hatred (for Brown, the syndicate boss) and desire (for Susan Lowell, Brown's lover) as it is by desire for justice.

The narrative of *The Big Heat* follows policeman Dave Bannion (Glenn Ford) as he investigates the case of a corrupt police officer who has committed suicide. As he uncovers evidence of syndicate involvement, the gang try to stop his investigation which results in the death of his wife. With her death, Bannion is cut adrift from the stability of the family and feminine constraints on masculinity. The remainder of the film explores the obsessional maleness that develops in Bannion outside these restraining structures. Several critics have focused on the domestic issues raised in the film (McArthur, 1992:57–8; Cohan, 1997:107–8; Gunning, 2000:421–2), directing attention toward the different embodiments of masculinity that Bannion displays both inside and outside the family. Initially, Bannion is represented within a secure domestic space. The first scene at home takes place in a kitchen-dining room, to emphasise the dominance of feminine controls on his life, and focuses on familial concerns in the discussion with his wife about their daughter. This contented home life, however, is interrupted by a telephone call from Lucy Chapman about the Duncan case introducing the external masculine world into the feminine space which is developed in the second scene at home where further disruptions to the family occur as a result of the entry of Bannion's masculine world. As Cohan argues, when Bannion adds a brick to the police station his daughter is building, he knocks it down, symbolically destroying the law and the family in the process (1997:107). A more obvious disruption occurs with the telephoned threat from the mob, as a result of which Bannion invades and disrupts Lagana's home. In the final family scene, Bannion is shown as a domesticated male doing the washing up and putting his daughter to bed while his wife, Katie, goes out to the car to be blown up by the bomb meant for Bannion which is followed by an image of Bannion's impotence as he fails to open the car door in an attempt to rescue his wife. From this point on, Bannion's masculinity is characterised by a lack of constraint and he becomes not just a rogue cop but a rogue male, operating outside the rules of the system which even the syndicate gangsters rely on. He becomes an agent of randomness and unpredictability that threatens the rationality and system of the syndicate. Thus, in the scene in the bar where he browbeats the psychopathic Vince (Lee Marvin) he is only able to do so because he is no longer governed by the rules of society and acceptable legitimate masculinity. Vince is cowed because, despite his own violent masculinity, he is still a part of the system (the syndicate which controls society) and governed by its rules, so that his own violence is constrained by the social law of the syndicate. In this scene the roles of policeman and gangster are reversed with Bannion as the potentially random agent of violence confronting the new policeman, the gang enforcer.

Vince is an interesting figure in opposition to Bannion. Bannion, as a rogue cop, apparently shares Vince's excessive and violent tendencies, but Vince's aggression is controlled by the system of the syndicate. Vince has a paradoxical representation in the film and he is shown as both servile and feminised as well as being uncontrolled and hypermasculine. His relationship with Debby (Gloria Grahame) is the key to this dichotomy. When Vince is first introduced it is in response to Debby calling him to the telephone to speak to Lagana, during which Debby makes kowtowing motions with her hand to express Vince's subservience to his boss. Later, when Lagana arrives to discuss the failure of car bomb Debby mimics a circus ringmaster putting horses through their paces to show how Lagana controls both Vince and Larry, prancing round the room saying 'Hup, Vince. Hup, Larry', though she is also aware that the process extends to her in her subservience to Lagana by looking at Vince to make sure she has flattered Lagana sufficiently before leaving the room saying: 'Now it's Debby. Hup Debby, hup.' This shows the gangsters as slaves of Lagana and that their aggressive masculinity belongs to him and can only be expressed on his orders. They are not in control of their own phallic desires and are thus effectively emasculated. The representation of Lagana is also split between feminisation and masculinity. As the head of the syndicate he embodies phallic power, but he is often represented as effete as when he takes a telephone call from Mrs Duncan and is shown lying prone on a bed as his henchman stands over him, suggesting a homo-erotic relationship. There is also an implication in the film that once Mrs Duncan has evidence of the syndicate's activities that she becomes the boss of the syndicate, reversing the ideological polarity of the early part of the film where femininity is attached to legitimate society and aggressive masculinity to the gangster syndicate, so that the syndicate becomes feminised resulting in its failure because too many controls are placed on Vince's violent enforcement of its rule.

The gangsters are represented as paradoxical figures, therefore, and Vince's male violence is either only expressed in the service of the mob, when his masculinity cannot be said to belong to him, or it occurs in the domination of Debby, which is a response to his transformation into a subservient drone and a substitute for real social power. When Vince throws a pot of boiling coffee in Debby's face, one of the most famous images of the film, there is an implication that such excessive violence is an overcompensation for his containment by the mob. Effectively, the syndicate has introduced so much discipline into the gangster world as a way of controlling gangster excess that it threatens the masculinities it has helped to create, diverting them from the enforcement of gang power to private acts of violence. Vince himself draws attention to the impression that syndicate law feminises him in his comment, after Larry's death, that things went wrong because he was forced to be too soft on Bannion. The syndicate fails because it is too restrained and rational and not excessive enough. Vince's final emasculation occurs at the hands of Debby who reciprocates his act of throwing coffee in her face, leaving him to crawl across the floor before begging to die at the hands of the police because this will allow him to regain his masculinity. Being left alive and disfigured is to be feminised because he has become like Debby: an object of violence not its agent. Ultimately, *The Big Heat* is a film that focuses on how America has been turned inside out as a result of gangster corruption of society. Social ideology does not allow any expressions of male individuality once the syndicate has established its rationalised system of control (because official society has 'othered' itself to the extent that it is no longer recognisable) and the only response is to go 'rogue' like Bannion and alienate oneself from any collectivity, community or social structure.

The Big Combo (Joseph H. Lewis, 1955) has many similarities to *The Big Heat* but exaggerates and stretches the definition of social aberrance because it becomes unclear whether anyone can be said to represent the official ideology of individuality.[5] Every character in the film is presented as 'perverse': the policeman, Diamond (Cornel Wilde), pursues the gangster Nick Brown (Richard Conte) in an obsessional vendetta that is fuelled by his sexual desire for Susan Lowell (Jean Wallace), Brown's girlfriend; Brown demonstrates a ruthlessness that is a product of his sadistic sexual potency; Susan displays a masochistic and suicidal desire for Brown; and McClure (Brian Donlevy) is shown as a Machiavellian schemer. It is suggested that individuality is only available through aberrant behaviour, though the film also suggests that expressing the self in such a way is a depersonalising process that turns people into things because they become a product of desires and instincts not thought and intellect. They are machines, in a cartesian definition, because there is nothing to distinguish them from the animal-machine that Descartes identified and they are as a consequence turned into unthinking objects by their desires, not thinking human subjects. *The Big Combo* maps the, by now, conventional opposition of the individual to the system of the syndicate but represents everyone as being inside the system. This is made evident early in film in a discussion between Diamond and his boss as he attempts to justify his reasons for spending all his time, and a great deal of taxpayers' money, on his pursuit of Brown. Brown is referred to not as a person but an 'organisation' and Diamond's definition in opposition to him highlights his unconventional and apparently individualistic behaviour, which is compounded by the fact that he is also defying higher authorities (the police system) in persisting in his quest. On the other hand, Brown, as the head of the syndicate, is envisaged as a dehumanised thing as is shown in the scene in the boxer's changing room when Brown is first introduced. Brown, in his discussion of what it takes to reach the top, is presented as an automata driven by desire for power. He asks a losing boxer why he and his henchman, McClure, who he has supplanted as gang boss, are different and why one is at the top and the other is a nobody (because 'second is nothing'). He argues that there is apparently no difference because both he and McClure eat the same steaks and stay at the same hotels, but then goes on to say that it is hate that makes the difference and that it is hate that has driven him to the top, which he then also links to sexual power. In this discussion, Brown implies it is desire that creates individuals, but the film takes the opposing view, seeing the expression of desire as a lack of thought which dehumanises, something that is shown a few moments later when Brown slaps the boxer simply to find out if he has enough hatred to fight back (and therefore prove he has the desire to be champion), a dehumanising act designed to prove Brown's power, but one that actually proves his own dehumanisation. The scene also implies an inversion of usual gangster relationship with his henchman. McClure is represented as the brains behind the syndicate and Brown the muscle, also imaged in the way in which Brown is introduced as a headless body, implying again that he is driven by desire not intellect. As the head of the syndicate Brown thus becomes the symbol of the depersonalisation that the syndicate creates.

The Big Combo generally presents people as things and technology plays an important role in the film, particularly McClure's hearing aid which is used memorably as an instrument of torture. Many other characters are referred to in terms of their objectification. Rita, Diamond's part-time girlfriend, is referred to as like a pair of 'old gloves' and acts as a substitute for Diamond's desire for Susan, effectively becoming a fetish object, a thing whose body substitutes for someone else's. Even Diamond, who seems to represent the individuated rogue cop, is objectified in the image when he kneels at Rita's feet to put her shoes on, implying that he is easily enslaved, while Susan is defined by her death driven desire and is referred to as simply a body when Diamond tells Brown what Habeas Corpus means. Diamond explains that it means 'You may have the body', saying this over Susan's semi-conscious form implying that, alive or dead, she is simply a body. In her masochistic desire for Brown, Susan allows herself to be turned into an object, not only in being enslaved by him, but also in allowing him to use her sexually despite a lack of willingness (and lack of will), as in a scene which implies oral sex when Brown begins kissing her on the shoulder before disappearing down her back. There is an impression overall that the syndicate creates unwilled subjects who are, therefore, simply objects, a complete inversion of the classic gangster who became a willed individual through the expression of his criminal and sexual desires. The syndicate, however, also acts as a metaphor for the dehumanising processes at large in society because the Big Combo is not simply a syndicate, but America itself. The public are passive objects in the face of the syndicate, as is the case with the ex-gangster Bettini who passively lies down to die when he thinks Diamond is his assassin. As a compensation for this and, in an attempt to assert his superiority to the depersonalised society around him, Brown is often shown as a feudal monarch, sitting on a throne, as in the hospital when he regally addresses Diamond using McClure as an intermediary or in Dreyer's shop when he also sits with his back to Diamond looking toward the camera to indicate that he is not only above the police officer but also above and outside the society he has created.

A final example of the obsessional individual reified by his desires for revenge is found in the late syndicate film, *Underworld USA* (Samuel Fuller, 1961), a film that also represents a transformation of the gangster genre into the 'modern' phase of the New American Cinema (Hardy, 1998b: 203) because it places no investment in the desires of its criminal hero, Tolly Devlin (Cliff Robertson) nor uses him as a focus for identification, but simply records his quest for revenge without comment. Even in *The Big Heat* and *The Big Combo* there is an implication that despite their obsessions, Bannion and Diamond are acting in the cause of wider society by extirpating the syndicate. In *Underworld USA* Tolly's quest is entirely personal and there is no sense that he either wants to, or can, rid society of the combine. This is partly because he is from the same criminal world and accepts the existence of the syndicate, but also because he simply wants revenge on the men who killed his father, after which the syndicate can carry on with its business because the syndicate and its boss, Connors, had nothing to do with his father's death. The film begins with Tolly as a young boy witnessing the death of his father. He recognises one of the killers and sets out to discover the identities of the others which involves him going 'undercover' by the unconventional means of getting himself a prison sentence after he discovers that the killer he recognised (Farrar) has been imprisoned himself. After eighteen years, mainly spent in jail, he finally catches up with Farrar and coaxes the names of the other killers out of him and goes after them on his release from prison, despite discovering that they are now big time racketeers, each with a different 'branch' in the syndicate: narcotics, labour, and prostitution. His battle now no longer seems to be simply a personal desire for revenge, but a public assault on the syndicate and yet Tolly still persists in seeing it as a personal quest. *Underworld USA* thus makes no judgement on the morality or un-Americanness of the syndicate, but simply accepts it as a fact of life that will not go away, so that even when Tolly does kill Connors the film implies that someone else will simply take the syndicate boss' place. *Underworld USA* ends the syndicate cycle with the values of the combine or organisation firmly embedded within society. It exaggerates the corporate imagery attached to the syndicate with Connors seeing himself as a CEO and referring to other cities in the Combine as shareholders. Similarly, the syndicate headquarters has a gleaming modernist design with a swimming pool on the roof which Gus, the syndicate assassin draws attention to, showing pride in the syndicate's place in legitimate society by mentioning both the Chamber of Commerce plaque praising the syndicate's philanthropic acts and how the pool is used for charitable purposes with special swimming days for the underprivileged. The syndicate is no longer therefore a perversion of American life but a fundamental part of it, so that when Connors states that despite police pressure on the Combine 'there'll always be people like us', he is no longer simply talking about gangsters, but about their status as businessmen who cannot be distinguished from the entrepreneurs of legitimate society. The transformation of gangster into businessmen could have signalled the end of the genre because with no gangsters (only business-men) there is no gangster genre. However, as will be seen in the final chapters, the genre has persisted in many forms, whether this is through retrospection, or through the replication or ironising of gangster conventions or by re-inventing or exaggerating them in new contexts.

6
Nostalgia and Renewal in the Post-Classical Gangster Film

The previous chapters in this account of the gangster film have high-lighted the dominant modes and cycles of the gangster genre within particular periods. Any study of a genre that attempts to periodise in this way will necessarily be slightly artificial, because it entails a process of selection that will always operate some kind of repression, whether this is of films which are anomalous in the context of general tendencies or do not fully fit the methodology (in the case of this study, the 'couple on the run' movie). This account has also, however, mapped the mutability of the gangster genre, in the context of which it is difficult to argue that the variation and fragmentation that develops within the gangster genre in the 1960s and 1970s is any more obvious than that already shown. Nevertheless, the 1960s and 1970s can be seen as the beginning of the dispersal and fragmentation of the genre in the context of new cultural concerns and new production processes such as the decline of the studio system, the development of 'post-classical' or New Hollywood Cinema,[1] new forms of mainstream production and distribution, the rise of the blockbuster, and the development of a more clearly defined 'independ-ent cinema'. Textually, post-classical Hollywood film creates a new ideo-logical positioning that entails either a reflection on, or revision of, the ideologies and generic structures that classical Hollywood cinema expressed, the most important of which for genre is the way in which it is transformed from an apparently transparent mode of expression to an object of representation.

Although the production axis of the gangster genre is a particularly significant aspect of its development in the period, the cultural context that accompanies the shift in cinematic modes of production is of equal import. Not only does the production of films occur within a changing society of countercultural protest and increased commodification, but transformations in the economic and cultural spheres make themselves heard within the meanings and formal structures of the films themselves. The period of the late 1960s and early 1970s can, in many ways, be seen as Hollywood's moment of modernism, although it can also be argued that this is actually Hollywood's second moment of modernism with the first more classically falling within the period of social and cultural modernity in the early years of cinema.[2] New Hollywood Cinema has a similarity to the experiments of aesthetic modernism in its development of 'auteur cinema' as both a practice and theory, its introduction of European art cinema aesthetics into the Hollywood film-making process, and in the experiments with form within film texts which partake of the same process as the experiments within literature, art, and music in the classical period of modernism. However, these cinematic developments are also accompanied by cultural developments that have come to be called 'postmodernism' which impacted on both the aesthetic and cultural circulation of texts of all kinds, whether literature, art, architecture, television, or cinema.[3] The features most often associated with postmodernism (a fuller discussion of which is included in Chapter Seven) are, culturally, simulation, the pervasion of the commodity, the death of the individual, and the death of grand narratives; while, aesthetically, postmodern texts are characterised by nostalgia, intertextuality (or 'pastiche'), the collapse of generic boundaries, the death of originality and self-reflexivity. Hollywood Cinema in the period is subject to competing cultural discourses of modernisation and postmodernisation, a tension that also characterises literary production at the same time with its dichotomies of experiment and nostalgic evocation and its formal twin strands of minimalist late modernism (in fiction by Ronald Sukenick, William Gass, and Raymond Federman) and a maximalist tendency to produce Epic works (in the novels of, for example, Thomas Pynchon and John Barth).

When examining gangster cinema in the period of the 1960s and 1970s similar concerns with competing discourses of modernism and postmodernism, system and fragmentation, or experiment and nostalgic replication can be found. This is not to say that all gangster films (or all Hollywood film production) in the period can be reduced to the parallel process of modernisation and postmodernisation, but that as an informing principle this helps to understand how gangster cinema in the period both reflects on (in its nostalgia) and revises (in its renewal) generic history.[4] Nor is this to argue that postmodernism only entails either the nostalgic re-evocation of prior 'originality' or the unconscious replication of its culture because, as is argued in the next chapter, its textual products can also have a refractive quality that comments on, or critiques, the cultural matrix that generates them even as they are simultaneously co-opted.[5] A film such as *Point Blank* thus both re-invokes its history in what could be seen as a nostalgic referentiality to both the syndicate and one-man-against-the-mob variations, but it also plays with the generic conventions that produce it, and renews them as they are refracted through its existential iciness, experimental editing, and fractured narrative. Similarly, the rise of the black gangster film in the 1970s is both a product of existing genre conventions (even, in the case of *Black Caesar*, invoking a specific ante-cedent) but also places these in the new context of African-American crime and social inequality. The effect is to re-invest the gangster film's origins in the ethnic struggle for success and assimilation with a new meaning by locating it within a cultural and economic milieu where these principles do not seem possible, even in the criminal sphere, thus generating within the genre an immediate and direct intervention into the social articulations of power along ethnic lines.

From retro to modern: gangsters in the 1960s

The gangster genre entered the 1960s with a cycle of films that reflected on and revisited its previous configurations in the shape of the nostalgic bio-pic in films such as *Baby Face Nelson* (1957), *Machine Gun Kelly* (1958), *The Bonnie Parker Story* (1958), *Al Capone* (1959), *The Rise and Fall of Legs Diamond* (1960), and *Pretty Boy Floyd* (1960) which were themselves to be re-visited in later manifestations such as *The St Valentine's Day Massacre* (1967), *Lucky Luciano* (1973), *Dillinger* (1973) and *Lepke* (1975). The historical evocation in these films is not postmod-ern nostalgia, with its desire to evoke a cultural cohesion or full individu-ality mythically located in the past, but an internalised generic nostalgia which both mythologises and demythologises historical gangster figures. The films were structured around a particular character trait in their gangster heroes and heroines which both singled them out as untypical individuals, thereby explaining their rise to success, but also identified these features as flaws that resulted in their ultimate downfall. A double process occurs in the exaggeration of the dominant psycho-logical or individual character trait so that although there is a tendency to mythologise the gangsters' untypical individuality, the films also demystify their gangsters by both emphasising the aberrance the dom-inant trait causes and stressing the anti-social behaviour that follows. These gangsters are more akin to the 'unnatural' psychopathic gangster of the 1940s with a one-dimensional quality that does not invoke any kind of tragic sympathy. Nor do the films, in their mise-en-scène and narrative style, contribute to any kind of identification, focusing as they do on the spectacle of action and violence in a 'thrills and spills' formula that was a product of the fact that many of them were cheap independent exploitation pictures designed for the drive-in teenage audience. There is a logic of excess within the cycle as each film tries to top its predecessors by making its character more excessive and ruthless. Thus, Baby Face Nelson is more psychopathic, Legs Diamond more invincible, Bonnie Parker wilder and more excessive, and Al Capone more ruthless.

Later examples of the nostalgic bio-pic are more interesting because of the way they exceed generic conventions even as they invoke them. In the cycle of the late 1950s and early 1960s the attempt to produce a hyper-realistic representation of historical gangsters results in an over-determination of the generic codes that foregrounds them as spectacles of entertainment rather than as documentary records. Later versions of the nostalgia cycle, *The St. Valentine's Day Massacre* (Roger Corman, 1967), *Bonnie and Clyde* (Arthur Penn, 1967) and *Dillinger* (John Milius, 1973) have more depth in their approach to the representation of history to the extent that they cannot be considered as part of the cycle. They use their accounts of historical figures to reflect on contemporary culture and articulations of power, generating both nostalgia and renewal in the process. This is particularly the case with *Bonnie and Clyde* and *Dillinger* which can be said to bookend the period of counter-cultural opposition in America offering similar tales of doomed gangsters but with differing cultural effect. Coming at the beginning of the counter-cultural protest of the 1960s, *Bonnie and Clyde* expresses a 'mainstreaming of deviancy' (Carr, 2000: 72) while also meditating on expressions of official coercion. The excessive force and violence that causes the deaths of the two lead characters is used to express an indignation at the coercive strategies represented by the State and the film locates itself within a culture of nascent protest, that shares the collective anger it expresses, and as a result helps to reinforce a mood of opposition already circulating in society. *Dillinger*, on the other hand, is released in the period of retrenchment in the early 1970s and, while it represents the same coercive force at work on the part of the State, is resigned to its perpetuation and even begins to legitimate its operation in the representation of the FBI agent, Melvin Purvis, as not just an avenging angel, but as one with legitimate power and righteousness on his side.

Before turning more fully to these two examples, a discussion of *The St Valentine's Day Massacre* will help illuminate the cinematic context within which the later historical gangster dramas develop. *The St Valentine's Day Massacre* appears to be a conventional example of the nostalgia cycle, but presents a self-conscious approach by utilising conventions of the gangster genre not for their own sake, but to reinterpret their meanings within a cultural context. The film is a meditation on old and new forms of gangsterism, which it makes most obvious in its opposition of Capone's corporate style of organisation with Moran's old-fashioned gangster. In rhyming scenes early in the film, Capone (Jason Robards) gives a speech to his mob that is represented as if it were taking place within a corporate board room while shortly after Moran (Ralph Meeker) gives a similar speech but set in the room of flophouse. While the scenes are intended to highlight relations of power in the gangster world, they also use their images of criminality to reflect on the differences between crime in the 1960s and crime in the 1920s. Capone is a very contemporary gangster, a syndicate boss doing business in a board room while Moran is of the past, an opposition that is also articulated in terms of the film's generic references, with Capone invoking the more contemporary syndicate film and Moran the classic gangster cycle. This is extended in quite direct references to the classic gangster film in the figure of Peter Gusenberg, who simulates the behaviour of Tom Powers in *The Public Enemy*, firstly by opening the beer taps in a rival speakeasy and then slapping a sandwich in his moll's face. These textual citations are not simply for the purpose of replicating generic influences or to meditate on the perceived authenticity of Moran's gang in opposition to Capone's soulless syndicate but are rather used to draw attention to the changing face of crime and its reality as a big business in the contemporary period. The film emphasises this with an early catalogue of the details of crime in Chicago (listing numbers of speakeasies and murders, as well as how much the bootleg business was worth in 1929) which is present to illustrate the corporatisation and pervasion of crime in the present rather than to record historical detail accurately. This use of the past also extends to the film's meditation on the death of the individual in a syndicalised society, which is represented as not just a gangster power arrangement, but one that the audience can recognise in society as a whole. This is also expressed when new characters are introduced in voice-over by their full name and with a personal history which seems to suggest their significance, but because there are so many instances of this device and because the characters' importance is as narrative functions, actually means that they become interchangeable and redundant. Even Capone is introduced in this way, despite his mythic status, as if the audience would have no knowledge of who he was, with the concomitant implication that he too is a cipher, empty of individuality, and is just another cigar-chomping corporate CEO. The film, however, is not nostalgic for a past where Moran's individuality is possible. In part, this is because Gusenberg's replication of Tom Powers' actions establishes him as a crude caricature of masculine individuality which the film also attributes to Powers himself. The film's lack of nostalgia is also shown in its presentation of violence and corruption as an everyday occurrence implying that as an endemic part of American society it is not the product of a distinct period, but pervades American history up to the present. In this vision, nostalgia is impossible and if anything *The St Valentine's Day Massacre* is an anti-nostalgic demythologisation of both its genre and its culture, re-invoking the one to reflect on the other, but locating value in neither.

.*Bonnie and Clyde* is even clearer in its references to the contemporary media and commodity culture (Leong, *et al.* 1997: 77), to the extent that its generic antecedents pale in comparison. The film is a seminal movie, not just in the gangster genre but in the Hollywood system of production itself, as Carr argues, because of the role it played in 'the demise of the Production Code' (2000:76–7). The film in its cultural vision also clearly roots itself in a culture of protest and opposition to the State and ideology, but mutes its counter-cultural vision by offering a politics of escape rather than a politics of social engagement and transformation of ideology and institutions. Nevertheless, its 'infusion of modernist elements into the classical paradigm' (Man, 1994: 8) re-articulates its historical setting in the Depression years of the 1930s to marshal comment on contemporary society, suggesting that the oppressions in 1960s America are the product of the same forms of capitalist exploitation that produced the Depression. The film reflects on the past to identify the same principles at work in the present by reiterating the State's hostility to its citizens and by offering a vision of the politics of dispossession in the Depression to make the same point about the 1960s. Clyde's comment to a dispossessed farmer that 'We rob banks' is not a statement of their criminality but becomes an identifying principle of their politics: opposition to capitalism, the State and their institutions. Bonnie and Clyde become romantic outlaws, gangsters with a social message of opposition, and they are presented as products of marginality from the outset (Clyde's criminal record is a badge of dispossession rather than a sign of criminal immorality), both yearning for something else, but something that society cannot provide. They are not, however, gangsters in the classic mould, and this is one of the areas where the film demythologises its forebears, because the classic gangster's goal is the achievement of the American Dream through illegitimate means. Crime in *Bonnie and Clyde* is presented, however, as simply emphasising marginality and distances Bonnie and Clyde ever further from the American Dream because it highlights their 'deviancy' and uncontainability within official ideologies. Crime is thus more an expression of oppositionality that leads nowhere rather than a positive response to social oppression, a configuration that also places the film within the road movie genre, epitomised by Clyde's statement that 'we ain't headin' nowheres, we're just runnin' from'.

This ambiguous response to society also manifests itself in contradictory images of crime in the film which is presented as a mode of social evasion, but also the way in which Bonnie and Clyde are co-opted.[6] Crime is on one level presented as an act of libidinous pleasure (and as a kind of sexual sublimation), a caper that displays many lighthearted Keystone Kops style moments, as when Blanche is scooped up into a speeding car as the gang make their escape from a shoot-out with the police or when Moss moves the getaway car because he sees a better parking space. Crime as pleasure entails a release from social constraints and has a 'carnivalesque' quality that becomes a way for the gang to express themselves outside social law. Crime becomes emblematic of the expression of individual freedom as with the joyride with Grizzard and his fianceé, which serves no purpose except as an expression of the ability of Bonnie and Clyde to act without prohibition. Crime, however, is also presented increasingly as a form of entrapment as when Bonnie comments on how they have nowhere to go and nothing to do except rob banks, suggesting the same replication of habitual mundanity found in legitimate expressions of 'labour', an image expressed toward the end when the gang are trapped by the police in a forest glade and drive purposelessly around in circles.[7] Crime, like life in official society, leads only to death and there is an increasingly hysterical representation of the gang's activities as they approach their end. Crime is also presented as a form of complicity in its representation as part of a media culture. The gang pose for photographs at several points in the film suggesting that they have an awareness of themselves as public identities and that they are part of society's circulation of images. Clyde initially persuades Bonnie to join him by foregrounding the image of their success and the fame it will bring, an articulation that locates them as commodified images whose identities exist in the dissemination of themselves as part of a cultural spectacle rather than as a product of their own subjectivities. The film can therefore be seen as having an ambiguous place in its re-use and de-mythologisation of generic forms and in its critique of culture, double-coding it as modernist inflected revisionism and as postmodern co-optation.

Dillinger, released in 1973, offers a similar sense of the impossibility of escaping society in its representation of the Dillinger gang gradually being hunted down by the implacable FBI agent, Melvin Purvis. Coming at the end of the counter-cultural period it can be placed in a context of the end of optimism in the ability to change society, with the outlaw inevitably being destroyed by the 'System'. The film is less certain in its representation of Dillinger as a 'romantic' figure. He is shown as an unpleasant snarling thug particularly in his violent 'seduction' of Billie Frechette which principally entails him calling her a 'whore'. In some respects the film demonises Dillinger as much as it mythologises him and sets out to debunk the myths of Dillinger as a public hero. Its revisionist tendencies, therefore, are not to challenge ideological representation, but to question popular myths of Dillinger as a Robin Hood style bandit hero. Like *Bonnie and Clyde* the film is also excessive in its portrayal of crime and violence but where in the former film the gang's actions are characterised by childlike exuberance, in *Dillinger* the criminal life is presented as creating chaos. The film almost invariably presents its violence as purposeless carnage as in the random shooting that characterises the East Chicago bank raid. The film's principle difference from *Bonnie and Clyde* is the ambiguity over whether it is Dillinger or Purvis who is the hero. In one scene, Purvis lectures a young boy over the moral rightness of the law when the boy expresses a desire to be like Dillinger rather than a policeman, but the film is uncertain in what it values: public duty or individual freedom. The latter is not fully legitimated because although the film articulates a lack of social freedom, the experience of freedom, when it occurs, is seen to create chaos. Nevertheless, Dillinger's death displays no sense of the moral superiority of the law in its representation as a judicial murder, with Dillinger effectively being killed by a firing squad. The result is a film that offers a revision of 1960s revisionism but in its uncertainty about where to locate value or authenticity more clearly points the way to a postmodern demythologisation of the notion of value itself.

Unlike other gangster films of the 1960s, *Point Blank* (John Boorman, 1967) presents a very modern vision of the new gangster economy. It is a film without nostalgia existing almost entirely within the present (a vision expressed in the disorienting editing of the film) with no sense that history has any part in its making, even though its structure is based on an opposition between the old fashioned individualist gangster, Walker (Lee Marvin), and the depersonalised corporate syndicate he takes on in his pursuit of the $93,000 they owe him. Walker is the 'last gangster' (Brode, 1995: 21), a reversion to a gangster ethos which sees the world in terms of personal relations and codes of honour in a world that does not attach any importance to the personal or the individual. The film is full of scenes which emphasise the depersonalisation and the isolation of the individual, whether it is a shot of Walker looking exposed when sitting on top of a fence dwarfed by the backdrop of Alcatraz, or images of shiny modernist architecture in the gang's corporate headquarters. The film, nevertheless, does cast a glance backward to *Underworld USA* in its representation of a pervasive corporate and legitimate gang syndicate and in its story of a man out for revenge on the new style gang, but places this within a landscape of existential isolation in which Tolly Devlin's desire for personal revenge becomes a de-personalised quest for money. Tolly Devlin lives in a world which still presents the façade of caring about the individual, but the world that Walker occupies owes allegiance to nothing but money. The gang as a syndicate treats people only as things and as far as they are concerned Walker is simply an accountancy problem rather than a real threat to their power. The syndicate is nothing but a capitalist enterprise (with Brewster describing himself as a 'corporate officer'), part of a matrix of capital that exists outside of itself in the global flows of money. The gang, in this form, has emptied itself out in a radical decentralisation of its operations. That Brewster carries no more than eleven dollars in his wallet, and that a dead gangster is revealed to have only credit cards in his, signifies the shift from a gang whose power is invested in a community of gangsters to an organisation where power exists not internally but in its dispersal through the circulation of money. This does, however, raise the question of whether the gang, and its officers, has any power any more or whether its dispersal means that power now resides only in an externalised flow of money, leaving the gang powerless and vulnerable to Walker's assault on them; as one of the syndicate assassins points out to Brewster: '[Walker's] just tearing you apart'.

Walker's position within the film is full of ambiguity. *Point Blank* has been seen as embodying a 1960s politics of the individual against the system (Hardy, 1998b: 258), but the overwhelming sense is that Walker has been drained of any kind of emotion and individual will. He is often portrayed as invulnerable or invincible, as in his swim from Alcatraz to San Francisco, or when he first enters the gang headquarters (dubbed 'Fort Knox') and defeats the gangsters with considerable ease. In these abilities, which seem more than human, he is placed in the context of the apparently invincible gangster of the past, such as Cody Jarrett (although there is also potentially a sly nod to the *Flint* series of which Marvin was the star). The film seems to imply by his abilities that he is the last of the individuals, which his alienation also seems to fore-ground, while his perplexity suggests a man clinging to past values that set him apart. He is often represented simply staring into the distance as if he is not a part of the 'reality' around him, as when he meets Yost/Fairfax on the boat trip to Alcatraz. He stands looking fixedly at Alcatraz, not noticing what is going on around him – even when a woman walks by and Yost/Fairfax looks at her, Walker simply does not notice she's there. His alienation and perplexity are so absolute, however, that, as Brode argues, he looks like he has 'just landed on another planet' (Brode, 1995: 21), although the images that show his lack of recognition of 'reality' more suggest the internalised solipsism of someone who has withdrawn into the self in the face of the lack of order he sees around him. His disorientation is so great that he cannot comprehend the new world of corporate gangs, as if it doesn't 'com-pute'. The resulting impression of Walker is that he is not superhuman, but non-human, effectively an automaton, but one who shows less life than the machines that Chris turns on to evoke some emotion in him. He does not therefore represent a return to the values and individuality of the classic gangster because he seemingly has no will, substituting instead a vestigial instinct that acts like a programme which cannot be shut down until its task is finished. Walker can arguably be seen not as the 'last gangster', but as the first 'post-human' gangster who in his implacable quest might be seen as a forebear of Yul Brynner's relentless android killer in *Westworld* who, in turn, also forms the model for Arnold Schwarzenegger's terminator. Walker simply becomes a 'thing', as the film finally reveals when it shows how Walker has been used by the crime boss, Fairfax, as a tool to rid himself of his conspiratorial subordinates. Walker is not an individual who achieves fulfillment by regaining his money, but an automaton set loose by Fairfax to do his work and he is thus simply an objectified tool in someone else's plans. Although he refuses Fairfax's offer of a place in the organisation, which might be read as an act of individualist authenticity, he is figured at the end in shadows, perpetually on the outside and thus perpetually in a state of loss.

The gangster film as epic: *The Godfather* trilogy

The first two instalments of *The Godfather* trilogy dominate the gangster movie in the 1970s not only in their critical reception and, in the case of the former, their box office success, but in the complexity of their narratives, their introduction of a new set of iconic images to the genre, and the stature they brought to the genre with their Epic scope and attention to detail. *The Godfather* has entered popular culture in a way that no other gangster movie has managed to the extent that the film no longer exists simply as a screen text but as part of popular consciousness in memories of any number of moments or images from the film: Marlon Brando's puffed out cheeks, the dead horse, the Don's chair, the Baptism sequence, the gun in the toilet or Luca Brasi's sleeping arrangements. This entry into popular culture is a product of the film's representation of an alternative cultural economy that shares so many features of everyday life experienced within the parameters of legitimate social ideology (the family, patriarchal power) but which is so radically different and so hermetically sealed as to effectively suggest that legitimate society and its ideologies are either redundant or non-existent within the world represented. The Mafia is thus both exotic and familiar, part of legitimate society but also a cultural enclave within it that both repels and attracts. The film's main focus therefore is its mapping of a tension in its vision of the Mafia as an entity that is distinct from the external world in its cultural ethos of the family and paternal hierarchies, but also embedded in society in its business activities. The film narrativises the transformation of the former into the latter in the Corleones' inability to keep the two separate as the 'family' becomes ever more porous and dissolves into the business of the 'Family'. Jameson discusses these two polarities in terms of the ideological (the Mafia as aberrant capitalism) and utopian (nostalgia for the family unit) functions of the film, suggesting that the two remain in tension until *Part II* deconstructs them and reveals their 'ideological content' which is that the Mafia is not a substitution for American business, but the very thing itself (Jameson, 1990: 33).

This deconstruction process, however, is already evident in *The Godfather*, even in the first two episodes of the film: Connie's wedding and Tom Hagen's extortion of Woltz in Hollywood. The wedding scenes initially establish the Corleones as a family in the private sphere, mapping familial relationships as part of a cultural structure that locates them within a set of historic traditions and origins. The image of the family as a close-knit community with a set of loyalties, a system of respect and honour, and a paternal hierarchy (all of which are found in the image of the Don receiving petitioners while the domestic event of the wedding goes on around him) emphasises the communal functions of the Corleone family. However, the Corleones also have a function outside the private family sphere in their public role as guarantors of social hierarchy, even though this is still represented in terms of a Sicilian heritage that locates them as in America but not of it. These images of a hermetically sealed world however are problematised as there are several images which show that the cultural space of the family has already been permeated by the Corleones' economic role as a criminal business. While the father's petition asking for justice for his daughter implies his return to traditional law after having experienced the failure of modern American law, the images of the photographer trying to breach security, the FBI examining licence plates, and the appearance of Michael (Al Pacino) in his army uniform imply not only that the family's real business is in the outside world, but that one of their members (Michael) is already more identified with external society than he is with the family; as he says: 'That's my family, Kay, not me.' Michael is shown as an outsider at the wedding, not simply because at this point he has apparently turned his back on the family-as-business, but because he will in the future effectively divest the Corleones of their function as a domestic unit and establish them entirely within the economic domain when he becomes Don.

The following episode, in which Hagen (Robert Duvall) travels to Hollywood to enforce the family law on the film producer, Woltz, compounds this vision of the Corleones existing beyond the local and private structures of power represented by the wedding and shows them enforcing their power externally and nationally. The family is already dispersed beyond the family unit and if any gangster film highlights both the physical and social reterritorialisation and deterritorialisation of the gang, it is *The Godfather*. Images of enclosed or fortified space are prevalent within the film, whether it is the hospital in which Don Vito is kept or the heavily protected family villa during the war with Sollozzo. These images represent the threat posed to the cultural unit of the family by the Corleones' business enterprises in the outside world, and it is no surprise that Don Vito is shot on the street, Apollonia blown up in a car outside the Sicilian villa, and Sonny (James Caan) is killed at the gate to the estate on the border of internal fortified space and unprotected external space. The images also show the 'gang' having a distinct physical space to call its territory and Don Vito's refusal to get involved in the drugs trade has less to do with moral objections, in this respect, than a fear that the family will become dispersed beyond this space and become fragmented by its entry into the global capitalist system. Hagen's visit to Hollywood has already established, however, that Don Vito's vision of the family as a coherent unit is a nostalgic fiction because the family are already dispersed and which same dissipation is suggested when Michael visits Fredo and Mo Green in Las Vegas. Here, Las Vegas represents both a mob enclave in opposition to external society and its intersection with wider capitalist flows of money. The fact that the Corleones are already partly involved, and that Michael wishes to extend their involvement, shows that they have already extended their territory beyond their local communal base and are part of a gang structure where 'territory' is notional or tied to the movements of money, of which Las Vegas is the symbol. As Man argues, this locates *The Godfather*'s gangsters within the ideological and economic systems of capitalism and not outside them trying to get in, as in the classic formulation of the gangster (Man, 1994: 133–4). At the end of the film, when Michael moves the family business to Nevada he allows another family to set itself up in the Corleones' place, apparently to maintain their power over a physical terrain (which also apparently reaffirms the family's position in historic traditions and reified feudal power structures in their right to grant the creation of a 'demesne' as a 'fief'), but this act emphasises the Corleone's deterritorialisation and dispersal as their control over their original base is now through surrogates, rather than being immediately and directly enforced by themselves. That *Part II* articulates the tensions in the relationship between the Corleones and a surrogate family points to the inability to guarantee power in the new deterritorialised structures.

What is interesting about this transformation of the Corleones is that it is through Michael and not through Sonny that the family becomes dispersed. In his desire to join Sollozzo in the drug trade Sonny represents a modernising tendency, but his difference from Michael is principally symbolised by the fact that he gives up his individual desires by surrendering to the will of his father which also represents the will of the family. Michael, on the other hand, is represented as being an outsider, despite the images of his future asccession when the family discuss what is to be done about Sollozzo and the police chief, McCluskey. Here, Michael is shown sitting centre-screen, in a chair, dispensing advice in the same way that the Don dispenses his wisdom to his petitioners. Michael, in his self-discipline, also symbolises a figure of order similar to his father so that the line of descent, passing to Michael, seems to guarantee the continuity of the family traditions, an image highlighted when Don Vito passes on his knowledge to Michael, ensuring that the patriarchal law of the family persists. However, having begun as an outsider Michael has been completely assimilated by the Corleone family, to the extent that he loses his identity in the process, not to the cultural family of Sicilian tradition, but to the criminal family and his assimilation into its economics of crime. His subsumption into the family-as-business entails his fragmentation within its externalised and deterritorialised spaces of operation, to the extent that his identity is utterly dispersed. In part, this is a product of assuming the mantle of the head of the family which means that although he has power, his identity, will and desires become invested in assuring the family's success rather than his own. Within the context of the new deterritorialised flows of the family, the power and will of his father no longer seem possible, although the move to Nevada can be seen as an attempt to both impose his will and to find a 'territory' within which it can be expressed.

There are two dominant images in the film that represent the tensions between the integrity of the self and its dissolution, both of which focus around the tensions between the private and public families. The first is the Don's chair which seems to guarantee the absolute purity of the Don's power while also, because it occupies a specially protected space, seeming to express the family as a physical territory as a separate enclave within society. It also, however, represents their extension across a larger external territory because this is the place where control over that territory originates. The *mise-en-scène* also contributes to this as representations of Vito and Michael both show them occupying centre-screen, effectively territorialising the screen space they occupy as their own. The Don's chair also represents the integrity of male power and identity, but as the metaphorical expression of the family's wider business and territory also entails the extension and dispersal of these. The second image is actually the Baptism montage at the end of the film which, while confirming Michael's status as family patriarch, in its juxtaposition with images of agents carrying out Michael's orders to kill enemies of the Corleones also represents his fragmentation. He is dispersed into each of the gangsters (who also cannot be said to have an identity because they are tools of the family's will) and scattered across America as a result. This dispersal also occurs because Michael is in the tradition of the 'cerebral gangster' whose power is not invested in his body but in his intellectual abilities to control others. Thus Michael's self is emptied as he is exteriorised into the bodies of others, dispersing himself by exercising control through his surrogates. While this seems to be an image of absolute power it also represents his deterritorialised self because, although his physical body may be in church his identity exists in the actions of the bodies that carry out his orders.

The Godfather, Part II (Francis Ford Coppola, 1974) has often been seen as a more 'scathing critique of American capitalist society' (Man,

1994: 121) than *The Godfather*, but it is more a continuation of this critique, extended spatially and temporally as it investigates the continued dispersal of the family across America and beyond (in the Cuba sequences). It also highlights the fact that the family as a cultural unit was always a myth in the sequences showing the early life of Don Vito which indicate that the family's Mafia origins were always as much a business enterprise as a protection of traditions. The dispersal and deterritorialisation of the family unit is represented in several forms. It occurs, for example, in the failure of Michael to guarantee traditional power structures in his relationship with the Corleones' surrogate family under Frankie Pentangeli because of Michael's involvement with Hyman Roth and the Rossato brothers in which capitalist principles are privileged over family codes of honour and loyalty. The relationship with Roth also draws Michael into a wider nexus of political and economic arrangements, including an abortive venture in Cuba, while the move to Las Vegas emphasises the family's location within a capitalist system of monetary exchange. The most obvious expression of the family's dispersal of traditional power structures and values is the murder of Fredo for his part in an attempt on Michael's life, but this is simply a confirmation of Michael's willingness to sacrifice family principles that was already shown with the killing of Carlo, Connie's husband, in *The Godfather*. These killings also foreground the hypocrisy of the family myth even as they seem to act in its defence. Michael kills Carlo and Fredo for betraying the family, but the fact that they betrayed it in the first place reveals that the structure of loyalties apparently embedded in the family is a simulation and that individual desire, as motivated by the greed articulated within capitalist economics, has always been a more dominant factor in the Corleones' construction of itself.

The complexity of the Corleones' economic and political relationships in Michael's narrative are foregrounded by the ambiguity over people's motives which itself acts to emphasise the blurring of distinctions in the dispersal of the family as it enters a wider international context. This complexity is seemingly juxtaposed to the simplicities of the past in the narrative of the young Don Vito (Robert De Niro) which focuses on the persistence of Sicilian traditions in their transferal to America and which apparently have less to do with monetary gain than with survival. Don Vito's rise and his revenge on a Sicilian Don for the murder of his father thus articulate a logical and comprehensible narrative, not only in terms of generic codes, but also within an identifiable social and cultural economy of vendetta. Although the two narratives seem to juxtapose the simplicity of tradition as located within the cultural unit of the family and the complexities of the deterritorialised economic unit of Michael's version of the family, the sequences that focus on Don Vito reveal that there was always a capitalist logic behind the foundation of the Corleones as a Mafia family. Although, in his dealings with people when he becomes Don, Vito seems to operate a favour economy outside monetary exchange, there is also an implication in the creation of Genco Import Co., as both a front for his criminal operations and as a sign of his Mafia status, that this is a fiction and that the real 'business' of the family is not social, but economic and that the logical result of this is the internationalisation and fragmentation of the family in Michael's present.

The Godfather, Part III (Francis Ford Coppola, 1990), although outside the period of the 1970s, is nevertheless more relevant as part of this chapter because it acts as a further extension of these issues in a global context, even while it partakes of a more contemporary postmodern nostalgia for tradition. In some respects this is simply a logical development of already existing narratives. *The Godfather, Part II* increasingly locates itself within a domain of political machination (not only in the figure of Senator Gehry), but also within the world of criminality with murder attempts taking on the appearance of political assassinations and with gangsters acting as diplomats and covert operatives. In *Part III* there is an apparent displacement away from the economic function of the family to a more political role, even while the film is motivated by Michael's involvement with the Vatican and the real estate holding company, Immobiliare, in which he has a stake. Michael becomes an international broker extending the territoriality of the Corleones even further by venturing into Europe and ultimately involving them in international political murders rather than gang killings. The Corleones become a globalised entity, operating effectively at the level of a nation state and far beyond the fortified enclave of *The Godfather*. Nevertheless, there is also a reversion to the family unit and a sense of internalisation as Michael becomes concerned both with continuing the family lineage and making the family a fully legitimate business by selling his gambling investments. The film represents an attempt to return to the mythic ideology of the family as a cultural rather than criminal entity, embedded in its Sicilian traditions where it simply has the function of a paternalistic agency of protection. That Michael fails in both these aims, while also causing the death of his daughter, is a product of the extension and dispersal of the criminal family function into global systems of capitalism and, although Michael dies in his Sicilian villa, suggesting a return to family origins and tradition, his death is also the death of the family as a cultural entity.

Gangsters on the margins: the gangster–loser film and blaxploitation

If *The Godfather* trilogy represented the institutionalisation of the mob and its increasing extension of social power, other developments in the early 1970s such as the 'gangster–loser' and blaxploitation film focused on the marginalised gangster outside the system of Mafia organised crime. The former type of narrative can be found in a crop of films all released in 1973 including *The Outfit* (John Flynn), *Charley Varrick* (Don Siegel), and *The Friends of Eddie Coyle* (Peter Yates) but also finds form in two later films, both directed by John Cassavetes, *The Killing of a Chinese Bookie* (1976) and *Gloria* (1980). The gangster genre also finds articulation in blaxploitation film, best exemplified by *Across 110th Street* (Barry Shear, 1972) and *Black Caesar* (Larry Cohen, 1973), but there are also gangster elements in the Shaft series, most notably *Shaft's Big Score!* (Gordon Parks, 1972). Often these films focused on small-time gangsters taking on the larger system of organised crime, through which they offered a parallel mapping of the control of the individual by the impersonal forces of legitimate society of corporations and government agencies. The world of the 'loser' gangster is a marginal culture where survival is the most important concern, but which is constantly threatened because of the pervasive hostility that is found in this world. In part, this is a product of the films' vision of an atomistic society where no one can be trusted, but also results from a sense of the indifference of distant governmental and social institutions to the plight of ordinary American citizens. This is most obvious in blaxploitation gansgter films where the dramatisation of urban space, in films predominantly set in New York, not only represents a horizontal stratification of spatial power in the opposition between wealthy downtown Manhattan and the impoverished urban wasteland of Harlem, but also takes metaphoric form in articulation of vertical relations of space. The films evoke the notion of an upper and lower city found in *Metropolis* with the world of the wealthy (including Mafia dons) occupying Upper East Side penthouses or the corporate offices of Wall Street skyscrapers while the gangsters who take on this elite world are territorialised in terms of derelict ghetto streets. The effect of this metaphoric cultural space is to emphasise the marginality of the gangsters and the impossibility of crossing over into the world of the establishment.

There are some exceptions to this articulation of power as, for example, in *Black Caesar* where the gangster, Tommy Gibbs, evicts his lawyer from his high-rise apartment and takes occupation of it on his mother's behalf but, in the main, the American Dream does not exist in these films and life is more about getting by or dreaming of escape. The films often resound with references to the heist movie of the 1950s, but place this within a bleaker representation of society while also offering a counter-cultural optimism about the possibility of escape. This is less the case in blaxploitation film, where power structures seem to be so embedded within institutionalised racism (as in *Across 100th Street* in the representation of power relations between whites and African-Americans within the police force) that failure is also embedded in the narrative structures, but both *The Outfit* and *Charley Varrick* show outsiders triumphing over the mob and effecting an escape even if the endings are ambiguous in exactly where it is the characters will go to escape the long reach of the Mafia. The gangster–loser film assumes that organised crime now effectively runs society and Charley Varrick's story of how big Combines moved in on the crop-dusting industry, marginalising small operators like himself, identifies the mob and corporations as the same entity. It is not simply that gangs are corporations, as in *Point Blank*, but that corporations are now society's gangsters. An element of opposition, in addition to the films' anti-corporate messages and their dreams of escape, can also be found in the ability of maverick individuals like Charley and the gangster partnership of Earl and Cody in *The Outfit* to outwit the rather lumbering mobs they challenge. Earl and Cody, for example, rob the Mafia with ease and there is an implication of decadence about the mob (as shown in the representation of the mob boss, Mailer, as a member of the landed gentry) that is also identified with corporations. The films therefore locate themselves within a distinctly American ideology of the pre-eminence of the rugged male individual, curtailing any real sense of political opposition by presenting corporatisation and its systematised social structures as perversions of America capitalism rather than its logical product.

Other examples of the gangster-loser film are less optimistic. *The Killing of a Chinese Bookie* presents an existential perspective in showing the individual as simply a cipher in an impersonal system with its story of a nightclub owner who owes money to the mob and who must obey their will by killing a Chinese bookie to pay off his debt.[8] The film ends ambiguously, showing its hero successful over the mob, but potentially mortally wounded, with the credits rolling before revealing whether he will live or die. *The Friends of Eddie Coyle* is uniformly bleak in telling the story of a petty criminal fighting a prison sentence by informing on a gang to whom he supplies guns. Eddie is simply a decoy the police use so that they can protect a more valuable informer – who in an act of grim irony, that fully expresses the desperation and pointlessness of the gangster–loser's life, is the man the mob use to kill Eddie. Organised crime as a metaphor for social entrapment is particularly obvious in the blaxploitation gangster movie. Although the Shaft series of films represents a hyper-masculine maverick figure triumphing over larger power systems, the social oppression of African-Americans forms the main focus. *Black Caesar*, which is modelled on *Little Caesar*, utilises the tragic downfall of its forebear to highlight the inability of the black gangster to triumph over society and find recognition. Although its hero, Tommy Gibbs, spends most of the film taking on the established mob and apparently winning, he is betrayed by his white lawyer and, although he still seems to overcome the odds, the film ends with an image of him being beaten by a group of black youths and left battered on a garbage heap. *Across 110th Street* shares the same doomed outlook in a narrative showing the destruction of a gang who rob a Mafia numbers bank. This is portrayed not only in the story of African-American gangster outsiders failing to beat the mob and the police, but also in the representation of power arrangements run on ethnic lines with Italian Mafia rulers and their African-American subjects in Harlem, an articulation that institutionalises power structures in a feudal territorialisation of urban space. All of these films represent the direct use of the gangster genre to foreground political issues so that even while they replicate existing generic formulae they re-define them through direct political comment on contemporary society and its inequalities of power. The gangster-loser and the African-American gangster represent the 'othering' of the individual and re-use the classic cycle's articulation of the American Dream to show that even in gangster form it is an impossibility.

A version of the gangster-loser film can be found in *Mean Streets* (Martin Scorsese, 1973), but where films such as *The Outfit* or the blaxploitation gangster film represent gangsters trying to operate outside the world of the mob, the characters in *Mean Streets* are both inside and outside. The film focuses on a loosely connected gang who engage in small-time crime or perform acts of enforcement for the local mob. The low level nature of their status is represented at several points, through the fact that Johnny Boy (Robert De Niro) only has $40 in his pockets but feels that this is an impressive amount of money or in Michael and Tony's scamming of two youths so that they can go to the cinema. Effectively, they are a group of Mafia hangers-on with no real place inside the mob system with the exception of Charlie (Harvey Keitel) who acts as an interface between the established Italian gang and the 'wannabe' gangsters of Johnny Boy, Michael, and Tony, but who nevertheless still performs only a small role as a collector for his uncle Giovanni. Charlie's status, as an interface, is to be outside both the organised mob and the group of gangster hangers-on, however, something that is expressed in two scenes, one where Charlie buys cigarettes from Michael and the other when he has dinner with Giovanni and one of his associates, Mario. In the former scene, Charlie is sitting ostensibly at the same table as Michael and Tony, but the scene is shot in such a way as to foreground Charlie so that it looks as if he is sitting separately. The scene expresses Charlie's distance from his own gang and also suggests that it is not a cohesive unit, but a loose affiliation of friendships. Part of the reason why Charlie is set apart from his own gang is that he is a part of the organised mob to which they can never belong (a situation that is highlighted when Giovanni dismisses Michael from his presence for interrupting a conversation with Charlie). The other reason is that Charlie stays loyal to Johnny Boy, who owes money to Michael, which is also why he is never fully on the inside of the local mob. In the scene when Charlie dines with Giovanni and Mario, Giovanni implies that he wants Charlie to avoid associating with Johnny, an observation that locates Charlie outside the gang system as part of the world of chaos and excess that Johnny represents.

The opposition between the local organised mob and the loose affiliation of Charlie and his friends operates in several systems of signification in the film. The film's narrative principally follows Charlie's spiritual anguish and his attempts to redeem Johnny, a redemption that takes two forms, one that is spiritual and one that will redeem Johnny in the eyes of his uncle and the mob. Both forms of redemption entail living responsibly and not 'beyond his means' which does not only mean economic responsibility, but also entails disciplining his behaviour. The film implies a gang structure not just of inside and outside, but of organised and 'un-organised' crime, the former associated with Giovanni and the system of order and discipline the mob imposes and the latter with Charlie's friends who, particularly in the form of Johnny, represent excess and chaos. Images of chaos and purposelessness attach to Johnny throughout the film (for example, randomly firing a gun from a rooftop) but also begin to affect Charlie, not only by association, but also in his actions as, for example, when he and Johnny begin to fight with dustbin lids. Charlie's redemption of Johnny is to bring him into the system of order that the local mob represent, but his association with Johnny allies him with chaos in their eyes – while Giovanni's disapproval of Charlie's relationship with Teresa is signified by her epilepsy, an uncontrollable form of behaviour. The mob's insistence on order is most obvious in the disciplining of the assassin who kills a man ostensibly to enforce gang codes, but principally to get noticed by the Mafia. This act signifies the way in which the mob, in its attempts to enforce law through its system of honour, actually creates random acts of violence, and the film strongly implies that the chaos created by Charlie's gang is a product of the mob system and not its inverse. Thus while the film articulates a vision that 'transposes the ideological emphasis of the classical gangster film by representing the Mafia not as a criminal "other" but as the dominant, patriarchal norm' (Grist, 2000: 95) where redemption and social order are identified with the mob (and not with ideology), it also locates this within a re-definition of the ideological framework found in *The Roaring Twenties*, so that criminality is a product not of the desire to assimilate into society, but to assimilate into the legitimacy represented by the mob. This is identified in the film by the restaurant that is promised to Charlie by Giovanni which represents assimilation and redemption from the chaotic fallen state of the street. It also represents a permanent territory that will identify Charlie as fully part of the system by giving him a base to operate from. In this, the film both re-uses and re-defines the gangster conventions of the 1930s by replicating the territorial imperative of the 1930s gangster, but problematising the signification of the street. Where occupation of the streets represented freedom of movement and control over social and cultural space in the 1930s classic cycle, here it represents marginality and failure within an atomised society which it comes to symbolise.

7
The Postmodern Spectacle of the Gangster

The beginning of the 1990s saw an upsurge in the production of gangster films after a slightly intermittent period of production in the 1980s with 1990 itself seeing the release of the Coen Brothers' *Miller's Crossing*, Scorsese's *Goodfellas*, Ferrara's *King of New York*, and Coppola's final installment of *The Godfather* trilogy. These films express the diversity of the genre as it has developed in recent years and include the postmodern retro style of *Miller's Crossing* and its recapitulation of gangster thematics through their simulation, the return to the foot-soldier in *Goodfellas*, the return of the big shot formula in *King of New York* and the reiteration of the Epic scope displayed by the gangster genre in *The Godfather Part III*. Subsequent years have seen further recapitulation and variation of gangster thematics in, for example, the 'gangsta' film (*New Jack City*, *Boyz n the Hood*, *Menace II Society* and *South Central*) which demonstrates both self-conscious referentiality in its re-visiting of blaxploitation and black gangster films of the 1970s, while also offering political engagement by placing African-American gangs in the realities of their social and cultural landscape. The 1990s has also seen further developments with the return to *noir* aesthetics (*Pulp Fiction*, *Killer*, *Kiss of Death*), the heist gang (*Heat*, *The Usual Suspects*), the nostalgic biopic (*Billy Bathgate*, *Bugsy*), the *exposé* variant (in the representation of the police as a syndicate in *L. A. Confidential*), urban realism (*Carlito's Way*), and the seemingly endless rise of the assassin genre which, although it has influences from other sources (existentialism, Japanese cinema and Hong Kong action movies), also has its roots in gangster stories of the mob hitman which it retains in films such as *Diary of a Hitman*, *Little Odessa*, *Leon*, and *Ghost Dog*.

The gangster film in the 1980s

The variety and diversity of the gangster film in the 1990s is in direct contrast to its history in the 1980s which is a rather fallow period for the genre. Notable contributions in the 1980s are *Scarface* and *Once Upon a Time in America* with *Prizzi's Honor* and *The Untouchables* deserving mention, but otherwise the decade can be characterised primarily in terms of the production of comedy gangster and nostalgia films of which *Prizzi's Honor* is the best of the former and *The Untouchables* the most interesting example of the latter. In some respects both these film styles are constructed less to extend and develop the genre than to reflect on its existing narratives and iconography and demonstrate how the codes of the genre have become embedded within popular cultural knowledge as measured through the audience's ability to recognise the originating iconography in its parody or replication. *Prizzi's Honor* (John Huston, 1985) places its parody of the gangster genre within the readily identifiable convention of the Italian family while also drawing on the hitman format, though here re-interpreted in the form of a female assassin. The film generates a tension between the old and the modern in the contrast between the tradition and code adopted by the Prizzi family and its representative, Charlie Partanna (Jack Nicholson), as it is placed in the context of a post-feminist modernity exemplified by Kathleen Turner's assassin, Irene Walker. This is not a simple opposition between old and new because the film also tracks further iconographic elements in the increasing corporatisation of the Italian crime family (initiated in *The Godfather*) showing how the traditions of honour that the Prizzi family value is ultimately shown to be entirely invested in money; as Irene comments, a Sicilian is more likely to part with his children than with money and 'you know how much Sicilians love their children'. Neverthless, the film does offer interesting observations on the entry of the crime family into the contemporary world, most notably in Irene and Charlie's marriage which is a union of both labour (assassination) and romance, before however, representing the triumph of tradition in Charlie's assassination of his own wife and the return to the family in the implicit union with Maeroso Prizzi which had been intended all along. Other comedy gangster films of the 1980s, *Johnny Dangerously* (1984), *City Heat* (1984), *Wise Guys* (1986), and *Married to the Mob* (1988) varied in their quality, depending on how successful they were in tapping into audience recognition of the generic codes.

   The nostalgia film's most notable entry in the 1980s was *Once Upon a Time in America* (Sergio Leone, 1984), but nostalgia is also present in examples such as *The Cotton Club* (1984), the story of the connection between crime and entertainment in the prohibition era and *Eight Men Out* (1988), which details the fixing of the 1919 World Series, while a film such as *Tough Guys* (1986) can also be placed partially within this 'retro' aesthetic with its story of two aging gangsters nostalgically trying to capture their younger days of glory. *Once Upon a Time in America* cannot be said to fully correspond with the nostalgia form partly because of its Epic historical scope which traverses a period from the 1930s to the late 1960s but also because it is less concerned with simply evoking a sense of historicity in its articulation of period imagery than with negotiating links between the past and the present. In this it also emphasises the connections between the social and the personal in its mapping of criminality's destruction of the bonds of loyalty and friendship through its exploration of the narratives of the two Jewish gangsters, Noodles (Robert De Niro) and Max (James Woods). The film begins by portraying the origins of the youth gang they form in order to protect themselves from the brutality of their environment. Over the course of the years, and through, a split narrative structure which alternates between Noodles' early years and his return, in old age, to his home, the film details their lives, through Noodles' imprisonment, his return to a now successful gang and his betrayal of the gang over a heist which he believes will result in their deaths. The film focuses on this act as a seminal event in the film, with the sound of a telephone permeating the film to continually remind the audience of Noodles' telephone call to the police betraying the gang. Noodles' treachery, however, is caused by noble intentions and his desire to save the gang from certain death represents the way in which the film shows how criminality has compromised morality and integrity in its fracturing of the social bonds of trust at a wider level. The complicity of individual action is also represented by Noodles' treatment of women, seen in the way his romantic idealisation of Deborah turns to sexual violence. The death of sociality and its resulting atomisation of society is symbolised by the loss of the gang's sense of honour and loyalty (represented by a suitcase of money, which none of them are allowed to touch except in lean times) in its betrayal, not by Noodles, who wants to retain the social bonds of the gang, but by Max, who planned the heist and the double-cross with the intention of fulfilling his personal ambition. The film in the present reveals that Max has planned the double-cross of the gang, in conjunction with Deborah, which places the film within gangster *noir* territory while also, within the film's Epic scope, extending the metaphor of the 'double-cross' to the level of American society which is revealed to be a culture of betrayal and complicity. In the social sphere, for example, the labour dispute the gang involves itself with is compromised by their help, leading to the co-optation of the union leader, Jimmy O'Donnell, who can only maintain union sociality with the aid of the gangsters he initially referred to as a 'plague'. *Once Upon a Time in America* maps a society where a depersonalised and hostile sociality cannot be transcended, but ultimately extends its ruthless logic. It is not criminality itself that creates betrayal because it is a simply a symptom of the atomisation represented by the sound of the telephone which punctuates the years and which describes the separation between people (as a telephone does even while it creates a temporary connection), ultimately returning individuals to the solipsism that Leone has articulated as the main vision of the film, isolated within their own 'inner reality' (Brode, 1995: 103).

A film that evokes a clearer sense of postmodern nostalgia and which simulates a specularisation of the gangster in its self-conscious facsimile of the genre is *The Untouchables* (Brian De Palma, 1987). *Where Once Upon a Time in America* articulates a historical vision to highlight larger social forces at work, *The Untouchables* is content to provide textualisations of the gangster and law enforcement within a simplistic cops-and-robbers format. The film places itself within its generic antecedents, most notably *G-Men*, in its story of the law turning to the ethos of the gangster to deal with Al Capone (Robert De Niro), as the veteran cop, Malone (Sean Connery) makes clear: 'He pulls a knife, you pull a gun. He sends one of yours to the hospital, you send one of his to the morgue'. Many of the film's textual references, however, are outside the genre and it is visually, narratively, and ideologically more resonant of the western, representing the Canadian border raid, for example, as the ride of the FBI 'posse'. The film also offers a quite basic good-evil opposition in its representation of the police and the gangster that marks an even less sophisticated vision than the Code enforced ideology of *G-Men*, exaggerating this with its sense that any action is justifiable on the part of the law if it is done in the name of justice, such as dropping a gangster from a building when he tells Ness (Kevin Costner) that he will beat the charges and walk free. The film is most interesting for its set-piece action, such as Capone's murder of a gangster with a baseball bat and the shoot-out at the railway station, the former having some reference to the gangster genre (in its discourse on teamwork to articulate the relationship between gangster and gang) while the latter predominantly evokes the spectacle of gangster violence in its undifferentiated self-reflexivity, as it makes reference to *Battleship Potemkin* (the Odessa

Steps sequence) and the spaghetti western (in its stylised slow motion violence), the result of which is a postmodern hybridisation of the gangster film where the gangster no longer resides within his genre, but is dispersed across generic boundaries.

Brian De Palma's *Scarface* (1983) can be seen as a similar pastiche in its re-invocation of film images. However, although the film stays close to the plot of its predecessor (the main difference being that the gangs have an international scope in their links with South American drugs cartels), it uses an approach more typical of 1970s post-classical cinema by re-invoking past traditions within a new context to reflect on the new conditions of 1980s free market capitalism. Although the film re-uses the original's 'The World is Yours' as an implied structure for its narrative, the motto of the film is better expressed by Elvira's comment to its hero, Tony Montana (Al Pacino), that 'Nothing succeeds like excess' a pointed, if slightly obvious, comment on Tony as a symbol of 1980s greed. The film is characterised by this excess, offering an exaggeration of generic concerns in the absence of any disciplining or prohibitive alternative in the film (although media comments, in the form of news reports, occasionally have this function). The violence has often been seen as excessively visceral and parodic (McCarty, 1993: 67), including the dismemberment of a man by chainsaw and the punctuation of the film with battle-zone style shoot-outs. This produces a iconographic spectacle of gangster representation in its exaggeration, but the effect is not simply surface style because the film consciously articulates this to critique a culture that is dominated by empty style. One articulation of this process is the way the sets tower over Tony to illustrate his insignificance because, rather than transcending the culture he inhabits, he has simply become another of its products, an ideological facsimile of the gangster individuality found in the movies. His own excessive behaviour, while typical of the original Scarface, also becomes an emblem of 1980s economic and cultural excess, as typified by the gigantic bath he sits in when Elvira makes her comment on how he embodies this culture. Tony's excess is a product of a sense of loss of his own selfhood and masculinity within this culture. His incestuous desire for his sister is re-figured in terms of the failure of masculinity and, although at one point he seems to suggest that he is embodied by his masculinity ('All I have in this world is my life and my balls'), he is also aware that it is money that buys sexual success, a displacement of masculinity outside his body and into capitalist production and ideology. His constant talk of money is an attempt to fill a lack that is most obviously exemplified when he is shown replacing the phallus with a machine gun in the final shoot-out. Ultimately his statement that capitalism is 'getting fucked' suggests that he is emasculated and feminised by the culture he symbolises, not empowered by a success that gives the appearance of power but leaves him (and by implication, anyone within 1980s capitalism) disempowered in an empty solipsistic isolation. He is the first post-social gangster in a post-social world with the gang (which is itself a place of atomisation in its internal fracturing) re-figured as an international cartel to represent the global dispersal of social bonds and the fragmentation of identity in the face of the competing loyalties that globalisation brings.

Postmodern inflections

What the tendencies in the 1980s do represent as a general process is a developing hybridity of the gangster genre as it begins to utilise conventions and iconography from elsewhere. This is not a new tendency in the genre, but is exaggerated in the context of cultural postmodernism, a further effect of which is that the gangster begins to lose his definition in the blurring of generic boundaries. Both the 'gangster' and the genre become polyvalent, the gangster finding cross-generic signification in his coding as an icon of deviance in contemporary film in general (as with the figure of Frank in *Blue Velvet*), but this is an axiomatic deviancy that could be applied to any figure who encapsulates contemporary America's cultural notions of marginality, for example, the serial killer or the rapist. The polyvalency of the genre occurs, for example, in the blurring of the gangster film into action-adventure in the era of the Hollywood high concept movie in which any film involving the spectacle of violence can be placed in the latter category. There are many features that can be attributed to postmodernist aesthetic practice some of which include: pastiche (or blank parody and its conscious reference to existing texts in order to highlight the textuality of the postmodern text); nostalgia or the retro-mode (articulating the death of originality in the re-circulation of already existing textual forms, while also offering nostalgic visions of a past cultural cohesion that does not seem possible in a fragmented postmodern culture), self-parody (in the internalised self-reflexivity of texts which also extends to generic self-consciousness in the postmodern irony of the *Scream* trilogy, for example); the mixing of codes; and generic hybridity.[1] All of these features insist on the textualised nature of the postmodernist text, articulating an inability to represent reality not because it cannot be adequately expressed, but because it does not exist. Only simulations (or copies without an original) are available in the endlessly recycled images and commodities of postmodern culture.

This process enacts the collapse of texts into culture, preventing the establishment of 'critical distance' and disavowing the possibility of a text ever making any critique of the culture that generates it. Although this implies that contemporary texts simply re-articulate their culture and its fragmented simulations it is possible to distinguish between two modes of cultural textualisation: the self-conscious and the unconscious, where the former entails knowingly articulating postmodernist strategies in some attempt to refract or map culture, while the latter involves the unconscious replication of cultural processes within the text. Such principles can be applied to the gangster genre, based as it is in a history of engagement with its culture, and contemporary gangster films can be studied in the types of strategy they utilise either to continue or problematise that tradition. This can be through identifiable postmodern aesthetic practices which refract contemporary culture and engage in some form of critique or through the use of realist modes to comment on a postmodern culture of commodification, simulation, and the spectacle of the image. Not all contemporary gangster films are postmodern, and the insistence on the resolutely urban context in the gangster film in this period can be seen as an attempt to offer some comment on contemporary social and cultural conditions. *Carlito's Way*, while utilising some aspects of pastiche, also explores a culture of commodified identity and free market capitalism and uses its urban setting to emphasise the impossibility of escape from contemporary social control. In such inflections, the gangster movie can be seen as both a parallel and opposition to the contemporary road movie in that both suggest that there is no outside and no escape, with the difference that the road movie still dreams an ideological fantasy of social transcendence even if it returns to the condition of an inescapable oppression. The gangster genre, on the other hand, often presents culture as an internalised space where there is no outside and where attempting to imagine something beyond the parameters of society and ideology is a dream made impossible by the cultural and material articulations of power and control.

Goodfellas (Martin Scorsese, 1990), one of the first of the 1990s revival of the gangster genre, is a film that plays with these images of gang life, presenting the gangster world as a place of opportunity, even perhaps the only place in contemporary society where the American Dream of freedom, individual power and the ability to consume is possible. The film follows Henry Hill (Ray Liotta) from his early years as a teenage runner for the mob to the achievement of his dream of becoming one of its members, as expressed in his first voice-over: 'As far back as I can remember I wanted to be a gangster.' This offers a self-conscious inversion of the ideological dreams of boys wanting to grow up to perform legitimate civic duties serving the State as policemen or firemen, and the failure of this ideology is pointedly shown in the beating of the mailman who suffers for his public service in order to allow Henry to miss school and work for the mob, an institution that is socially more significant than the State. In Henry's words, dreams within the ideological parameters of the State are dreams of 'nobodies' who will never achieve the American Dream because it is not possible within the sphere of legitimate cultures. It is only possible for the gangster who 'is a somebody in a neighbourhood of nobodies' and who operates without prohibition, playing cards without police intervention and double parking in front of fire hydrants. Although these are trivial freedoms, the film proceeds to catalogue them as the main reason why 'being a gangster is better than being President of the United States'. The life of the gangster is a life of privilege and to be a gangster is almost to be a proletarian aristocrat, a status that allows access to spaces that others are not able to enter. Control of space (both physical and social) is foregrounded when Henry takes Karen on a date and is escorted to the front of a night club floor and given a specially laid out table, but it is shown as not having legitimate sanction because he has entered through the kitchen. As well as emphasising both the 'proletarian' and 'aristocratic' qualities of the gangster (the unofficial entry to privileged space) this scene also demonstrates that legitimate sanction and prohibition are meaningless. They have no impact on everyday life which is now the domain of the mob who become the real, if unofficial, power within society. Assimilation by legitimisation, the dream of the classic gangster (and replayed in DePalma's *Scarface*), is an anachronism because control of legitimate society is to have only the semblance of power. In its observation of the triumph of gangster ideology, *Goodfellas* does not, however, offer any moral or ideological comment on the activities of its gangsters, using editing and camerawork (particularly the subjective camera technique used to focalise the film's narrative through Henry's perspective) simply to record them while also drawing the audience into the pleasures of the gangster life. The resulting effect is the creation of an internalised self-reflexive gangster culture which, like the postmodernist text's lack of reference to reality, not only pays no attention to official codes of society ('reality'), but displaces them.

The film does not, however, open with Henry's evocation of, and tribute to, the life of the gangster, but with an image of violence that represents the way in which the freedoms of gangster culture can become unrestrained excess if not properly governed (or disciplined).The opening image shows Henry and his fellow gang members, Jimmy Conway (Robert De Niro) and Tommy DeVito (Joe Pesci) driving in a car when they hear noises from the trunk, followed by the revelation that the sounds emanate from the body of a man believed to be dead and then by the trio's violence as they stab and shoot him repeatedly to finish him off. This is an image of brutality which is not placed in its context until later in the film when it is revealed that he is Billy Batts, a 'made-man', who Tommy has killed without permission from the mob, an excessive act in itself because it goes against the mob's prohibition. The opening images dramatise the tensions of the mob world that the film proceeds to catalogue in its episodic chronology following Henry from the 1950s to the present. These tensions are between the glamour of the pleasures provided by the gangster world and the reality of the violence with which this is inextricably entwined, and between the licence the gang grants its individual members and the prohibitions it enforces. The most important and paradoxical figure within these relationships (because he embodies all their facets) is the figure of Tommy, an affectless psychopathic gangster in the mould of Tom Udo from *Kiss of Death*. Two scenes highlight the tensions as they are located within Tommy and show how they are not just a product of individual desire for gratification, but are generated from the same system of prohibition, the gangster code of honour, that seeks to control them. The first scene shows Tommy entertaining a group of gangsters in a restaurant, including Henry, who Tommy begins to taunt for questioning his honour before finally revealing that he has been joking. The scene shows the gangster life of pleasure in the entertainment Tommy provides, but then follows this with a moment of abrupt violence when the owner comes over to ask for money. This, to Tommy, is not empty of meaning and represents a genuine slur on his honour for which he disciplines the owner by beating him. However, he then turns to his fellow gangsters and holds out his hands as if he has just performed a trick, turning random violence into a pleasurable act which has no meaning. The second scene involves the wounding and killing of a young waiter in which Tommy firstly mimics a cowboy and shoots at the waiter's foot to make him dance (inadvertently wounding him) before killing him when Jimmy jokingly points out that the waiter has disrespected Tommy.[2] The scenes locate pleasure and violence together in the gangster lifestyle and suggest that the two generate each other in a self-destructive logic when it goes beyond the licence the gang grants the individual gangster. In these examples, Tommy is acting within the gang's licence (and his acts of personal gratification are thereby sanctioned), but his killing of Batts is in excess of the rights the gang grants and he is consequently disciplined (by being 'whacked') for his breach of the gang's own code.

The gang is a paradoxical place because of its configuration as a force for prohibition and discipline that follows the same patterns as legitimate authority. The gang, in its creation of a set of codes of behaviour, is as ideological as legitimate society and Henry's voice-over notes how the mob 'offers protection for people who can't go to the cops', suggesting it acts as a guarantor of rights like the State, but expects submission to its laws in return. In operation, this entails Paulie (Paul Sorvino) prohibiting Henry's drug trafficking or Jimmy, after the Lufhansa heist, disciplining the excessive consumption of his gang who have bought cars and fur coats for their wives, before extending this by having them 'whacked'. The tension of the discipline of mob law and the licence and rights it grants for the individual gangster is foregrounded in a scene after Henry has left his wife, Karen. He is visited by Paulie and Jimmy who tell him that 'Nobody says that you can't do what you want to do', but that he *must* return to his wife. When Henry turns informer he does so not because he fears the law but because he fears mob vengeance for his breach of its laws. Henry breaks the prohibition because, like Tommy, he exceeds the licence the gang grants him and indulges in the excessive gratification of desire, as represented by the cocaine business which creates him as an increasingly isolated psychotic cut off from reality and from the mob. Nevertheless, although the gang is a paradoxical place representing both freedom and restraint, the most memorable images of the film are those embodying the lack of restraint, and this is how the film ends, juxtaposing the failed masculinity of Henry the 'schnook' (now that he has entered legitimate society as part of the Witness Protection Scheme after he has broken the ultimate mob prohibition to never 'rat on a friend') with a shot of Tommy firing a gun point blank to the soundtrack of Sid Vicious' version of 'My Way'. The film thus ends with an image of a gruesome punk parody of the kind of individual that the gang can create, an individual who does nothing but destroy, and counterpoints this with Henry's emptied self now that he is no longer part of the gang which guaranteed him individuality despite its prohibitions.

Postmodern gangsters: spectacle and simulation

If *Goodfellas* maps a self-reflexive internalised gang culture, *Miller's Crossing* (Joel Coen, 1990) offers a postmodern textual self-reflexivity in its account of the gangster world with an internalisation of generic conventions (Horst, 1998: 98) that articulates no engagement with any kind of social reality. The film's 'reality' is another text, *The Glass Key*, but it also utilises other elements from the gangster genre and, in its self-conscious use of these conventions without re-interpreting or varying them, can be seen as a postmodern spectacle of the gangster film that simply puts generic codes on display. The most memorable image of the film foregrounds this spectacle of textual 'gangster-ness': the Tommy gun scene in which gang boss, Leo (Albert Finney) wipes out the hired assassins from a rival gang. The scene is formally perfect, beginning with a match cut through the window of Verna's apartment to the window of Leo's house while also having a circular logic, beginning and ending with fire (from the burning newspaper to the burning car), resonating with the return of the cigar to Leo's mouth that he had stubbed out at the beginning of the scene. The scene also presents a violence that is only possible within its textualisation in the image of Leo shooting a man through the window with a torrent of bullets, followed by a shot to show the man having an epileptic fit as the bullets hit him, the conjunction of images implying that he is only being held up by their force as they enter his body. All the while, the scene is accompanied with the diegetic and then non-diegetic use of 'Danny Boy'. In this example, the scene highlights the textualised spectacle of gangster violence, which is compounded when the scene cuts to a henchman saying 'Leo sure is an artist with the Thompson' to internally emphasise the display of the aesthetics of violence. This scene highlights the film's textuality but there are many others including a street shoot-out that is reminiscent of the various representations of an attempted machine gunning of Al Capone (seen in films such as *Al Capone* and *The Saint Valentine's Day Massacre*) when the Sons of Erin Club, one of Leo's bases, is effectively razed by a volley of police machine-gun fire.

This can suggest that the film is simply a depthless simulation, a reading that the film itself plays with when Verna attempts a Freudian explanation of why Tom is worried about losing his hat, but which he dismisses, suggesting that it has no meaning. The film focuses on the surface of the gangster look without apparently examining the ideological, moral or emotional significations that have attached to the

genre. There is no ideology of freedom or oppression, no moral judgement on gangster corruption or criminality, nor engagement with characters' emotions which are here presented as cold postmodern desire:
whether this is Verna's *femme fatale* manipulation of Leo or Dane's
homosexual attachment to Mink. In this depthlessness, *Miller's Crossing*
offers a postmodern spectacle of generic imagery and attaches this to the
foregrounding of its iconography. The representation of the hero, Tom
Reagan (Gabriel Byrne) does, however, offer a new version of the gangster, albeit one created out of the fragmentations and depthlessness of
postmodern culture itself. Tom is represented as a drifter and as an
affectless gangster, not in the psychopathic mode of Tommy DeVito,
but in terms of his inertia and lack of emotion as characterised in his
response to Bernie's plea to 'Look in your heart', to which he replies
'What heart?' In this he can be seen as a parody of the classic gangster
figure's energy, but the film does have generic antecedents for his representation in figures such as the listless Shubunka from *The Gangster* or
Jeff Hartnett, the alcoholic dreamer and thinker from *Johnny Eager*.
Tom's life follows no linear narrative and his actions are accidental
(his relationship with Verna, for example) and ambiguous in their
motive. Unlike Beaumont in *The Glass Key* who joins Varna with the
aim of exonerating Madvig, it is unclear whether Tom's motives in
joining Caspar are deliberate betrayal, an undercover operation
designed to subvert Caspar's organisation, or simply an accident as he
drifts from one outfit to another. Tom is a 'cerebral gangster', like
Beaumont, but with no long terms plans, seemingly existing in a per-
petual present unable to connect events over time. Thus, his stratagems,
while they may be part of a long term plan, are also as much a product of
a momentary thought designed to preserve himself, as with his ability to
persuade Caspar to kill Dane, or his tricking of the former to his death.
Although much is made in the film of Tom's dream of, and concern
with, the loss of his hat, an image that is apparently without meaning, it
is the representation of his hairstyle that perhaps has more importance
for Tom's identity. His hair is folded down at the sides on his forehead to
give the impression that he has horns and which give him a devilish
quality that implies a Machiavellian interiority. However, this image
also meshes with the satanic imagery of the film as a whole (particularly
fire and the invocation of hell when Caspar kills Dane) so that it becomes as much a matter of style as an indication of psychological depth.
The image also contributes to the persistent ambiguity about Tom's
gangster motivations and whether he is an authentic Machiavellian
who simulates loyalty to Leo or inauthentic in his scheming because

he is maintaining an authentic loyalty to his boss. Either interpretation entails a simulation and casts doubt on any notion of Tom having an authentic self beneath his passive façade with the result that only the simulation remains. Tom becomes the gangster as postmodern subject, empty of identity but simulating a façade of selfhood, of which his hat might be a symbol and its blowing through the woods in his dream a symbol of the purposelessness at the heart of the vibrant urban world he inhabits which, because of the film's self-conscious textualisation, is not Prohibition era America, but postmodernity.

Reservoir Dogs (Quentin Tarantino, 1991) is another postmodern film that locates itself self-consciously within the traditions of the gangster genre in its re-enactment of a failed heist and the subsequent fragmentation of the gang. The film also offers self-reflexive pastiche in mixing 'various genres, such as Gangster, Black comedy/parody, Horror and B-movie' while also utilising images from specific texts such as the posse in *The Magnificent Seven*, the use of colours for names (*The Taking of Pelham 123*), and including references to the gangster lifestyle of *Goodfellas* (Holding, 1997: 21). The film also partakes of the cops-and-robbers formula in featuring an undercover cop, Mr Orange (Tim Roth) which the combination of heist and undercover variations maps the implicit sense of failure that attaches to the representation of the characters. The opening scene with its discussion of the meaning of Madonna songs and tipping offers itself as a postmodern pastiche of the pleasures of gangster lifestyle found in *Goodfellas*, but in a 'proletarian' version (focusing on acts of everyday consumption and the argument over a dollar tip) featuring marginalised gangsters whose black suits code them only as simulations of gangster style and class. This is compounded by the image of the gangsters over the credits which apparently glamorises them in its reference to a similar image of the Rat Pack from *Ocean's Eleven*, but which also has reference to the black suited losers of *The Blues Brothers*. Instead of focusing on their successful incarnation of gangsterdom, the image emphasises their aspirations to gangster authenticity and their failure to achieve anything other than its style. The film, however, is ambiguous in its representation of the gang as losers and it is unclear whether this is done for the purpose of articulating a vision of the 'reality' of the contemporary gangster world or to direct attention to the film's cinematic influences and its self-conscious fictional status. The same can be said of its opposition between Mr White's code of honour and Mr Blonde's desire based psychopathic violence, two radically distinct gangster identities which return to key thematics articulated within the gangster genre (discipline and integrity as opposed to excess and selfish desire) but both representations also gesture towards a postmodern construction. It could be argued that Mr White represents a nostalgic vision of the gangster individual and Mr Blonde a postmodern affectless death of individuality, but both figures have a history within the genre that implies their iconic re-articulation is a depthless simulation performed for the sake of aesthetic formalism. The film also offers itself as a postmodern spectacle of gangster codes in its implied violence (Mr Blonde slicing off the ear of a policeman) and its set-pieces (the Mexican standoffs) and the fact that much of the violence is actually absent exaggerates the film's postmodern self-reflexivity by displacing its textualised spectacle off screen into the codes of the genre that are being invoked.

The 'gangsta' film: spectacle and urban realism

A group of gangster films that utilises this spectacle of postmodern violence and recodes it in terms of urban realism is the contemporary 'gangsta' or 'hood' movie, found in films such as *New Jack City* (Mario Van Peebles, 1991), *Menace II Society* (Allen and Albert Hughes, 1993) and *Boyz 'n the Hood* (John Singleton, 1991) which, however, is more a rites of passage film. The latter film is most important within the gangster genre for its evocation of the gang wars in South Central and the endless and self-destructive cycle of violence created by institutionalised racism, lack of opportunity, drug use and the hostile warlike attitude of the Los Angeles police. As Davis notes, the reality of the postmodern experience for African-Americans in Los Angeles, as *Boyz 'n the Hood* affirms, is a 'carceral city' dominated by the enclosure of space in gated communities and the offensive strategies of the police force and city government.[3] Like early post-war gangster films, *Boyz 'n the Hood* maps a 'fatherless' society for African-Americans, cut off from State and social structures and left to fend for themselves in a world that is better characterised by Hobbesian brutality than by Social Darwinist discourses of the American Dream that formed the context for gangster films of the pre-war years.[4] The film's focus on youth gangs acts as a metaphor for this social articulation, but the film does offer the return of the father in the form of Furious Styles (Larry Fishburne) who attempts to instill in his son, Tre (Cuba Gooding Jr), a sense of responsibility that re-affirms the ideology of the American Dream even while it maps an environment where the achievement of liberation seems impossible.[5]

Boyz 'n the Hood is part of a return to what Munby suggests is the roots of the gangster genre in the experiences of non-white ethnic groups in the United States, a return that locates 'gangsta' cinema in its seditious generic history.[6] Munby argues, however, that in 'gangsta' cinema the ghetto is 'both real and imagined' (1999: 225) and that the ' "American-ization" or *embourgeoisement*' that was available to ethnic whites is not available to African-Americans and does not therefore manifest itself as a concern.[7] Nevertheless, he argues that 'the black recourse to the gangster image is part of a long history of struggle, both black and white, to use the weapons of confinement against the grain and communicate (visibly and audibly) across the race and class line – to dramatize an enduring collective sense of grievance' (226). *New Jack City* does not immediately seem to conform to this view, adopting an 'exploitation – entertainment' approach to its gangster material (Brode, 1995: 185). The film has a cops-and-robbers formula, opposing maverick cops, one black (played by gangsta rapper, Ice T) and one white, to a charismatic villain, Nino Brown (Wesley Snipes). The film follows the rise of Brown's yuppified gangster as he breaks free from the established mob and sets up a drugs operation more vicious than anything previously known. His gang is called the Cash Money Brothers, emphasising both its place in a capital-ist economy and its location within an African-American communality. *New Jack City* is primarily interesting for two things: its representation of the black gangster Brown and of the apartment block he occupies in order to effect his plan of cornering the drug market in the ghetto. Brown corresponds with the genre's image of the consumerist gangster in his sharp clothes and his postmodern apartment (a mix of minimal modernist and Gothic styles) and the adoption of such 'style' accoutre-ments codes a move upmarket as he challenges the establishment. Brown's threat is not just that he challenges the existing Italian mob organisation, but that his activities threaten the existing social order in his mimicry of the corporate strategies of society in his centralisation of production in the Carter apartments.[8] Brown, however, transgresses generic definition in the other images that attach to him. At one point he is described as a 'mad scientist', but he is also represented as an inner city Bond villain, complete with self-destruct mechanism for his head-quarters when it is assaulted. The film also visualises him as a dictator presiding over the apartment block as if it were a small independent republic. Cutting the gang off from the mob is presented as a declaration of UDI and the mob war that follows is a colonialist attempt to repossess territory and to extirpate the upstart rebels. The Carter apartments are imagined as an independent oppressed post-colonial nation which seemingly draws parallels between oppressions caused by white cultural imperialism abroad and the deprivation in the inner city caused by institutional racism which results in intra-ethnic oppression. The apartments become territorialised as a prison space, a metaphor for the carceral inner city, while also being a fortress designed to keep both the zombified inmates in and the hostile police force out.

Menace II Society less obviously places itself within generic conventions but does make reference to De Palma's *Scarface* and Scorsese's *Goodfellas* (Yaquinto, 1998: 199) and offers a more original vision of the African-American gangster. The film is more obviously concerned to highlight the social oppression that creates youth gangs suggesting that there is no life but the gangster life for young underprivileged African-Americans and that this experience is one of self-destructiveness, as the viscerality of the violence in the film confirms. The film opens with a random murder spree in a Korean shop which is a product of racist paranoias that represent the re-direction of racism to its expression between marginalised groups. This is then placed within a context of the oppression of African-Americans with footage of the Watts Riots and the statement that the riots were followed by the arrival of drugs to suggest that the latter are not a release from the misery of poverty, but another way in which oppression is experienced. McKelly has commented that this expresses 'the inextricability of criminality and the legitimate institutions of commerical and legal order' (*McKelly*, 1998: 38) contributing to the overall impression that the dreams of inclusion found in De Palma's *Scarface* are entirely absent from *Menace II Society*. The film as a whole follows an episodic fragmented format in the manner of *Goodfellas* to enact a sense of purposelessness, but also utilises the voice-over of its hero, Caine, as a way of holding the narrative together. Caine, however, admits his own perplexity at experience in the 'hood, saying after the robbery of the Korean store that 'this don't even make sense' and the film proceeds to map the chaotic and atomistic consciousness that results from African-American experiences of their oppression. Events happen at random and with no motivation, as with Harold's death or with Caine's revenge which his voice-over says doesn't make him 'feel good . . . feel anything'. The characters in the film experience a postmodern schizophrenia, in Jameson's definition (Jameson, 1985: 118–20), unable to connect random events together into a linear cause and effect structure and the result is the same waning of affect that Caine experiences in his inability to 'feel anything' or O'Dog expresses in his repeated viewing of the surveillance tape he takes from the store which shows his murder of the owner. This is waning of affect for the dispossessed, however, not the affectlessness that Jameson argues is the product of the repeated consumption of commodities (a luxury of the privileged) with the result that O'Dog's repeated consumption of an image of death maps his consumption of himself, leading to an enervated solipsism which prevents him from adequately engaging with society and its oppressions. It does, however, seem to provide a structure to his experiences, something that is lacking in the film as a whole, because social institutions are represented as alternative versions of ideology and oppression. Some structures of order are presented in opposition to the randomness of gang-life, in Sharif's Black Muslim beliefs but, with his death at the end of the film, there is a sense that this too is not a route out of oppression, but simply an explanation of it.

Fantasies of escape: *Carlito's Way* and *True Romance*

A film that shares concerns with social environment and which presents gangster criminality as a code for wider social forms of oppression is *Carlito's Way* (Brian De Palma, 1993), a film that also maps the attempt of its hero, Carlito Brigante (Al Pacino) to transcend this environment.[9] The film highlights the intersection of criminality with the fragmented culture generated by rampant free market capitalist forces, emphasising the pervasion of crime by the latter during the period that Carlito has been in prison. The film references *High Sierra*, representing Carlito as someone who dreams of escape. Like Roy Earle, in *High Sierra*, he is also a nostalgic gangster who stands by his code while others around him abandon any sense of loyalty or, like the lawyer, Dave Kleinfeld (Sean Penn), in his treatment of Carlito, perceive of other people simply as commodities, signifying Carlito's reduction in gangster status from big shot to consumer product. Like Roy Earle, Carlito looks back to the structures of the old days in opposition to the contemporary landscape where there 'ain't no rackets...just a bunch of cowboys ripping each other off'. Contemporary culture is characterised as a culture of randomness and fragmentation, absent of any controlling force without the effective presence of either the police (whose impotence is emphasised by the fact that they have to resort to illegal techniques to enforce justice) or the rackets to guarantee order. In response to this, Carlito attempts to distance himself from the chaos around him while he dreams of escape to the Bahamas. He plans to put this into effect in the company of his girlfriend Gail, who, however, represents the absolute inability to transcend this environment and live out one's dreams in her transformation from aspiring dancer to night-club stripper. The night-club is the dominant articulation of space in the film and represents this paradoxical culture which encourages fantasies, but offers only entrapment. The night-club (like the theme-park) is a site of pleasure where escape from everyday life is possible on a temporary basis, but which requires the return to the oppressions of society. Night-clubs, however, are predominantly articulated as places of sleaze (the strip joint) or emblematic of capitalist fragmentation and economic servitude, represented in the former case with the tension created by Benny Blanco's appearances at the club Carlito runs and in the latter case by Saso's debts. The club itself is a form of debt for Carlito and is not the opportunity that Dave represents it as, but entrapment for Carlito as he is drawn into a set of obligations (particularly to Dave) which root him in the corruption and fragmentation from which he seeks to escape.

As a response to this Carlito dreams of escape but his deferral of this act implies his ineluctable and unavoidable co-option back into social control. When he takes control of the night-club, Carlito refers to himself as like Humphrey Bogart (in *Casablanca*) and like Rick he believes he can distance himself from the corruption and chaos around him. Rick, however, is also a figure who is made complicit by his acceptance of exactly the same processes he distances himself from. He is also ultimately forced to engage with the world, but this does not result in the achievement of his dreams, only the fulfillment of others. Of more importance to the representation of Carlito is, as noted, Roy Earle with whom he shares a similar doomed quality and who from the outset faces only death. *High Sierra* prefigures Roy's death by opening with a shot of the mountain on which Roy will die. *Carlito's Way* represents this doom more overtly by opening with an image of Carlito lying on a stretcher waiting to die. The scene is shot in black and white, but cuts to a poster saying 'Escape to Paradise' advertising tropical holidays, an image that is shot in colour, before cutting back to Carlito in black and white with a smile on his face as he imagines a scene only shown at the end of the film: the visualisation of Gail's escape as she enters the landscape of the poster and is seen dancing within it. In his opening interior monologue, Carlito maintains that he still has hope for escape and can dream of a life outside society. He misrecognises his situation in his belief that he can still think outside the ideological parameters of society, but the ensuing narrative reveals his vision as a fiction, by showing that ideology is also a material practice that allows the subject to recognise the failures of society but does not allow the possibility of ever achieving dreams of transcendence.

Carlito's code of honour is another example of the way in which an ideological effect leads to his material oppression and causes his further entrapment, particularly in the way that Dave exploits it (by involving him in the attempt to spring Taglialucci, but more importantly by creating Benny Blanco's vendetta) to make him more complicit in the world of criminality. Carlito's personal code becomes abstracted and externalised and although it allows him occasional triumphs over the self interest and fragmentation associated with the world of the street punks (as in an early shoot-out in a pool room) he is ultimately destroyed by it. His mythic gangster integrity is in opposition to the world of the gangster in their contemporary 'street punk' form, but Carlito is still of his environment as well as distanced from it.[10] In the court scene before his release, he argues that he could claim that it was external forces and events (his mother's death) that created his criminality but that 'I was already a mean little bastard when my mother was alive', highlighting the internal generation of his aberrance. He is both typical and untypical in this respect, typical because he shares the same desires as other gangsters, but untypical because he still has his code. He is thus isolated from his criminal context and is an aberrant gangster like the gangsters of *noir* who are of the rackets but whose aberrance is not measured in their difference from legitimate society, but their difference from the general ethos of the criminal underworld. The film does not locate this complicity and oppression within gangster society, however, because its representations of Dave and Gail highlight the social nexus of ideological control. Dave in his obsession with criminality shares the same dreams as Carlito, locating his 'escape' from society in a sense of belonging and the power that involvement with the mob will entail. In this, he represents an opposition between the glamour attached to his image of crime and its reality in the form of the obligations and criminal machinations that ensnare him. Gail's transformation into a stripper is also emblematic of wider oppression and becomes an image of Carlito's submersion into the grim reality of contemporary society and an image that this is not just an internalised film about how crime submerges dreams and desires, but how contemporary society as a whole does so.

A film that offers similar fantasies of escape from the mob and the social reality of oppression it represents is *True Romance* (Tony Scott, 1993). The film locates its hero, Clarence Wurley (Christian Slater) in the grim post-industrial urban wasteland of Detroit but shows him dreaming of escape in his mental occupation of a world of comic books and kung fu movies. The possibility of escape arrives, firstly in the form of the prostitute, Alabama (Patricia Arquette), who represents a dream of another life (coded by her Florida origins), and then by providing him with the opportunity of leaving reality behind with the suitcase of cocaine he inadvertently takes after he has killed Alabama's pimp, Drexl. In the process, he also helps to draw Alabama out of her life of female oppression by replacing the commodification of the female body in prostitution with the romance of marriage. His killing of Drexl represents his and her escape from the realities of the urban criminal world, something that is imaged in the shift of the narrative focus from Detroit's grime to the sun of Los Angeles. The film, however, shows that escape has not yet been achieved, firstly by a reversion to its earlier setting, in the scene where the gangster boss, Vincenzo Coccotti (Christopher Walken) interrogates, tortures and finally kills Clarence's father (Dennis Hopper) and then by showing the arrival of the mob in Los Angeles in a disturbing scene in which Alabama is gruesomely tortured by a mob assassin, a scene that represents the return of the repressed life she thought she had left behind, represented here by physical violence to the female body rather than sexual exploitation of it. The film finally shows the transcendence of the couple, in an ending which reversed Tarantino's original script (Tarantino, 1995: 133–4), as Clarence comes back from the dead and is finally shown in soft focus walking on a Mexico beach with his son. Although, the film is not ostensibly of the gangster genre, it nevertheless has resonance in terms of the postmodern double coding of the gangster figure as both iconic of a world of oppression and lack of opportunity and as an image of desire in terms of the lifestyle he represents. The gangster offers a way out of the everyday consumption of trash culture, represented by Clarence's comics, Alabama's fake leopard clothes and their purple Cadillac, but he also acts as a figure representing the power structures that submerge people like Clarence and Alabama within this world of the serial commodity. The film has an ambiguous attitude to this trash culture, not least because the gangster is one of its products. *True Romance* places value in the everyday by mythologising objects such as the Zippo lighter or the burgers that Clarence eats after he has murdered Drexl, but also sees it as a place to be escaped because consumption only promises an image of power without delivering the actuality. It is only through Clarence's simulation of a gangster persona, made possible by his expropriation of the found object of the cocaine, that allows escape, although the scripted ending, in which Clarence dies, suggests that this can only ever be a fantasy or simulation.

Pulp Fiction and after: postmodern gangsters or postmodern film

With *Pulp Fiction* (Quentin Tarantino, 1994) it can be argued that the codes of the gangster genre have become so diffuse that it is not possible to talk of it as a distinct genre any more with the film articulating the semiotic codes of the gangster genre to map identity or lifestyle as a form of cultural expression as opposed to using them to explore the psychology of the gangster and the social reality he inhabits. The language and dress of the gangster are more important in their generation of an alternative semiotic system or cultural economy that, like *Goodfellas*, sets the gangster apart (and gives him a means and a language by which a vision of the world he inhabits can be enunciated) not just as an opposition to legitimate ideology and society, but as a way of displacing them entirely. The codes of the genre form the main narrative of the film, not as postmodern pastiche, but as a way of directing attention to the pervasion of official cultural and semiotic codes by those of the gangster. The film is not an ideological comment on the gangster's moral and economic corruption of society, as was represented in previous incarnations such as the syndicate film, but identifies the gangster with the cultural 'corruption' of society in his role as a symbol of popular and mass culture. Thus, a gangster discoursing on the 'Royale with cheese', as he drives to a hit, is inappropriate in terms of film iconographies of the gangster, but appropriate in terms of the world he both inhabits and symbolises. In this respect, the film is as paradigmatic of its genre as it is of its postmodern cultural production because it recognises the gangster's ideological function in the way in which he has been used to demonise mass culture. The film, however, does not adopt this ideological position because it attaches no value to popular culture: like the gangster, it simply exists and it is inescapable. The commodity and the screen image have entered and displaced 'reality', most obvious in the Jackrabbit Slim's section, but also in the articulation of the iconic figure of the gangster who has stepped from the screen into reality and back again (in the film's re-articulation of his cultural embodiment). The film enacts a society where the semiotic codes of the gangster do not just exist on screen, but have become the norms of everyday behaviour so that the gangster is no longer aberrant, but typical.

Pulp Fiction, however, does not just locate itself within the gangster genre, but enunciates references from a range of texts and popular cultural artefacts, suggesting that the film utilises the gangster as a symptom of the collapse of screen and commodity into culture. *Like Reservoir Dogs*, *Pulp Fiction* has an abundance of images from the 1970s, including John Travolta's self-reflexive gangster version of his role in *Saturday Night Fever* which de-hierarchises the gangster genre and shows that as the gangster genre has pervaded popular culture it has been pervaded in reverse. The film thus uses the gangster figure more as a style or a representation of a glamorised simulation of individuality, but this is also inflected and hybridised by wider cultural reference in the form of the gangster as samurai warrior, adopted by Jules (Samuel L Jackson) which itself influenced the hitman or assassin genre, most obviously in *Ghost Dog: The Way of the Samurai* (Jim Jarmusch, 1999) and *Leon* (Luc Besson, 1994), where the mob assassins both adopt a similar distant existential lifestyle as both a form of identity and as a means to effect their job more efficiently, to the extent that the former begins to displace the latter. Such referentiality also locates the film outside a distinctly American culture, so that with its references to Japanese and Hong Kong cinema it becomes a global gangster film rather than a specifically American incarnation. The film, therefore, represents a radical hybridisation of both film texts and culture, to the extent that 'it has no specific location or setting' (Brooker and Brooker, 1996: 143). *Pulp Fiction* articulates a problematic that afflicts the study of genre in a postmodern culture, in this case whether there is such a thing as the 'postmodern gangster' film or just postmodern film. It transgresses genre boundaries so often, most notably when Jules and Vincent abandon their iconic black suits after the accidental killing of Marvin (itself a non-generic and parodic act) for un-iconic beach wear, that it is potentially meaningless to discuss it in terms of its generic reference.

In the context of this hybridisation of generic discourses, *Pulp Fiction* could have signalled the end of the genre in its diffusion of gangster codes in a postmodern play of images. In some respects, it has had the reverse effect, generating many imitators, both in the United states (*Things to Do in Denver When You're Dead*, *Two Days in the Valley*) and abroad (*Lock, Stock, and Two Smoking Barrels*). Although these replicate the same kinds of postmodern play that *Pulp Fiction* represents, the gangster genre has continued in the post-*Pulp Fiction* era in different forms, not least because the cultural and ideological concerns and the iconography of the genre express the condition of living in modernity and postmodernity on an everyday basis. The genre's concern with the ideology of the individual, occupation of physical and cultural space, social relations, and the creation of alternate cultural and social economies to capitalism are all social articulations that find form in the gangster genre and are still relevant in the contemporary period. The gangster genre does increasingly reflect on its postmodern textual and cultural production, most notably in *Donnie Brasco* (Mike Newell, 1997) which similarly emphasises style and the gangster code. The film articulates these to suggest that to be a gangster is to live through and express the self as part of an alternative semiotic system, even while existing within the codes of everyday society, the latter being expressed, for example, in Lefty's fondness for wild-life programmes, which could have been used as a metaphor for the survival of the fittest ethos of the underworld, but is here presented as an expression of Lefty's taste which is empty of any wider signification. The film, however, re-defines *Pulp Fiction*'s vision of gangsters by presenting them as both ordinary people (symbolised by the secondhand clothes they wear and the prevalence of brown) and untypical because of the alternative culture they live in, but this is more on the lines of their creation of a sub-culture as opposed to an alternative economy that entails radical questioning of American ideology.

Casino (Martin Scorsese, 1995) maps a similar domain in its story of gambling in Las Vegas, but reverses the polarities, by representing the displacement of gangster culture by big business and, unlike both *Pulp Fiction* and *Donnie Brasco*, still identifies the possibility of authenticity existing, attached to the gangster world (even if it is a nostalgic authenticity) in opposition to the big corporations who take over Las Vegas. The film, however, ultimately shows the displacement of the 'street guys' who see Las Vegas as offering the fulfillment of dreams that *Carlito's Way* finds impossible, but ends ambiguously with the end of the dream, but also the survival of its hero, still successful and re-invoking the dream of the 'good old days'. The gangster genre also finds expression in other postmodern forms, as in the *exposé* variation of *L. A. Confidential* (Curtis Hanson, 1997) which redefines the 1950's version by representing the police as a syndicate who not only have more muscle than the mob but are more organised and can command stronger loyalties. The film also partakes of the demystification of gangster *noir* in its analysis of the corruption of society and the extension of gangster economics and values into the establishment. The heist variation of the genre also finds expression in *Heat* (Michael Mann, 1995) and *The Usual Suspects* (Bryan Singer, 1995) with the former being more conventional in its cops-and-robbers format, despite not taking sides, while the latter might be better located within the postmodern suspense thriller with a self-reflexive structure that ultimately questions whether any of the events have actually happened or are just a story made up by Verbal Kint. The film, however, maps a loosely affiliated gang in the heist format while also using the syndicate codes of the secret organisation run by a criminal mastermind (Keyser Soze). The film, thus re-articulates the problematic generated by *Pulp Fiction* because it shares the same mixing of codes (heist, syndicate, conspiracy, suspense) and foregrounds its self-reflexivity to such an extent that its textualisation of its events becomes its narrative. In the context of such pastiche operations of the genre, it is perhaps no surprise that the contemporary gangster film has returned in recent years to an even more exaggerated postmodern re-articulation of its codes with the revival of the comedy gangster movie (*Eight Heads in a Duffel Bag, Analyse This, Mickey Blue Eyes*), a replication of already replicated conventions that seems to suggest a form of generic self-consumption from which, at least for the moment, there seems to be no escape.

Notes

1 Modernity and the Classic Gangster Film

1 For a fuller discussion of the gangster film in the silent era, see McCarty (1993:1–49) and Everson (1998:227–34).
2 See Griffith, 1976:111–18 for a discussion of the role of the production cycle in classic Hollywood production.
3 Mitchell, (1995:203) discusses the gangster genre in exactly this way because, he argues, all genres need to be studied in terms of their 'repetitive patterning'.
4 Studies of modernity have produced contradictory responses as a result of this diversity. Giddens argues that modernity entails the creation of systems that can control risk and unpredictability (Giddens, 1991:3) while Lyon sees it as a sphere of plurality (Lyon, 1994:30).
5 For further discussion and analysis of the *flaneur*, see Tester (1994) and for discussions of the predominantly male gendering of the *flaneur* figure, see Friedberg (1993:33–7) and Wilson (1992:90–100).
6 Ruth (1996:74) also comments on the way in which the gangster's social 'mixing with refined men and women from the upper echelons of society' suggests a similar 'upheaval in a social order that . . . had seemed stable and enduring'.
7 See Clarens (1980:88–92) and Munby (1999:58–61) for details of the censorship of the film by the Hays Office.
8 See Ruth (1996:90) for a discussion of the ambiguous gendering of gangster consumption.
9 See Clarens (1980:84) for details of the production process.

2 The Post-Code Gangster

1 The classic cycle's influence is so pervasive that the gangster film in the post-Code era of the 1930s has received scant critical attention. Only Yaquinto (1998:48–64); Roddick (1983:107–16, 121–43; and Clarens (1980:116–59) cover the period of the late 1930s in any detail. Munby (1996:101–18; 1999:66–82) offers detailed discussion of *Manhattan Melodrama*; McCarty (1993:102–5) discusses *The Petrified Forest*; Schatz (1981:99–102) offers some discussion of *Manhattan Melodrama*, *G-Men* and *Angels with Dirty Faces*; and Shadoian (1977) ignores the period between the classic cycle and *The Roaring Twenties* entirely.
2 See Neale (2000:78–9) for an analysis of the critical tendency that raises the early cycle to 'classic' rather than 'generic' status with the effect of marginalising other variations.
3 Joseph Breen took over as director of the Production Code Administration in 1934.

4   See Doherty (1999:156–7) and Black (1994:107–32) for details of the role of the Legion of Decency in the censorship of the gangster movie in the early 1930s.
5   See Roddick (1983:112), for a discussion of this motif in *Bullets or Ballots*.
6   Of all the gang's crimes kidnapping was the one that signalled their absolute evil for audiences in the 1930s who would have the Lindbergh case in mind as they watched. Kidnapping was 'a crime so distasteful to the Hays Office that it had been barred from the screen since early in 1934, when Paramount had tried to cash in on the Lindbergh case with *Miss Fane's Baby Is Stolen*' (Clarens, 1980:125).
7   *Invisible Stripes* is also interesting as a generic variation because it articulates a trope that was to become popular, and which was also used in *Each Dawn I Die* (1939): the gangster as guarantor of official and heterosexual society (generated by the hero's self-sacrificing death which gifts his younger brother the money he needs to establish his own business and to marry his sweetheart). Later films that used this device include *The Big Shot, Johnny Eager* and *The Glass Key*.
8   Coppola drew extensively on *The Roaring Twenties* in creating the Epic dimensions of *The Godfather* trilogy, while the film influenced Scorsese from the beginning of his directorial career; see Grist (2000:16).
9   Many critics have noted these aspects of the film. Clarens (1980:155) notes the film's 'romantic revisionism', Krutnik (1991:198) its 'summing-up of the conventions of the early 1930's', while Hardy (1998b:90) comments on its influence on *film noir*.

3   The Death of the Big Shot

1   For a discussion of genre trends in wartime Hollywood, see Schatz (1997:221–32).
2   See Neale (2000:78–9) for an analysis of the critical trend which sees the classic narrative cycle of the early 1930s as effectively the only available expression of the gangster film aesthetic.
3   As well as re-visiting the family plot in its representation of the gangster trying to blackmail legitimate society into giving it its sanction, *Johnny Eager*, like *The Glass Key*, offers an image of the cerebral gangster who thinks and schemes rather than using his body, a gun, or his will to assert authority over others.
4   See Marling (1995:201–2) for a discussion of the this cross-social corruption in Chandler's *The Big Sleep*.
5   McArthur (1972:26), for example, notes how Cagney's ruthless physical dynamism was re-interpreted as 'psychotic' when it entered the post-war years.
6   This act of subsuming the self in undercover work became quite prevalent in *film noir* versions of the undercover narrative, most notably in *T-Men* when one of the undercover agents has to deny his 'real' self by pretending not to know his wife when he meets her on the street.
7   Shadoian (1977:199) notes how Fallon resembles an automaton, so drained is he of identity.

4   Outside Society, Outside the Gang

1   For an analysis of the function of the narrative dominant, see Todorov (1990:36–8).

2   See Neale (2000:151) for further details of the history of *film noir* criticism.

3   The articulation of desire also works the other way, as Krutnik (1982:34) notes in relation to the novels of James M Cain: 'narrative disruption is desire itself, manifested through the hero's reaction to the body of the woman'.

4   See Davis (1990:38–41) for a discussion of both the bourgeois and left wing tendencies of *noir* fiction and *film noir* and Jameson (1993:37) for an analysis of the reactionary politics embedded in Raymond Chandler's version of the *noir* aesthetic.

5   See Neve (1992:145–70) for a fuller account of the relationship between *film noir* and society.

6   See Huyssen (1986:44–55) for an analysis of modernism's relationship to a feminised mass cultural space and Dekoven (1991:32–7) for a discussion of modernism's fears of the feminine cultural flows that assail male identity and threaten to fracture it.

7   It can be argued that the syndicate film, while being a development of *film noir* is also its inversion in that while *noir* focuses on the collapse of system in post-war culture and suggests the end of modernity and the onset of a post-industrial, or even postmodern, society, the syndicate film offers a nightmare of modernist systematisation where there is too much structure and too little freedom. The two forms thus articulate contradictory responses to modernity, one seeing nothing but chaos and the other seeing nothing but system.

8   See Woodiwiss (1988:14), for a discussion of the endemic violence that seemed to afflict eastern cities, Chicago in particular.

9   Doris' role also places the film within its generic history because she represents the saintly woman from the silent gangster melodramas who redeems the criminal hero. In this respect, the seminal position of *Force of Evil* stems from its re-capitulation of previous gangster narratives (the rackets, the rise of the gangster, one-man-against-the-mob, the family narrative, and the Cain and Abel formula) and because it draws attention to the fact that all of them are derived from capitalist ideology (the legitimation of capitalist rules of acquisition, the American Dream, the ideology of the individual, the paternalism of the family, or the ideology of individual choice respectively).

10 The film again stars John Garfield and also involves Polonsky, this time as scriptwriter.

11 Two other gangster-boxing films share similar *noir* concerns: *The Set Up* (1949), a small town version of *Body and Soul*, in which an aging boxer wins a fight without knowing that his manager has agreed a fix and suffers punishment for an unwitting crime against the mob as a result; and *Killer's Kiss* (1955) which is more interested, like *Gun Crazy*, in mapping the sexuality of criminality and violence.

5   Order and Chaos, Syndicates and Heists

1   As a result these cycles have sometimes been ignored in accounts of the gangster film. Shadoian (1977) mentions the existence of the heist and syndicate variations in the 1950s, but offers no discussion of individual films, preferring to discuss relatively minor films in the classic tradition (*The Brothers Rico*) or examining the pseudo-gangster genre, the *exposé* film (*The Phenix City Story*, *The Captive City*).

2   Heist films also often articulate a nostalgia for the lost American values of self-reliance in the face of a totalising corporatisation of society, as is the case with the character of Dix in *The Asphalt Jungle* who represents a yearning for Jeffersonian ideals in his desire to return to his rural roots. Syndicate films, on the other hand, often express the triumph of un-American ideas and are not only a response to corporatisation or the Kefauver hearings, but also locate themselves in a culture of paranoia created by the earlier HUAC investigations so that syndicates come to embody the totalitarian principles attributed to Communism.

3   The expression of desire, for example, is what causes the downfall of Doc whose predilection for teenage girls prevents his getaway when he waits too long in a diner to watch a girl dance.

4   Implicit within this is a link between death and money which the film flirts with but ultimately represses because while it wants to highlight the aberrance of killing for money it does not want to suggest that capitalism itself is deathly.

5   See Kerr (1983:59) for a discussion of the importance of *The Big Heat* as an influence on *The Big Combo*.

6   Post-Classical Gangster Film: Nostalgia and Renewal

1   The phenomenon of New Hollywood Cinema is a contested affair, some critics associating it with the rise of the blockbuster (Schatz, 1993:17–25) while others identify it with auteur cinema and a new generation of maverick directors (Cook, 1998:11–37).

2   See Everson (1998) for an account of the American Silent Cinema and the development of film grammar and genre structures.

3   Many cultural theorists locate the origins of postmodernism within this period, Jameson (1992:125–51) arguing that the fragmentation of culture and the rise of the commodity in the 1960s marks its inception, while Harvey and Jencks both locate the rise of postmodernism in the 1970s, Jencks (1987:9) and Harvey (1989:141–59).

4   For a discussion of the parallel processes of modernisation and postmodernisation in the spheres of culture and economics, see Crook *et al.* (1992). For a counterview which argues that there is a distinct shift from modern to postmodern production principles, see Harvey (1989).

5   The issue at stake in postmodernist texts' ability to comment on culture is whether, because of the loss of textual critical distance, there can ever be a postmodern avant-garde or whether the avant-garde is the domain only of modernism. See Best and Kellner (1997:135) for a discussion of the difficulty of distinguishing between modernism and postmodernism in their avant-garde modes.

6   See Carr (2000:86) and Leong *et al.* (1997:77) for a discussion of a similar process that co-opted the film itself through its cultural commodification.

7   See Man (1994:13–18) for a discussion of the way that the modulation of this shift from optimism to disappointment is focalised through 'subjective realism' as the narrative mimics the mood of the characters.

8   See Brode (1995:85) for further discussion of the film's existential outlook.

7 The Postmodern Spectacle of the Gangster

1   For fuller accounts of postmodern aesthetics and cultural forms, see Connor, (1989); Wakefield (1990) (Denzin) (1991) Jameson (1991) Best and Kellner (1997).

2   See Brode (1995:169) for a discussion of the self-reflexive qualities of this scene.

3   See Davis (1990:265–323; 1993:29–54) for a discussion of the postmodern fragmentation of space in Los Angeles which, he argues, results in a new form of 'postmodern feudal indenture system' for those living outside the contemporary American dream of unlimited consumption (African-Americans and Chicanos).

4   See Dyson (1993:215, 219–22) for a discussion of masculinity in the film which, he argues, marginalises the female role in holding black communities together by placing such a high stake on the importance of the return of patriarchal values.

5   *Hoodlum* (Bill Duke, 1997) offers a similar vision in its historically based representation of the black gangster, ending with the redemption of the criminal and his return to official society with the image of his arrival at church.

6   A comparable development in the gangster genre, in the aftermath of the Cold War, was an interest in new white ethnic immigration, in the form of Russian gangs in *Romeo Is Bleeding* (Peter Medak, 1994) and *Little Odessa* (James Gray, 1994). The former represents the intersection of legitimate and gangster society with the story of a corrupt police officer being hired to murder a mob assassin while the latter features another assassin, Joshua, who returns to his childhood home to perform a hit.

7   For a fuller discussion of the taxonomy, history, and sources of the black gangster film, see Reid (1995:456–73).

8   This is actually a metaphorical displacement on the part of the film to foreground the monolithic nature of Brown's racket, as corporate strategy in a contemporary globalised and postmodern economy is to decentralise rather than to centralise; see Waters (1995:13–19 133–57) for a discussion of corporate 'differentiation' and the cultural fragmentation this produces.

9   Critics have implicity noted this by commenting on the film as a gangster version of *Hamlet* (Brode 1995:227; Yaquinto, 1998:231), a figuration contributed to by the interior monologue conducted in voice-over which expresses Carlito's desire to distance himself from the society around him.

10 See Brode (1995:227) for a discussion of Carlito's historic roots in the honest gangster who lives by his code.

Bibliography

Arrojo, José, ed. (2000) *Action/Spectacle Cinema: A Sight and Sound Reader*, London: BFI.

Ashbrook, John, ed. (1997) *The 'Crime Time' Filmbook: The Year in Crime Films*, Harpenden: No Exit.

Balio, Tino, ed. (1993) *Grand Design: Hollywood as a Modern Business Enterprise, 1930–1939*, Berkeley: University of California Press.

Baudrillard, Jean (1983) *Simulations*, New York: Semiotext(e).

Bell, Daniel (1974) *The Coming of Post-Industrial Society*, London: Heinemann.

Bell, Daniel (1976) *The Cultural Contradictions of Capitalism*, London: Heinemann.

Bergman, Andrew (1992) *We're in the Money: Depression America and Its Films*, Chicago: Elephant.

Benjamin, Walter (1968) *Illuminations: Essays and Reflections*, trans. by Hannah Arendt, New York: Schocken.

Benjamin, Walter (1985) *One Way Street and Other Writings*, London: Verso.

Berman, Marshall (1983) *All That Is Solid Melts into Air: the Experience of Modernity*, London: Verso.

Best, Stephen and Kellner, Douglas (1997) *The Postmodern Turn*, London: Guilford Press.

Biskind, Peter (1983) *Seeing Is Believing: How Hollywood Taught Us to Stop Worrying and Love the Fifties*, London: Pluto.

Black, Gregory D. (1994) *Hollywood Censored: Morality Codes, Catholics, and the Movies*, Cambridge and New York: Cambridge University Press.

Black, Gregory D. (1997) *The Catholic Crusade Against the Movies, 1940–1975*, Cambridge and New York: Cambridge University Press.

Brode, Douglas (1995) *Money, Women, and Guns: Crime Movies from 'Bonnie and Clyde' to the Present*, New York: Citadel.

Brookeman, Christopher (1984) *American Culture and Society Since the 1930's*, London and Basingstoke: Macmillan Brooker – now Palgrave Macmillan.

Brooker, Peter and Will (1997) 'Pulpmodernism: Tarantino's Affirmative Action', in Cartmell *et al* (1996:135–51).

Browne, Nick, ed. (2000) *Francis Ford Coppola's 'The Godfather Trilogy'*, Cambridge: Cambridge University Press.

Buchsbaum, Jonathan (1992) 'Tame Wolves and Phoney Claims: Paranoia and Film Noir', in Cameron (1992:88–97).

Buscombe, Edward (1995) 'The Idea of Genre in American Cinema', in Grant (1995:11–25).

Cameron, Ian, ed. (1992) *The Movie Book of Film Noir*, London: Studio Vista.

Carr, Steven Alan (2000) 'From "Fucking Cops" to "Fucking Media!": *Bonnie and Clyde* for a Sixties America', in Friedman (2000:70–100).

Carroll, Peter N., and Noble, David W. (1988) *The Free and the Unfree: A New History of the United States*, 2nd edn, Harmondsworth: Penguin.

Bibliography 171

Cartmell, Deborah, Hunter, I. Q., Kaye, Heidi and Whelehan, Imelda, eds (1996) *Pulping Fictions: Consuming Culture Across the Literature/Media Divide*, London: Pluto.

Cawelti, John G (1976) *Adventure, Mystery and Romance*, Chicago: University of Chicago Press.

Christopher, Nicholas (1997) *Somewhere in the Night: Film Noir and the American City*, New York: Henry Holt.

Clarens, Carlos (1980) *Crime Movies: An Illustrated History*, London: Secker & Warburg.

Clarke, David C., ed. (1997) *The Cinematic City*, London and New York: Routledge.

Cochran, David (2000) *America Noir: Underground Writers and Filmmakers of the Postwar Era*, Washington: Smithsonian Institution Press.

Cohan, Steven (1997) *Masked Men: Masculinity and the Movies in the Fifties*, Bloomington and Indianapolis: Indiana University Press.

Cohan, Steven, and Hark, Ina Rae, eds (1997) *The Road Movie Book*, London and New York: Routledge.

Collins, Jim, Radner, Hilary and Collins, Ava Preacher, eds (1993) *Film Theory Goes to the Movies*, New York and London: Routledge.

Connor, Steven (1989) *Postmodernist Culture*, Oxford: Blackwell.

Cook, David A. (1998) 'Auteur Cinema and the "Film Generation" in 1970s Hollywood', in Lewis (1998:11–37).

Cook, Pam, ed. (1985) *The Cinema Book*, London: BFI.

Copjec, Joan, ed. (1993) *Shades of Noir: A Reader*, London: Verso.

Corrigan, Timothy (1991) *A Cinema Without Walls: Movies and Culture After Vietnam*, New Brunswick, NJ: Rutgers University Press.

Cowie, Elizabeth, 'Film Noir and Women', in Copjec (1993:121–66).

Crook, Stephen, Pakulski, Jan and Waters, Malcolm (1992) *Post modernization: Change in Advanced Society*, London: Sage.

Dargis, Manohla (1996) 'Dark Side of the Dream', *Sight and Sound*, 6: 8 (1996:22–4).

Davis, Mike (1990) *City of Quartz*, London: Verso.

Davis, Mike (1993) 'Who Killed Los Angeles? Part Two: The Verdict is Given', *New Left Review*, 199 (1993:29–54).

DeKoven, Marianne (1991) *Rich and Strange: Gender, History, Modernism*, Princeton: University of Princeton Press.

Deleuze, Gilles and Guattari, Félix (1984) *Anti-Oedipus: Capitalism and Schizophrenia*, London: Athlone.

Deleuze, Gilles and Guattari, Félix (1987) *A Thousand Plateaus: Capitalism and Schizophrenia*, Minneapolis and London: University of Minnesota Press.

Denzin, Norman K (1991) *Images of Postmodern Society: Social Theory and Contemporary Cinema*, London: Sage.

Dika, Vera (2000) 'The Representation of Ethnicity in *The Godfather*', in Browne (2000:76–108).

Doherty, Thomas (1999) *Pre-Code Hollywood: Sex, Immorality, and Insurrection in American Cinema, 1930–1934*, New York: Columbia University Press.

Dyson, Michael Eric (1993) 'Between Apocalypse and Redemption: John Singleton's Boyz N The Hood' in Collins *et al.* (1993, 209–26).

Ellis, John (1982) *Visible Fictions*, London: Routledge and Kegan Paul.

Everson, William K. (1998) *American Silent Film*, New York: Da Capo Press.

172   *Bibliography*

Foster, Hal, ed. (1985) *Postmodern Culture*, London: Pluto.

Friedberg, Anne (1993) *Window Shopping: Cinema and the Postmodern*, Berkeley, Los Angeles, and London: University of California Press.

Friedman, Lester D., ed. (2000) *Arthur Penn's 'Bonnie and Clyde'*, Cambridge: Cambridge University Press.

Friedrich, Otto (1986) *City of Nets: A Portrait of Hollywood in the 1940's*, London: Headline.

Giddens, Anthony (1991) *Modernity and Self-Identity: Self and Society in the Late Modern Age*, Cambridge: Polity Press.

Gledhill, Christine (1985) 'The gangster/crime film', in Cook (1985:85–92).

Grant, Barry Keith, ed. (1986) *The Film Genre Reader*, Austin: University of Texas Press.

Grant, Barry Keith, ed. (1995) *Film Genre Reader II*, Austin: University of Texas Press.

Griffith, Richard (1976) 'Cycles and Genres', in Nichols (1976:111–18).

Grist, Leighton (1992) '*Out of the Past* a.k.a. *Build My Gallows High*', in Cameron (1992, 203–12).

Grist, Leighton (2000) *The Films of Martin Scorsese 1963–77: Authorship and Context*, Basingstoke: Macmillan – now Palgrave Macmillan.

Gunning, Tom (2000) *The Films of Fritz Lang: Allegories of Vision and Modernity*, London: BFI.

Hardy, Phil (1998a) *The BFI Companion to Crime*, London: BFI.

Hardy, Phil, ed. (1998b) *The Overlook Film Encyclopedia: The Gangster Film*, Woodstock, NY: Overlook.

Harvey, David (1989) *The Condition of Postmodernity*, Oxford: Blackwell.

Harvey, Sylvia (1978) 'Woman's Place: The Absent Family in Film Noir', in Kaplan (1978:22–34).

Hess, John (1976) '*Godfather II*: A Deal Coppola Couldn't Refuse', in Nichols (1976:81–90).

Heynen, Hilde (1999) *Architecture and Modernity: A Critique*, Cambridge, Mass: MIT Press.

Hirsch, Foster (1981) *Film Noir: The Dark Side of the Screen*, New York: Da Capo Press.

Holding, Chris (1997) '*Reservoir Dogs*: Let's Go to Work' in Ashbrook (1997:20–6).

Horst, Sabine (1998) '*Miller's Crossing*', in Körte and Seesslen (1998:87–114).

Huyssen, Andreas (1986) *After the Great Divide: Modernism, Mass Culture, and Postmodernism*, Basingstoke: Macmillan – now Palgrave Macmillan.

Jameson, Fredric (1984) 'Postmodernism, or The Cultural Logic of Late Capitalism', *New Left Review*, 146 (1984:53–92).

Jameson, Fredric (1985) 'Postmodernism and Consumer Society', in Foster (1985:111–25).

Jameson, Fredric (1990) *Signatures of the Visible*, New York and London: Routledge.

Jameson, Fredric (1991) *Postmodernism or, The Cultural Logic of Late Capitalism*, London and New York: Verso.

Jameson, Fredric (1992) 'Periodising the Sixties', in Waugh (1992:125–51).

Jameson, Fredric (1993) 'The Synoptic Chandler', in Copjec, (1993:33–56).

Jameson, Richard T. (1994) *They Went Thataway: Redefining Film Genres*, San Francisco: Mercury House.

Jancovich, Mark (1996) *Rational Fears: Horror in the 1950's*, Manchester: Manchester University Press.
Jencks, Charles (1987) *The Language of Post-Modern Architecture*, 5th edn, London: Academy.
Jencks, Charles (1989) *What Is Postmodernism?*, 3rd edn, London: St. Martin's Press.
Jones, Emrys (1990) *Metropolis: The World's Great Cities*, Oxford: Oxford University Press.
Kaplan, E Ann, ed. (1978) *Women in Film Noir*, London: BFI.
Karpf, Stephen L. (1973) *The Gangster Film: Emergence, Variation and Decay of a Genre, 1930–1940*, New York: Arno Press.
Kern, Stephen (1983) *The Culture of Time and Space, 1880–1918*, Cambridge, Mass: Harvard University Press.
Kerr, Paul (1983) 'My Name is Joseph H Lewis', *Screen*, 24: 4–5 (1983): 49–67.
Körte, Peter and Seesslen, eds (1999) *Joel and Ethan Coen*, London: Titan.
Krutnik, Frank (1982) 'Desire, Transgression and James M. Cain', *Screen*, 23: 1 (1982):31–44.
Krutnik, Frank (1991) *In a Lonely Street: Film Noir, Genre, Masculinity*, London and New York: Routledge.
Krutnik, Frank (1997) 'Something More Than Night: Tales of the *Noir* City', in Clarke (1997:83–109).
Langman, Larry and Finn, Daniel (1995a) *A Guide to American Crime Films of the Thirties*, Westport, Conn. and London: Greenwood.
Langman, Larry and Finn, Daniel (1995b) *A Guide to American Crime Films of the Forties and Fifties*, Westport, Conn. and London: Greenwood.
Leitch, Thomas (2002) *Crime Films*, Cambridge: Cambridge University Press.
Leong, Ian, Sell, Mike and Thomas, Kelly (1997) 'Mad Love, Mobile Homes, and Dysfunctional Dicks: On the Road with Bonnie and Clyde', in Cohan and Hark (1997:70–89).
Lewis, Jon, ed. (1998) *The New American Cinema*, Durham, NC and London: Duke University Press.
Lyon, David (1994) *Postmodernity*, Buckingham: Open University Press.
McArthur, Colin (1972) *Underworld U.S.A.*, London: Secker and Warburg.
McArthur, Colin (1992) *The Big Heat*, London: BFI.
McArthur, Colin (1997) 'Chinese Boxes and Russian Dolls: Tracking the Elusive Cinematic City', in Clarke (1997:19–45).
McCarty, John (1993) *Hollywood Gangland: The Movies' Love Affair with the Mob*, New York: St. Martin's Press.
McKelly, James (1998) 'Raising Caine in a down Eden: *Menace II Society* and the death of Signifyin(g)', *Screen*, 39: 1 (1998):36–52.
Maltby, Richard (1993) 'The Production Code and the Hays Office', in Balio (1993:37–72).
Maltby, Richard (1995) *Hollywood Cinema: An Introduction*, Oxford: Blackwell.
Man, Glenn (1994) *Radical Visions: American Film Renaissance, 1967–1976*, Westport, Conn: Greenwood Press.
Man, Glenn (2000) 'Ideology and Genre in the *Godfather* Films', in Browne (2000:109–32).
Marling, William (1995) *The American Roman Noir: Hammett, Cain and Chandler*, Athens, Ga. and London: University of Georgia Press.

May, Lary (2000) *The Big Tomorrow: Hollywood and the Politics of the American Way*, Chicago and London: University of Chicago Press.

Merritt, Greg (2000) *Celluloid Mavericks: A History of American Independent Cinema*, New York: Thunder's Mouth Press.

Miller, Stephen Paul (1999) *The Seventies Now: Culture as Surveillance*, Durham, NC: Duke University Press.

Mitchell, Edward (1995) 'Apes and Essences: Some Sources of Significance in the American Gangster Film', in Grant (1995:203–12).

Mottram, Eric (1989) *Blood on the Nash Ambassador: Investigations in American Culture*, London: Hutchinson Radius.

Munby, Jonathan (1996) '*Manhattan Melodrama*'s Art of the Weak: Telling History from the Other Side in the 1930's Talking Gangster Film', *Journal of American Studies*, 30: 1 (1996):101–118.

Munby, Jonathan (1999) *Public Enemies, Public Heroes: Screening the Gangster from 'Little Caesar' to 'Force of Evil'*, Chicago and London: University of Chicago Press.

Naremore, James (1998) *More than Night: Film Noir in Its Contexts*, Berkeley and Los Angeles: University of California Press.

Neale, Steve (1980) *Genre*, London: BFI.

Neale, Steve (2000) *Genre and Hollywood*, London and New York: Routledge.

Neve, Brian (1992) *Film and Politics in America: A Social Tradition*, London and New York: Routledge.

Nichols, Bill, ed. (1976) *Movies and Methods*, Volume I, Berkeley and Los Angeles: University of California Press.

Palmer, R-Barton (1994) *Hollywood's Dark Cinema: The American Film Noir*, New York: Twayne.

Rafter, Nicole (2000) *Shots in the Mirror: Crime Films and Society*, Oxford: Oxford University Press.

Reid, David and Walker, Jayne L. (1993) 'Strange Pursuit: Cornell Woolrich and the Abandoned City of the Forties', in Copjec (1993:57–96).

Reid, Mark A. (1995) 'The Black Gangster Film', in Grant (1995: 456–73).

Roddick, Nick (1983) *A New Deal in Entertainment: Warner Brothers in the 1930's*, London: BFI.

Rosow, Eugene (1978) *Born to Lose: The Gangster Film in America*, New York: Oxford University Press.

Ruth, David E. (1996) *Inventing the Public Enemy: The Gangster in American Culture, 1918–1935*, Chicago and London: University of Chicago Press.

Schatz, Thomas (1981) *Hollywood Genres: Formulas, Film-making, and the Studio System*, New York: McGraw-Hill.

Schatz, Thomas (1993) 'The New Hollywood', in Collins *et al.* (1993):8–36.

Schatz, Thomas (1996) *The Genius of the System: Hollywood Film-making in the Studio Era*, London: Faber and Faber.

Schatz, Thomas (1997) *Boom and Bust: American Cinema in the 1940s*, Berkeley: University of California Press.

Shadoian, Jack (1977) *Dreams and Dead Ends: The American Gangster/Crime Film*, Cambridge, Mass. and London: MIT Press.

Schrader, Paul (1995) 'Notes on Film Noir', in Grant (1995:213–26).

Short, Martin (1984) *Crime Inc: The Story of Organized Crime*, London: Thames Methuen.

Silver, Alain and Ward, Elizabeth, eds (1992) *Film Noir: An Encyclopedic Reference to the American Style*, Woodstock, Overlook.

Silver, Alain and Ursini, James, eds (1996) *Film Noir Reader*, New York: Limelight.

Sklar, Robert (1992) *City Boys: Cagney, Bogart, Garfield*, Princeton, NJ: Princeton University Press.

Spicer, Andrew (2002) *Film Noir*, Harlow: Longman.

Straw, Will (1997) 'Urban Confidential: The Lurid City of the 1950s', in Clarke (1997:110–28).

Tarantino, Quentin (1995) *True Romance*, London: Faber.

Telotte, J. P. (1989) *Voices in the Dark: The Narrative Patterns of 'Film Noir'*, Urbana and Chicago: University of Illinois Press.

Tester, Keith (1994) *The Flaneur*, London: Routledge.

Todorov, Tzvetan (1990) *Genres in Discourse*, Cambridge: Cambridge University Press.

Tudor, Andrew (1995) 'Genre', in Grant (1995:3–10).

Wakefield, Neville (1990) *Postmodernism: The Twilight of the Real*, London: Pluto.

Walker, Michael (1992) 'Film Noir: An Introduction', in Cameron (1992:8–38).

Warshow, Robert (1977) 'The Gangster as Tragic Hero' in *The Immediate Experience*, New York: Atheneum, 127–33.

Waters, Malcolm (1995) *Globalization*, London and New York: Routledge.

Waugh, Patricia, ed. (1992) *Postmodernism: A Reader*, London: Edward Arnold.

Whyte, William H. (1960) *The Organisation Man*, Harmondsworth: Penguin.

Wilson, Elizabeth (1992) 'The Invisible Flaneur', *New Left Review*, 191 (1992:90–110).

Woodiwiss, Michael (1988) *Crime Crusades and Corruption: Prohibitions in the United States, 1900–1987*, London: Pinter.

Woodiwiss, Anthony (1993) *Postmodernity USA*, London: Sage.

Yaquinto, Marilyn (1998) *Pump 'Em Full of Lead: A Look at Gangsters on Film*, New York: Twayne.

Index